JUDAH'S TAMAR

JUDAH'S TAMAR

In Her Shoes (Trials)

DEIDRA BYNUM

XULON PRESS

Xulon Press
2301 Lucien Way #415
Maitland, FL 32751
407.339.4217
www.xulonpress.com

Unless otherwise indicated, Scripture quotations taken from the New American Standard Bible (NASB). Copyright © 1960, 1962, 1963, 1968, 1971, 1972, 1973, 1975, 1977, 1995 by The Lockman Foundation. Used by permission. All rights reserved.

Paperback ISBN-13: 978-1-6322-1781-3

Ebook ISBN-13: 978-1-6322-1782-0

Dedication:

To my beloved family, thank you for your constant love and support. To my dearest big sister Felecia, you are a great woman of God, His precious gift to me. Thank you for always teaching and encouraging me in love through Christ.

I would also like to acknowledge two very special women who have been a blessing to our family. Lorraine Ford and Lagail Milton, thank you for your unconditional love, service, and friendship. May God continue to richly bless you, for you are "Angels, On Assignment."

Deidra

TABLE OF CONTENTS

Part One

Judah's Tamar Introduction...

T amar, twice the daughter-in-law of Judah, was a wife with an innate desire to be a mother. Marrying into a family that had three sons, she was guaranteed customarily by the "Levirate Marriage Law" that in the event of her husband's death, she would with no doubt (in this case), have two other opportunities to marry, giving her two additional chances at becoming pregnant and giving birth to an heir.

Undoubtedly, that was not what she had planned when she married Judah's eldest son. Still, it was a nice insurance policy where she was the named beneficiary. Tamar had no idea of the challenges she would face in attempting to benefit from the clause documented in the established law after the death of her husband, Er.

Here in her story, despair, and desperation meeting; conquer fear and fraud by using the weapons of desire and deception. Sounds oxymoronic? In this fascinating story, it is not. Tamar is being identified as an "Unsung woman of the Bible" because of her deliberate discretion in acting. She exercised patience and wisdom in achieving her desired goal.

For anyone who has ever been defrauded, cheated out of something owed or promised, and feel retaliation laced in malice for the demise and destruction of the culprit is the answer; allow Tamar's story, depicted here to show you how she chose to answer her problem in disguise.

With God on her side, she chose a sure-fire strategy of desire, to recover what rightfully belonged to her and divinely belonged to God.

Executing her plan in the most unorthodox way, she also secured for herself the opportunity to respond to her offender in the manner of her choosing.

In the words of John Adams:

"Every problem is an opportunity in disguise."

Felecia's Mocked Trial...

Having some previous knowledge and experience working as a courtroom clerk, after praying, the next thing Felecia needed to do was set the stage for her #38 courtroom drama. Since this story derives from the Book of Genesis, chapter 38, found in the Bible, she decided that assigned number would be appropriate. Presiding over this case, she chose to borrow none other than the prestigious, honorable Judge Deborah from the Bible's Book of Judges (chapter 4). In Hebrew, her name means "Bee." As history denotes, she was known to be a well-equipped "Stinger" against the Canaanite armies.

Documented, a great "Shero" and Prophetess under her Commander-in-Chief Barak, she led an army of Israelites against the Canaanites, destroying them for their cruel treatment of the Israelites while holding God's people in captivity. She was honored by God and identified as a strong, fearless woman with great integrity. Not bias, there would be no need for her to recuse herself from this trial. Though Tamar is a Canaanite woman, in Judge Deborah's courtroom, indicatively, she is recognized as the "Plaintiff." Judge Deborah is bringing along her comrade, Jael, to act as her trusted courtroom reporter.

The bailiffs employed are soldiers selected from the armies of Israel to guard over this proceeding. Seated in the jury box are twelve carefully chosen men, one from each of the tribes of Israel (Rueben, Simeon, Levi,

Dan, Naphtali, Gad, Asher, Issachar, Zebulun, Benjamin, Manasseh, and Ephraim) excluded here is the tribe of Judah, for obvious reasons. Among the witnesses summoned to testify are Hirah the Adullamite (Judah's companion and friend), and Shelah, Judah's third-born son.

Also set to testify are Tamar's father, her unnamed spy, the message carrier, and her midwife. Like most great trials, reserved for last, a star witness. Only a few spectators from the public are allowed to occupy the seats in the gallery. Finally, seated in courtroom #38 on the left side, waiting for her case to be called, is the plaintiff, Tamar, and on the right side, the accused, the defendant, Judah. With all the players in place, armed with her personal knowledge and experience along with a countless number of hours watching her favorite famous television attorney, "Perry Mason" Felecia announces, "Court is now in session."

All Rise,

Court is now in session; the honorable Judge Deborah will be presiding over this matter:

When the chief bailiff made the announcement for everyone in the courtroom to rise (stand up), in unison, everyone did. In walked the Iconic figure, Judge Deborah. Strolling over to her high bench with her hair pinned up, all could see she was there for business, not glamour. Still, she was glamorous in a different kind of way. Draped in her long black robe, radiating power, the color alone commanded the utmost respect.

She wore eyeglasses that appeared to be specifically designed to shield her eyes, allowing her to look out into the sea of souls in her courtroom but not granting access for those seated before her to look back into the window of her soul. Once she sat down, everyone else in the courtroom followed suit. The silence in the courtroom echoing silence was broken by movement when the courtroom clerk (considered an officer of the court) dressed in a beautiful brown skirt suit approached the judge's bench to provide her with her calendar of cases slated for the day.

From where Tamar was sitting, this was moving to watch. The female clerk was allowed to walk up to this powerful judge and not be retrained or have weapons drawn on her. If anyone else in the room, especially her had tried that, her case for fraud would have quickly turned into an open and shut, case of justified homicide. Judge Deborah would be protected at all cost. The thought of that scared her; she could not afford any outbursts. She was a female victim with a good case, prepared to be disputed before a fair, female Judge of good character, and as far as she was concerned, the accused was a misguided male!

This was not the time for her to be hormonal. She needed to calm her nerves so that when her turn came to speak, representing herself, she would remember why she was there and what was at stake. She needed to tell her story in such a compelling manner, that she would be declared "the winner!" Once the roll was taken, with everyone responding by saying, I, Here, or Present. All parties present for the cases being heard that day, were called by the clerk in no specific order. Only glancing over at Judah sitting next to his witness (and friend) Hirah a few times, Tamar's focus was drawn to and engulfed in the other cases called and heard before hers.

For the plaintiffs who represented themselves, she learned very quickly what to do and what not do. For those who had attorneys and expert witnesses, their cases were handled professionally, rendering their client a dismissal, or a reduction in fines or sentencing. Every time the judge slammed her gavel, whatever her ruling; it was final.

Watching the previous cases in real time, mentally she added what she witnessed (courtroom jargon and etiquette) to her offense.

With no other cases besides hers left to be heard, docket number #10 (her case) was the last one called. Tamar watched as the judge beckoned the courtroom clerk to come. While speaking with the clerk, she placed one hand over her powerful microphone as they exchanged words. After they finished, the verdict from that conversation was rendered; they were recessed for lunch.

The judge said she also wanted to review some additional facts listed in Tamar's complaint, and that court would reconvene at 2.30.p.m. It was noon. Once the judge slammed the gavel down, declaring dismissal, everyone scattered from the courtroom. Tamar decided she would use the time to run to the law library to check and double check a few important things she felt she might have overlooked. Those findings would prove crucial in her pending case.

Scene: Courtroom #38

Time: 2:15 p.m.

Tamar slid back into the courtroom at a quarter past two. Sitting there in the courtroom watching person after person file in, started messing with her stomach and her head. Since the other complainant's and their witnesses from the morning session had no reason to return, it could reasonably be assumed, everyone coming in now was there to participate in or hear her case.

Instead of bowing to "FEAR" (F) alse (E) vidence (A) ppearing (R) eal), she closed her eyes and bowed her head to "POP!" In the (P) ower (O) f (P) rayer, the illusions that were attempting to form in her head and heart were chased away. After quietly saying Amen, she heard the announcement.

All Rise..

After the judge entered and was seated, Tamar only had a few minutes to gather herself, her papers and her courage before her case was called. The clerk speaking clearly said; Docket #10, case #25-5 Tamar vs. Judah, are all parties in attendance? The shaking in her voice could not be mistaken when she responded, "Here." Judah, on the other hand, responded with a strong, "Present!"

His resounding confidence made her question herself in a split second. Why was she was there representing herself. Doubling down, the same voice, in a whisper, asked why she was even there at all, since everything thing had worked out in the end. She recognized it was the voice of the enemy when he continued in a whisper, saying, "You have the power to shut this down by simply withdrawing your complaint."

Preparing to agree and verbalize those words, the judge interrupting her mental battle speaking said; "I see you are here representing yourself. I know you might be a bit nervous. I want you to take a moment and breath. I have cleared my calendar for the remainder of the afternoon to hear this remarkable case. When you are ready, you may start from the beginning and tell us your story." To further assist her preparation, the judge turned to one of the bailiffs and told him to get her (Tamar) a bottle of water.

The whispers from the enemy were replaced with a voice of care, then confidence. This great judge saw something in her and her story, ruling it "remarkable." Resonating, this reminded Tamar why she was there;

to set the record straight concerning what happened to her, why she did what she did, and did not do what she could have done.

After she took a sip of the literal water, the refreshing living water in her spirit began to flow. The judge electing to skip the request for an opening argument from Tamar and a plea from Judah (because she could) leaned back in her chair and said:

"Tamar, please proceed with your story."

Tamar straightened her posture, then began to speak; this is what she said:

"Good afternoon to you, Judge Deborah, to your distinguished colleagues, jurors, witnesses, and guest."

Turning to Judah, she said, "and to you too, honorable Sir Judah." Everyone looked at Judah as he responded to her high honor of him by lowering his head.

There was a moment of silence as invisible respect paraded, then faded in the air. Tamar's voice broke in as she started her story. The judge told her not to start with an opening argument, having the floor, she began with an opening statement; "I am here today for the world to know who I am and what I was chosen by God to do.

My name is Tamar. I am a Canaanite Woman. I am currently a resident of Canaan. You see, it was known to us when Judah left his father and brothers and came to live among our people he did so in vain, separating himself from his people, the Israelites. Upon entering Canaan, he met and quickly became friends with Hirah, an Adullamite (she pointed at him), sitting there next to him. It wasn't long before Judah's eyes found Shua's (a Canaanite resident) beautiful daughter. Though he was an Israelite, and she was a Canaanite woman, he married her.

This mixed marriage was something his people, especially his father Jacob, frowned upon. Married and settled in Canaan, three sons were produced from their union. The eldest was, Er, their second born, Onan, and their youngest, Shelah, sitting over there (she pointed at him). To further establish himself in our community, upon determining his eldest son Er was ready for marriage, he sought out a wife for him and selected me. I was a young woman living in my father's house the day I was handpicked by Judah and presented to his son to wed. Shortly after our nuptials, sadly, my husband, Judah's son Er, died. Only God knows why. (ref; Gen 38:7)

After everyone had properly mourned the death of Er, Judah, though living in our community, chose to observe the Israelite's "Levirate Law." I have a copy of it here, exhibit #1. I would like to have it entered into the record as evidence, along with exhibits #2, #3, #4 and #5." Tamar gave the bailiff everything, who, in turn, handed exhibit #1 to the judge. Taking a couple of minutes to examine the documents, the judge responded by saying, "I'll allow it." Then she said, "please continue." Continuing, Tamar said, "In accordance with the "Levirate Law" Judah promptly sent his second son Onan to me out of duty observing their existing law.

Onan inheriting me and all the rights of Er, lessened his monetary share as a full, next in line kin. Onan on behalf of his deceased brother by law, had to wed, then bed me. Though he never said it, I could sense his reluctance. He did not want to impregnate me with his seed to raise up an heir for his brother Er. If I wasn't sure about it in my private thoughts, it was proven the moment we were intimate. Instead of releasing his seed inside of me, he withdrew himself and spilled his seed on the ground, therefore only enjoying the pleasure of the deed with no transfer of seed."

Looking over at Judah, he lowered his head, this time shaking it from side to side as if it was possible; this was the first time he was hearing this news. Tamar clarifying, looked in the direction of the jurors and said, "I believe his father did not know this." There would be no objection. Tamar, speaking again, said, "After Onan enjoyed intimacy with me, then spilled generations (seeds), he died. His death was sudden. The cause of it, like with Er, was unknown to man, again only God knows why (ref; Gen 38: 9-10)."

Looking at the judge she said "Your Honor, though you may strike it from the record, I need to say this. If I had to guess, I believe he angered the God of Israel because he toyed with and violated the "Levirate Law" by not fulfilling the act of surrogacy on behalf of his deceased older brother.

Tamar waited to hear the words she heard earlier in one particular case, "move to strike that last statement" those words were not spoken, so she continued,

"Your Honor, after Onan was laid to rest, Judah discreetly approached me. He told me it was best if I went back to my father's house as a widow and remain there until Shelah, his youngest son, was old enough to wed, then bed me to raise up seed as an heir for my first husband, his firstborn son, Er. My father-in-law, without regard for my feelings, insinuated I was cursed by telling me he was doing this to protect his only remaining son.

> "Then said Judah to Tamar his daughter-in-law: 'Remain a widow in thy father's house, till Shelah my son be grown up'; for he said: 'Lest he also die, like his brethren.'

(Gen 38:11 Hebrew Bible)"

Tamar went on to say, "My father-in-law was not the only one making comments about me. It was speculated and rumored that I had indirectly killed two men with my intimacy. This was hurtful, none-the-less, I found solace in the thought of my future marriage to Shelah, the last of Judah's sons. I was told, all I had to do was wait until he became of age. So, with that great hope, I returned to my father's house as advised by my father-in-law and commenced to waiting.

Secluding myself, I waited, and waited. Occasionally I went out for fresh air or to visit my friend over there (she pointed at her witness; the spy). Keeping her eyes and ears open for me, between us, I found out Judah's wife (Shua's daughter) had died. My father-in-law mourned her death. Afterwards he was comforted. Shortly thereafter, I observed for myself, Shelah had grown up and appeared to be more than eligible to fulfill the law and Judah's promise to me.

Giving the defendant the benefit of the doubt, I waited a little longer. When it became clear to me, my father-in-law had reneged on his promise, I was heartbroken. I cried day and night. I could not understand why he had chosen to deceive me in the manner he did. What he did not know was there was a voice crying from a place deep within me, a call even. I was promised a baby for me, and more importantly, an heir for my husband Er's honor.

Not only had we been wronged; I had been boxed in, unnecessarily. You see Your Honor, after researching the "Levirate Law" again, I discovered the sons of Judah, by blood identify as Israelites. As a result of that, in accordance with an exemption clause, Onan and Shelah could have chosen to opt-out of having a child with me on behalf of their deceased brother. Your Honor, there was an out found in exhibit #1, section 7, part B, which states;

> "But if the man does not desire to take his brother's wife, then his brother's wife shall go up to the gate to the elders and say, 'My husband's brother refuses to establish a name for his brother in Israel; he is not willing to perform the duty of a husband's brother to me.' Then the elders of his city shall summon him and speak to him. And if he persists and says, 'I do not desire to take her,' then his brother's wife shall come to him in the sight of the elders and pull his sandal off his foot and spit in his face; and she shall declare, 'Thus it is done to the man who does not build up his brother's house.' In Israel, his name shall be called, 'The house of him whose sandal is removed.' (Deut 25:5

"My question is, why weren't we extended the opportunity to take advantage of this option? Onan would have been free of his obligation and would probably still be alive." Pointing at Shelah, she said, "Shelah, too, he could have been absolved of this responsibility as well. We would have all been free. Instead, I was left in limbo."

Looking in the direction of the Israelite jury pool, she said, "I suppose Judah did not want to have to go back to Israel to hold open court on the matter. I believe he did not want to deal with the embarrassment and shame it would have caused him and his sons before the elders of Israel, especially since he left without their blessing. He cared about him and his son's image and reputation, not mine. It did not matter that I was ostracized and thought to be a cursed woman.

Still, I waited to have my good name exonerated by an executed vow of matrimony. Because I was chosen by Judah for his eldest son Er, then passed down per the "Levirate Law," I was under the headship of my father-in-law. He was the only one who could select a new husband for me or release me. To that end, I slept with two confusing questions. "This being Canaan, why is Judah trying to exercise the "Levirate Law" here? And why was the law being ignored? The day my source told me Judah was on his way to Timnah with Hirah for their sheep shearing feast, acting fast, this is what I did;

> "If Shelah wasn't going to be given to me to wed and bed, then for the sake of his son Er's legacy, Judah's seed would have to do instead.

> I laid aside my sacred widow's garment to dress the part of a veiled temple harlot.

I waited for him to return full from the feast, where surely good food and much wine made him want to satisfy his inner beast.

Seductively I sat in the entranceway, and enticed my deceased husband's father to come and lay.

Once we agreed to do the deed, I calmly told him what I would need.

I asked, what will you pay me for my good wine? He said on my word; you will receive a kid goat by tomorrow this time.

I asked if he would give me something of his to hold instead; his seal, cord, and staff was the negotiated suitable pledge.

He agreed then handed them over to me, and when the deed was done, I left with his i.d.

More importantly, my deceased husband DNA had been deposited inside of me."

We parted ways after the deal, with my identity safely concealed but for Judah, months later, his deeds would be revealed."

Looking around the courtroom, it appeared everyone was holding their breath. Tamar waited for them to exhale before she continued. She resumed the telling of her story by saying, "I ran back to my father's house stripped off-exhibit #2 (the harlot's garment) and hid it. I put

my widow's garment back on and went back to doing what I had previously been doing, waiting.

This time the wait was with great hope and expectation, pregnant, I was
finally in the beginning stages of gestation.

In the meantime, the defendant (Judah), more concerned about
honoring his word to an unknown, perceived prostitute rather than
his known daughter-in-law, me, sent Hirah to retrieve his pledge by
bringing the kid (goat) he had promised, in his moment of purchased
pleasure. Hirah wasted his time.

The woman he sought was not there; neither was she known to the
other men there because that woman was me. I was not a temple prostitute. I was a widow who got tired of waiting on a promise. The kid
(goat) Judah was prepared to offer the woman in disguise did not compare to the kid (baby) he promised me years ago that I was now carrying inside. Impaired, indirectly, he made good on his promise. His
debt to both women had been paid in full."

> "My plan worked, I could finally smile, when it was
> confirmed, I was with child!" Soon after my smile
> started to show, it wasn't long after that my stomach
> started to grow. That's when the real trouble, started.

In a surprise move, the judge asked Tamar to pause her story; she
wanted to hear from a few witnesses. She stated that since Tamar
and Judah were representing themselves in her courtroom, she would
be conducting the questioning. She advised all who were called on
to answer her questions briefly and truthfully. She asked all the witnesses to stand and be sworn in simultaneously. Jael's recorded report
reflected this exchange:

Officially under oath Judge Deborah began her questioning:

Judge: "I call Shelah to the stand."

(Shelah takes the stand)

Judge: Are you Judah's third son?

Shelah: Yes, Your Honor.

Judge: Did you marry your sister-in-law per the "Levirate Marriage Law?"

Shelah: No, Your Honor.

Judge: Why?

Shelah: My father did not tell me to.

Judge: Thank you, you may step down.

Judge: I call Tamar's unnamed spy to the stand.

(Spy takes the stand)

Judge: is it your testimony that you spied for Tamar and supplied her with information?

Spy: Yes, Your Honor.

Judge: Why did you feel the need to do that?

Spy: I felt sorry for her. People were saying ugly things about her. I did not believe she was cursed. I also knew she was waiting on the promise to be wed to Shelah to have children. She was not just looking to have seed for her first husband but also to have children to take care of her. That is an important duty in our community.

Judge: Thank you, you may step down.

Judge: I call Tamar's father to the stand.

(Tamar's father takes the stand)

Judge: Thank you for appearing here in my courtroom today. I know it must have been difficult to watch your daughter go through what she has, so I will be brief.

Judge: Did Judah or his first born deceased son pick Tamar to wed?

Tamar's Father: Judah selected my daughter for his firstborn son.

Judge: After Er, died, did your daughter come back home?

Tamar's father: No, after her husband Er died, she was given to the next brother in line, Onan, to fulfill the "Levirate Law."

Judge: After Onan's sudden death, did she stay and become the wife of her deceased husband's youngest brother, and if not, what did she do?

Tamar's father: No, Your Honor, she did not stay. She was told by her father-in-law to come back to my house, remain a widow, and wait for Shelah to get older before marrying him. Judah expressed his fear that his youngest son might die like his other two sons if he was given to her too soon, so she came home and waited.

Between the deaths of her husbands and so many ugly rumors, she was not in a good place. The only thing that gave her a glimmer of hope was being betrothed to young Shelah, guaranteeing her she would still be a wife, allowing her to have seed raised up for her husband Er. She wanted to honor his legacy and have her own children to take care of her. Though legally Judah was responsible for her, living in my home, I provided for her.

Judge: I have one last question; were you aware of your daughter's plan to secure Judah's seed?

Tamar's father: No, Your Honor, I was not aware of my daughter's plan. I believe my daughter, out of desperation, acted alone. The craving in her belly spilled over into her heart. My daughter wanted to obtain what was promised to her by any means necessary. Judah became her mark for the fulfillment of that promise.

Judge: Thank you for your testimony; you may return to your seat.

Judge: I would like to call one last witness; for now, I call Hirah the Adullamite to the stand.

(Hirah takes the stand)

Judge: Hirah, are you friends with Judah, and if so, do you think you are a loyal friend?

Hirah: Yes, I am Judah's friend, and yes, I am loyal to him.

Judge: The day you returned with Judah from the sheep-shearing festival, what can you tell me about the exchange between Judah and the perceived harlot he encountered that day and beyond?

Hirah: (with a smirk on his face, answered) Yes, I did accompany him; however, I was not close enough to them to hear their private discussion.

Judge: Alright, I can see you are loyal, so let me re-phrase the question. First, let me have the court reporter read back Tamar's testimony concerning her being told you returned to retrieve Judah's pledge, exhibits #3, #4 and #5.

Jael: "In the meantime, the defendant (Judah) was more concerned about honoring his word to an unknown perceived prostitute, rather than me, his known daughter-in-law, concerning my pending marriage to Shelah. Judah sent Hirah to retrieve his pledge by bringing the kid (goat) he had promised, in his moment of discretion. Hirah wasted his time. The woman he sought was not there; neither was she known to other men because that woman was me. I was not a temple prostitute."

Judge: So Hirah, where you may not be able to speak on the conversation between Judah and the perceived harlot the day of the event, it is apparent in the eyes of this court that you at some point were made privy to what transpired. Now I asked you again, what happened when Judah did not go himself, but sent you back to pay his debt and retrieve his pledge? And let me remind you, Hirah, you are under oath and are now considered a hostile witness. Let me warn you, we are here for the truth, and if in your loyalty you perjure yourself, you will be held you in contempt of court! Do you understand?

Hirah: Yes, Your Honor.

Hirah's truthfully testifying covered the following:

> "When Judah sent the young goat by his friend (Hirah) the Adullamite, to receive the pledge from the woman's hand, he did not find her. He asked the men of her place, saying, "Where is the temple prostitute who was by the road at Enaim?" But they said, "There has been no temple prostitute here."
>
> So he returned to Judah, and said, "I did not find her; and furthermore, the men of the place said, 'There has been no temple prostitute here.'" Then Judah said, "Let her keep them, otherwise we will become a laughingstock. After all, I sent this young goat, but you did not find her."

(Gen 38:20-23)

Judge: So, it's your testimony that when you inquired of the men who frequented the Enaim location, they told you, no prostitute had been there?

Hirah: Yes, Your Honor, they were not familiar with the woman I described.

Judge: So, is it your testimony, when you told Judah the woman he had been intimate with was not there for you to make the exchange, you're saying he told you to let her keep his credentials so that both of you would not be thought of as fools, because you were tricked by a perceived temple harlot?

Hirah: Umm, Yes, Your Honor.

Judge: Last question; as Judah's close friend, would you agree it was important to him to make good on his promise to the woman he laid with?

Hirah: Yes, Your Honor. She had his seal, cord, and staff; they were important to him.

Judge: Really? You just testified that your friend willingly opted to forgo a search for the woman who had his, in your word, "important" seal, cord, and staff. I would have thought Judah would have done the opposite by putting out an APB (All Points Bulletin) on her, possibly offering a reward for his items.

What if his items were found later? How do you think he would have explained being separated from them?

Hirah: I don't know, Your Honor.

Judge: Thank you, you may step down.

When Hirah finished testifying, he was escorted back to his seat by a bailiff.

The courtroom was quiet for a couple of minutes as the judge conferred with Jael, her court reporter. Once they came out of their huddle, the judge advised everyone there would be a fifteen-minute recess. She advised everyone when they returned, Tamar would be allowed to finish her story. The judge also told them a few other witnesses would be called to include the defendant, Judah. She further stated deliberations would occur after that, and her ruling would be handed down.

Fifteen minutes later, court was back in session...

Tamar stood up with confidence and jumped into the second half of her story:

"After three months had passed. My baby bump started to show. What was spectacular to me was speculated and whispered about by others. According to the rumors, while outplaying the harlot, I got pregnant by an unknown, unnamed man. This time I did not care what others were saying about me. Not only did I know the truth, I had the proof! My outlook on life had changed. Things were fine; my focus was on preparing for the arrival of my baby, my husband's heir. I had a smile on face and joy in my heart.

I could tell by the smug look on the faces of others; it would be just a matter of time before I was confronted. I was right. One day there was a knock at my father's door. My father- in- law sent men to seize me. Rumors surrounding my pregnancy had gotten back to him. He believed them. From what I could gather, he was furious! Without witnesses to my alleged crime, he ordered them to make a citizen's arrest and bring me before him and our community's council; there would be no trial. Seized, I was sentenced to be burned immediately. Before leaving, I begged if I could retrieve something from my quarters.

Granted the opportunity, I got what I needed, returned, raised my head high in honor, and with my hands tucked under my widow's garment, I walked out of my father's house. Before leaving, I whispered in my crying father's ear. I said, "Father, please trust me.

Do not worry at all, I promise you; I'll be back before nightfall." As the men hurried me down the road to my pending death, I thought very carefully to myself how convenient it would have been for the men of our community (especially my father-in-law) to watch me be killed in the manner chosen.

My death by burning would send a message to the women in my predicament, not to do what I was being accused of doing. As for the co-signing men of our community, because it was not known among them, who had fathered my child, this act would surely burn up the evidence of their own indiscretions before my child had a chance to be born with the face and DNA of its' father.

However, the two who stood to gain the most by my death were Shelah and my father-in-law, Judah. Young Shelah was off the hook; he was no longer obligated by the "Levirate Law" to marry me. He was free to marry another. This, among other things, was a relief to my father-in-law.

Not sure if I was cursed or not, he would no longer have to be afraid or tossed in his emotions as to whether to send Shelah to me or not and, I would no longer be tied to him. He would no longer have to live with the guilt of not taking care of me or betraying me. Sending my child and me up in smoke would also ensure he would not have to see every day what his deception led my desperation to do. My father-in-law was a man of great pride. Talk about a cover-up; the answer to his problem would have been, me and my baby's ashes.

Your Honor, the closer I got to the council's circle, I could see smoke going up and hear the voices of the people. Sounding like an angry mob, they were shouting, "Burn, her! Burn her! Burn that harlot! I was calm because I knew I would not burn, once my message reached Judah, everything would turn! When I got within earshot range of my father-in-law, I covertly removed his credentials from under my widow's covering and gave them to his messenger along with a message. And well, this is what happen:

"It was while she (Tamar) was being brought out that she sent to her father-in-law, saying, "I am with child by the man to whom these things belong." And she said, "Please examine and see, whose signet ring and cords and staff are these?"

(Gen 38:25)

"Your Honor, the color immediately rushed out of my father-in-law's face, when he recognized the seal, cord, and staff to be his."

Everyone in the courtroom looked directly at Judah. This caused him to bury his face in his hands. Not sure what Tamar was going say next, he began to weep. He remembered that day. Tamar turned to the judge and said,

Your Honor,

> Judah recognized them, and said, "She is more righteous
> than I, in as much as I did not give her to my son Shelah."
> And he did not have relations with her again."

(Gen 38:26)

After Judah made his announcement, the fire on the ground was immediately stamped out. However, the angry faces and shouts from the mob (especially Hirah) to burn me up, dissipating, was replaced with a different kind of follow-up; "ash" (a)we (s)hock and (h)ow did this happen?

Running to my side, my father -in-law personally and profusely apologized to me. I was not cursed. He was living proof. He had unknowingly been intimate, with me and lived. He vowed that day to never have relations with me again and to take good care of me and our child. This time when we walked away from each other, what was once concealed, had been revealed, to heal.

After releasing me, I was safely escorted back to my father's house. I arrived before nightfall, just as I promised. Meeting me at the door, I explained everything to him, he wept for joy. Approximately six months later, I gave birth to twin boys. My midwife is here in the courtroom if you wish to call on her for that account.

Judge: Yes, I would, Midwife will you please take the stand, and remember you are under oath.

(Tamar's Midwife takes the stand)

Judge: Good afternoon. Were you present at the birth, and if so, can you tell the court what happened?

> Midwife: Well, Your Honor, "It came about at the time she was giving birth, that behold, there were twins in her womb, moreover, it took place while she was giving birth, one put out a hand, and the midwife took and tied a scarlet thread on his hand, saying, "This one came out first." But it came about as he drew back his hand, that behold, his brother came out. Then she said, "What a breach you have made for yourself!" So, he was named Perez. Afterward, his brother came out who had the scarlet thread on his hand; and he was named Zerah."

(Gen 38:27-30)

Judge: Thank you for your testimony. You may step down.

Judge: Sir Judah, it appears Tamar is almost finished with her testimony; please prepare yourself to speak when she is done.

Tamar looking up at the judge with her eyes exposed said, "Your Honor, thank you for allowing me to speak today. In closing, I would like to acknowledge my father-in-law.

Changing her tone, she said; "Your Honor, although my father-in-law defrauded me with his son Shelah, the day he had me seized and brought to him, after he recognized his credentials, I looked into the soul of his eyes, I saw and felt his embarrassment, pain, and appreciation that I had not exposed him publicly. I also saw his repentance. His immediate response of love covered me against the people who were prepared to burn me and my unborn alive without cause. Looking in his eyes that day, it was as if everything he had done wrong was standing in front of him embodied in me.

Mirrored in me, he saw his own reflection. His soul through his eyes was an open book, with messages bookmarked from his earlier days when he left his father Israel and his brothers, to calling for me to be brought before him to be burned, not stoned, which is the actual punishment by law for the crime I was accused of. And what about him? Accordingly, as my accomplice, he should have been sentenced to death too. (ref: Deut Chapter 22)

For thinking I was cursed because of the death of his two sons, it was as though he realized at that moment; the guilty had to be his sons and not me. Otherwise, how was he was still standing among us in the land of living after not only laying with me but impregnating me? I almost thought I saw him pinch himself. You see, what he did not know was seated in the core of my heart's crave, were graves and an unfulfilled promise. A promise I suspect that even in our dysfunction, is a part of God's divine purpose and plans to come, way beyond our years.

My father-in-law is a great man of God, favored and honored among men. Finally, Your Honor, let the record show, I am not here today for revenge or to slander his good name. Er, was my first husband, and I had a responsibility to cooperate with the law of his land on his behalf. I wanted to ensure there would be seed for his legacy. As it turns out, Judah's seed appropriated, proved to be the better choice than his sons. If I stand accused of anything, it is that I manipulated their law, to fulfill it.

"Waving her hand, signaling the bailiff to open the back doors of the courtroom, Tamar turned to the Judge, then to Judah. With a smile of gratitude to God on her face, she watched the fruit of her faith and accomplishment be wheeled into the courtroom in their double-seated stroller.

Pointing at them, she said, "Your Honor, these are my star witnesses, Zerah and Perez. They, too, are the sons of Judah! Judge Deborah stood up and took a good look at their faces, raised her gavel, and pronounced from the highest seat in the courtroom, "Judah, you are the father!" Everyone started cheering aloud. The repeated banging from the judge's gavel and the command in her voice for order in the court, simmered things down. Although she was smiling, she reminded everyone court was still in session. Judge Deborah looking over at Judah, asked if he was ready to present his defense. It took him a couple of minutes to collect himself. Overwhelmed, the judge patiently waited for his response. Standing to his feet, it appeared he was struggling with what to say or if he should even speak.

Once he found his voice, this is what he said:

> "Thank you, Judge, for allowing me to speak. I did not prepare an argument or a defense because I have none, so I will speak from my heart. Everything my daughter-in-law stood before you today and said is accurate. I want to say a few things to clarify and support her testimony. First, let me say, my daughter-in-law is an amazing woman and mother. Only God can see through our actions to the core of our heart.
>
> He saw the full content of hers. Tamar was protecting my deceased son Er's legacy. Advocating for us all, she stayed willing to do what needed to be done to fulfill the" Levirate Law" for us in her homeland. Her

faithfulness led her to strategize. She chose to go about things in a different way, still, she was more honorable than I. Understanding God works through willing individuals; she was the willing one in our crisis. When my second son Onan died, I was sore afraid. The scent of Shelah, possibly dying too, was as strong as the smell of ammonia, so I sent her back to her father's house under the guise of a widow in waiting.

Then when my wife died, my world was completely shattered. I was afraid. All I had left was my youngest son. I did not want to lose him too. I despised my dilemma. I made the decision not to send Shelah to Tamar. It was my choice, not his. I also had no plans of releasing her by letting her have her day in court before the elders of Israel.

I was ashamed and did not want to run the risk of inquiry or their rightfully so, "I told you so." Your Honor, my daughter-in-law, would have been well within her rights to accused Onan and Shelah before them, spit in their faces, remove their sandals and have it declared; 'In Israel, his name shall be called, 'The house of him whose sandal is removed.' (ref: Deut 25:5-10)

I was thinking about how bad this would have made me look, too. Everything changed the day I unknowingly proposition her by the roadside. Although she knew who I was, I did not know who she was. My daughter-in-law was not a harlot; she was a widow seeking justice. When Hirah went to pay my debt and retrieve my pledge, she was nowhere to be found. You were right, Your Honor. I was embarrassed and did not want it to get out that I had been tricked by a phantom temple harlot.

Rather than go and find the perceived prostitute myself, I was willing to walk around without identification, than be thought a fool. If my credentials were to show up later, I was prepared to say I had lost them. Covertly serving my need, I unknowingly fulfilled hers. Focused, she used finesse, not force, to achieve her end. When she was thought to be an unknown harlot to me, I used her, and when I was told she had played the harlot for someone else and was pregnant, I judge her. I was prepared to honor my vow to a perceived temple prostitute, over my word to my daughter-in-law, and for that; I am truly sorry.

In tears, Judah turned to Tamar and said:

"I violated you emotionally and criminally. Guilty, I broke the law! Though I tried to vilify you, how you chose to deal with the abandonment and offense you received at my hand was a wake-up call for me. The day I embarrassed you, no doubt, having you removed from your home and brought to the public square with plans to have you and the babies you were carrying burned, that unbeknownst to me were my sons, my heirs, you responded with love, grace, and mercy.

Using extreme discretion, you made me aware in private, that by way of my indiscretion, I was the father.

Instead of exposing me publicly, you did for me, what I should have done for you. My dear, you covered me. You did not expose me, but my God did. That is why publicly, I needed to apologize to you for the wrong you suffered for my poor decisions. I spoke highly of you then and now because even at that moment, your focus was honor, not just for Er, but for my unborn sons and me. At the door of death, your priority was to protect our family's name and legacy.

Thank you for your faith and steadfastness. You are a great asset to our family. Though I lost two sons, Er and Onan, God through you have blessed me with two more. Zerah and Perez are my beloved sons, who I believed are destined for greatness. Thank you, Tamar. I honor you and your sacrifice. You are a humble yet fiercely courageous woman. You will be honored throughout the ages. Thank You, Your Honor, for allowing me to respond by sharing my testimony."

Looking over at the twelve jurors, this what Judge Deborah said:

"Jurors, thank you for traveling from the "House of Israel." Thank you for responding to do your civic duty. However, there will be no need for deliberations. Judah, of his own accord, has declared his guilt, and Tamar has stated she wishes not to seek revenge or punishment. Let this be entered into record and let that record publicly show; their agreed disposition will serve as the verdict.

Judge: Judah and Tamar, please approach the bench...

"To you both, let me say, it has been my distinct honor and pleasure to preside over this case. You have given us all an opportunity to see your story from a different vantage point, and for that, I say, "Thank You."

Tamar, you are a phenomenal young woman. During my research, I discovered your name means "PALM TREE." Judging this case out of biblical history, for me, has the feel of Prophecy!

"Now Deborah, a prophetess, the wife of Lappidoth, was judging Israel at that time. She used to sit under the "PALM TREE" of Deborah between Ramah and Bethel in the hill country of Ephraim; and the sons of Israel came up to her for judgment."

(Judges 4:4-5)

Thank you for the courage and love you displayed in my courtroom today. May the commitment you continue to demonstrate on behalf of your family go down in history as a beckon of light in spirit for those who feel hopeless. May they be encouraged to pray and persevere with the understanding that God will make a way...

Sir Judah, Tamar said it best, you are a great man of honor. Thank you for publicly repenting on behalf of your daughter-in-law, covering her, and recovering your family. May others draw strength from your humility and love. Let me also take this time to remind you of something else that is vastly important." Standing up Judge Deborah said:

Look around this courtroom. Your family is here, including your kinsmen. Please take the time after court to greet one another in love.

You may disagree on where to live or even how to live, but as you can see from the hearing today, family is of the utmost importance, it is the bedrock of who we are. Judah, your name means "Praise." Just as your mother, Leah, realized she had much to be thankful to God for, so do you. Therefore, you should lift your hands to God in total "Praise!"

> "And she conceived again and bore a son and said, "This time I will praise the Lord." Therefore, she named him Judah. Then she stopped bearing."

(Genesis 29:35)

Finally, I would like to share this remarkable find...

> "During my lunch hour, I did some research on the "Levirate Law." I found a specific clause I want to illuminate. Tamar, your midwife's testimony in part was:

> "This one came out first, Zerah." But it came about as he drew back his hand, that behold, his brother came out. Then she said, "What a BREACH you have made for yourself!" So, he was named Perez."

BREACH means:

"To break or act contrary to a law or promise, denoting in some way the breaking of a rule or order, upsetting the normal or desired state."

Tamar, if you look at what happened during the birthing order of your sons, your babies tell a unique story of what happened between you, and your father-in-law. "Zerah," like you Judah, attempting to lead and do things your way, stuck his hand out first. Identified and marked, he "drew back his hand." He is technically the firstborn son slated to fulfill the seed legacy for your late son Er.

Tamar, you, wrestled in "your wound" and "Perez" like you, wrestled in "your womb." Creating a BREACH, both of you em (Er) ging, OVERCAME, and PREVAILED! You became a mother and honored your late husband, and Perez being the last, fully entered the world first! I believe this will be of great spiritual significance in the years to come.

"So the last shall be first, and the first last."

(Matthew 20:16)

As for the clauses I am referencing, in the "Levirate Law," it states:

> "It shall be that the firstborn whom she bears shall assume the name of his dead brother so that his name will not be blotted out from Israel."

(Deut 25: 6)

Judah and Tamar, as God would have it, Er's name and legacy are not honored once but twice (Z'Er'ah and P'Er'ez). He has given you, "Double for your Trouble!"

> "Now to Him who is able to do far more abundantly beyond all that we ask or think, according to the power that works within us, to Him be the glory in the church and in Christ Jesus to all generations for-ever. Amen."

(Ephesians 3:20-21)

Court is adjourned...

And it is so...

All Mysteries Belong to Sovereign God...

"Out of this mess, came a message that brought us the MESSIAH!"

Hallelujah to the Lamb of God!

"Let (His)tory reflect, all were chosen to be in the lineage of Christ. May God Be Glorified, in the Highest!"

Recorded in the Genealogy of the Messiah, Yeshua, Jesus the Christ:

> "The record of the genealogy of Jesus the Messiah, the son of David, the son of Abraham: Abraham was the father of Isaac, Isaac, the father of Jacob, and Jacob the father of Judah and his brothers. JUDAH, the father of PEREZ and ZERAH by TAMAR, Perez was the father of Hezron, and Hezron, the father of Ram." (ref: Matthew 1:1-3 in part)

And...

> "So, the last shall be first, and the first last."

(Matthew 20:16)

THE SUMMARY...

This story is a wonderful example of God's Sovereign Grace. Despite their deeds of the flesh, Judah and Tamar were selected to be in the lineage of the Messiah, God's PLAN of REDEMPTION.

> "The Lord Almighty has sworn, "Surely, as I have planned, so it will BE, and as I have purposed, so it will HAPPEN." (Isa 14:24 NIV)

> "Then I began to weep greatly because no one was found worthy to open the book or to look into it; and one of the elders *said to me, "Stop weeping; behold, the LION that is FROM THE TRIBE OF JUDAH, the Root of David, has overcome so as to open the book and its seven seals."

(Revelation 5:4-5)

In choosing to separate from his father, Israel, and his brothers, Judah wanted to make a life for himself in Canaan. Not long after arriving, he saw and married a Canaanite woman and fathered three sons with her. We can gather from that he had plans to stay and thrive among the Canaanites. When tragedy strikes, not once, not twice, but three times, losing two of his three sons back-to-back and then his wife, it is understandable why he would be afraid to release his last son, his only remaining heir. In losing his sons and his wife, it does not appear he entertained the idea; he might be the one who was cursed. After all, he was the common denominator. He was the one who went against his father's wishes and chose to live among the Canaanites, then marry a Canaanite woman.

He also selected a Canaanite woman for his eldest son, Tamar. Her only crime was her hope and cooperation, which eventually became her father-in-law's conflict and contradiction. Onan, his second son in choosing to spill his seed before the Eyes of God was offensive and the equivalent to the spilling of generations! Because of Tamar's discretion concerning the matter, instead of exposing him, she chose to wait for her father-in-law's decision and timing as she was betrothed to her late husband's next in line brother, Shelah.

This was in accordance with the law of his people (Israelites), not hers. After waiting and waiting, she did what she felt she had to do. Determining her father-in-law had obviously changed his mind, her focus, her mission, her need, was for seed, not greed, and Judah would have to do. Selecting the perfect time after the sheep shearing festival when Judah returning, would pass by her way, likely happy from drinking, and ready to lay and play, Tamar veiled, positioned herself and waited.

The deal was made and the deed was done, with the price temporarily being a promissory note (his seal, cord, and staff). I ask you, who would trust a prostitute with their credentials (identification, credit cards etc...)? I'm not surprised when Hirah went to exchange Judah's items for him; the woman he had laid with was not there and when Judah was told about Tamar's indiscretion, he saw the perfect opportunity to be rid of her. Judging her and requesting she be burned immediately would take care of two problems with one burn; He could blame her publicly for being impatient and cursed for sinning.

That would possibly validate suspicions in their community surrounding her and the deaths of his two sons. Therefore, making it appear, he had used great wisdom in withholding Shelah from her. Most of all, he would be absolved of his responsibility to her and for her. He would never have to see her face again. Having their exposure covered by love, wisdom, mercy, and grace, Judah repents, and Tamar is honored. Her mission would not be aborted but rather celebrated.

This portion reminds me of the woman in John, chapter eight, who was caught in adultery. The scribe and the Pharisees brought her to Jesus while he was teaching, testing Him; they demanded she be stoned for being caught in the act of adultery. Jesus using His finger, responded by bending down and writing something on the ground.

Because they persisted, He stood up and said, "He who is without sin among you, let him be the first to throw a stone at her" (In Tamar's case, it would have been he who is without sin, let him strike the first match!) Stooping down again, Jesus began to write. One by one, starting with the oldest of her accusers, they walked away. Where was the one, she was caught in the act with? And who among her accusers were guilty of laying with her at some point? Speculating, it's highly possible it was their names that were written on the ground. Left standing alone with Jesus, vindicated, He admonishes her to go and sin no more. (ref; John 8 3-11)

Vindicated, Tamar, a Canaanite woman married into the family of Judah, "grafted in," she became one with his family. During the birthing process, Zerah sticking his hand out first, was identified and marked. However, Perez is described as bulldozing past him to enter the world fully, first, therefore seizing the birthright, by emerging completely. This is a case where "Almost doesn't count."

Consider by some to be the weaker of the twins, he (Perez) was strong where he needed to be, the womb, a place of incubation. The takeaway lessons from this story for the believer in Christ; we must learn never to underestimate the purposes found and fought in tight places. In them, we grow, become healthier, wiser, or the opposite. Sometimes, in need of learning patience, discipline, or gratitude, in tight places, we are reduced in strength, restricted to shed fear or pride. Becoming humble, we emerge, walking in completeness, in Christ.

> "Transformation only becomes a tragedy when patience is not allowed to have her perfect work."

> "But let patience have her perfect work, that ye may be perfect and entire, wanting nothing." (James 1:4)

God bless you,
Deidra

SPIRITED LIFE (IN PART) BY ANDREW WILSON...

The line-jumper is named Perez, which means breach or break-through. The one with the scarlet cord is called Zerah, which means dawn or rising. In those two names is found the heart of the gospel.

The world looks for a Zerah. We want a king who rises up and shines like the dawn. We want the firstborn, with a mark of royalty on his fist. But God chooses Perez, the boy of the breach, the child of break-through. He wants the sort of king we never would choose: a younger, weaker boy, without the obvious ...

Sum of it all...

> "But God has chosen the foolish things of the world to shame the wise, and God has chosen the WEAK things of the world to shame the things which are strong and the base things of the world and the despised God has chosen, the things that are not, so that He may nullify the things that are, so that no man may boast before God." (1 Corinthians 1:27-29)

PART TWO

IN HER SHOES
(TRIALS)

#1

CODE BLUE

"Code Blue! Code Blue! There's an emergency in room #222! Erlene was on top of Gigi beating her black and blue! Don't call for the doctor don't call for the nurse; call for the police, a priest, and possibly a hearse!"

Jude Johnson and Erlene met in college when they were both eighteen. Sitting in orientation with over five thousand other excited new freshmen, they spotted each other seated on the same row at the same time. Most of the introduction and instructions from Dean Howard speaking from the podium was wasted on Erlene's ears, she was distracted. She did hear Dean Howard raise her voice and say, "While you are here, your helicopter parents are not! You will be responsible, for being responsible. You will meet new people, make lifelong friends, join sororities, and be introduced to many new things.

Some of you will even meet your spouse here." Erlene was excited and afraid to look at the handsome young man on her row. She thought if she was looking at him, he was probably still looking at her. Giving her an excuse, Dean Howard, instructing everyone, said, "Turn around and look at the person behind you, on both sides of you, then down your row in each direction."

After pausing for about thirty seconds, she removed the microphone from its stand, stepped from behind the podium, and said, "At the end of this semester, one-fourth of you will not be here. Furthermore, by the beginning of your senior year, that number will have increased to half." As far as Erlene was concerned, the Dean could have dropped the mic after that mind-blowing prediction. She went from not paying attention to the speaker to being slightly spooked by her words.

Following Dean Howard's instructions, giving and receiving uncertain looks from her peers, she determined she was not going to make up those fractions. An only child, her parents had saved over the years for her college education. She had done her part in working hard to get there, too. She would not let herself or them down. Erlene decided in that moment; she would stay focus and finish well, by any means necessary. Just as she thought to think what could possibly cause the speaker to predict such a massive exodus, Dean Howard offered her explanation in the form of a shortlist; academic failure, failure to pay, and failure to behave.

Looking over the room, she gave a specific warning to the female freshmen; "failure to protect themselves!" The last thing on her list seem to have a personal feel to it. Erlene determined she would work on figuring that out later, though there would be no need. Dean Howard explained that too. Shev shared that over the years she had witnessed many promising "filly freshmen" women come from all over the world in pursuit of an education. Unfortunately, they ended up leaving prematurely because they had gotten caught up with a wild stallion, got pregnant, and chose to drop out. The room was quiet. The girls who were previously scanning the room inconspicuously, eyeing all the cute guys, were mentally slapped into reality, including Erlene.

The guys on the other hand looked straight ahead, appearing not to identify as a stallion, the one to cause such a fate to befall the female, freshmen, fillies. The Dean ending her talk, told everyone her door was always open if they ever needed to talk. For Erlene, during her first three years, it was a revolving door. Jude Johnson, like most of the other male freshmen and upper-level students, gave the new female freshmen a few weeks to get settled in their dorms, discover their newfound freedom, and forget Dean Howard's stern warnings.

Petite and cute, Erlene had her share of campus stalkers. They came in all shapes, sizes, and colors. No one stalked her harder than the guy she locked eyes with during orientation, Jude Johnson. He was tall and fine. He had a pair of hazel eyes that made up twenty-five percent of his charm; he was a walking one-fourth threat. Erlene determining not to forfeit her education, spent a lot of time talking to Dean Howard. Between talking to the Dean and watching her predictions come true, by the beginning of her fourth year of college, Erlene felt safe enough to agree to a date with Jude Johnson.

She had dated a few other guys over the years, but because she wasn't attracted to them, she was able to kill a few birds with one unmovable stone. She partied, made new friends, and kissed a few guys and liked it, but the promise she made to herself when she entered college, she kept. Erlene remembered asking Dean Howard why (during orientation) she referred to female freshmen as fillies. The Dean told her she had come from a family who raised horses, and she found them to be beautiful, gracefully, impressionable creatures. To her, they were gentle, smart, but vulnerable. However, when allowed to grow properly, they become strong enough to carry loads, trot for miles, gallop pristinely or run as fast as a high horse-powered sports car. In a race, coming around the stretch, neck, and neck, they would fight to the finish and win. Correlating the two, Dean Howard explained:

"A filly is a female horse under four years old. A mare is an adult female horse." She further educated her by telling her a young male horse is considered a colt and adult males come in two categories, horses (castrated), and stallions (not castrated), with the latter being preserved for breeding.

Looking around in "awe" at the beautiful paintings of all sorts of horses on Dean Howard's walls in different stages of their lives, Erlene asked her if she had painted them? She told Erlene her seventeen- year-old niece was the up-and-coming artist. Locking her eyes on a particular painting, Dean Howard walked over and explained that it was one of her favorites. It was a painting of a group female fillies grazing together, undisturbed. She told Erlene it reminded her of how essential the first three years of college for freshmen females are.

Discovery, and discarding occurs in that season. Making room for new cultivations and growth, they are positioned to choose new paths or hold on to old ones. Transformed they follow their voices, affecting chosen change in their lives. She also told Erlene, that most students (male and female), by the end of their third year of college, have matured emotionally and socially and in most most cases, have identified their career paths, choosing to further their education, or pursue a career in their major or minor studies.

Erlene saw herself in that painting. By her fourth year of college, no longer a filly, but compared to a mare, Jude Johnson pursued who and what he had majored in the previous three years, her. Sweeping her off her feet, they made plans to be each other's graduation present. After their class walked across the stage and received their diplomas, some walked back into school, furthering their education. Many walked into jobs waiting for them, while some drove off in new cars and others enjoyed elaborate graduation parties.

Jude and Erlene walked into each other's arms. Prancing their way down the justice of the peace, they got married. They eloped, then galloped, happily side by side down their trail into the next twenty-seven years of marriage. One day while stepping out the barn and roaming in the pasture, Mr. Johnson spotted another young wild filly standing idly by on his track, swishing her tail back and forth. Literally catching his eye, he chose to trot after her.

Code Blue! Code Blue!

There's an emergency in room #222! Erlene was on top of Gigi beating her black and blue! Don't call for the doctor, don't call for the nurse; call for the police, a priest, and possibly a hearse! The police needed to come because two grown women were tussling in room #222. They needed a priest because the paralyzed patient they were fighting in front of looked like he was coding and turning blue!

The horrid look in the eyes of the man lying in bed who could not speak held overwhelming evidence; his trespassing and treason was the reason for the smackdown brawl. Two hospital security guards entered the room and tried but failed miserably at any attempt to separate the women. Each were screaming at the other; they had a right to be there! In walked Angela, the nurse on duty assigned to Mr. Johnson.

Standing a little over 4ft tall, weighing in at around 115 pounds, soaking wet, she threw her hands up in the air and yelled, "Silence!" Silence immediately filled the air. Minus the heavy breathing from the women and the security guards, you could hear the drip-drop, coming from Mr. Johnson's I.V. Taking command of the room, she ordered everybody out! The two women walked out on their own, with the security guards following close behind them in a single file line. Mr. Johnson could still hear the women outside his room.

Though they had calmed down, given what he had just witnessed, that state of calm would be temporary at best. After adjusting his pillow, nurse Angela looking at him and shook her head. Mr. Johnson knew why. Within minutes, just as he predicted, the women's voices started to climb again.

Angela bending over her patient as if they were in a football huddle, told him he needed to call the next play. Knowing he could not speak, she looked at him and said, "Now Mr. Johnson, one of them will have to leave. Which one do you want to stay? By law, your spouse has the right to be here; she is legally your next of kin, unless you have made other documented arrangements.

However, if you want the woman you have been with for the last two years to stay, I will speak with your wife and explain your wishes. Respectfully, I can ask the one you choose to leave if they would like to come back tomorrow." Looking in his eyes, she told him to blink once for his wife and twice for his co-habiting girlfriend. Instead, he blinked frantically, squeezing out tears. She gathered his tears resulted from her identifying Gigi, the woman he had lived with for the last couple of years, as his "co-habitant girlfriend."

He hadn't thought about describing her that way. Steady tears fell from his eyes, and because Angela could not get a read on who he wanted to stay and who he wanted to go, she told him she would decide. Mr. Johnson appeared to have exhaled. He trusted his nurse to make the right decision. After all, he had just watched this little powerhouse nurse single handily quiet, then clear his room.

Because she had spoken with both women separately: at one time, or another, with the insight she had, he knew she would handle the situation. He was glad he didn't have to choose. After checking his vital signs and comfort level, she turned and left him lying in his bed to deal with the lies compiled in his head. Far from dead, it was time for him to deal with his runaway truth instead. There was no need for a priest.

A steady stream of tears fell from his eyes as he thought about the physical altercation, he had just witnessed between his longtime mare (wife) and his two-year filly (girlfriend). It was all his fault. Taking longer than expected for one of the women to come back into his room, his mind replayed the words they screamed at each other during their fight. Dialoguing with himself, he allowed his mind to travel back in time to the day he first saw a beautiful young woman he decided within minutes was going to be his wife.

He pursued her for three years before she consented to date him. He finally wore her down. Putting his best foot forward, he treated her like a queen. Not wanting to lose her because she was so fine, he wined and dined her, until finally, she signed. Married in court by the "Justice of the Peace" on their graduation day, he remembered how excited Erlene was. She didn't care who saw her elation.

As predicted by Dean Howard, they were among the small fraction of students who had met their spouse in college. As far as she was concerned, she had met and married the love of her life. He was not a wealthy man, but his pursuit of her was priceless. He had watched her blossom from a filly to a mare, and when she had fulfilled her promise of obtaining a degree in early childhood education, he was right there. After they married, he went back to graduate school.

He worked two jobs to put himself through school and to help take care of their young marriage. Aware of who she was, as far as Erlene was concerned, he had netted a great catch too! She landed a job in her major, "Early Childhood Education." Though her job did not pay much, being around little people, helping them develop their young minds was her reward. Jude loved her because she was LOVING, KIND, BEAUTIFUL, FUNNY, SMART, STRONG, RESOURCEFUL, and a FIGHTER.

She lived and thrived well in those first four qualities in the first twenty-six years of their marriage. However, in their twenty-seventh year, the last four qualities, is where she found herself grazing.

SMART, STRONG, RESOURCEFUL, and a FIGHTER, those were the qualities his behavior challenged in her in their upcoming changing years. Jude Johnson remembered standing not once but twice next to her at the altar to be married. First, in front of the magistrate when they eloped as young adults and again for their twenty-fifth silver anniversary when they renewed their vows in the wedding of her dreams.

After their twenty-six years of marriage, with no children born out of their union, he remembered, his mind started to wonder. Not long afterward, his eyes began to wander. He loved his wife but was aware their chances of having the baby he had promised her had evaporated. Erlene knew her husband loved her. She, too, remembered him telling her when they married, he was looking forward to having a son who looked like him, a daughter who looked like her, or both.

Erlene smiling, said she wanted that too. When he married her, on their wedding night, he was surprised to discover he was her first, though they both knew she was not his first. Having experienced more than his share of women, he felt he had been given a gift, a virtuous wife. Laying in his hospital bed, he found himself reciting their vows in his head;

"I take thee Erlene to be my lawfully wedded wife, to have and to hold, from this day forward, for better, for worse, for richer, for poorer, in sickness and in health, to love and to cherish, till death do us part, according to God's holy ordinance; I pledge myself to you."

Most of that vow for most of their marriage, he honored. He did love his wife, but there was no child(ren) to solidify their union. Per their spoken vow, they held each other in good times and bad (for better and worst). Their love was the glue that held them together in poor times when they first married. Growing together made it easy to celebrate their love during their rich (financially comfortable) season. Both had been through bouts of sickness and good health over the years and was always there to take care of one another.

Examining their vows closer, he could not ignore the three things from his vow he did not keep and the one major thing that remained: He did not cherish her, death had not occurred for them to be apart, and to his God, he did not keep the promise he made in accordance to God's holy ordinance; the pledging of himself to her only. And then there was the one thing that remained, completely tipping the scale. His nurse was right, lawfully, and legally; Erlene was still his wife.

After some time had passed, the door opened. In walked nurse Angela. Singing one of her gospel hymns to herself, she checked his vitals, changed his bedpan and his I.V. The whole time, he was attempting to get her attention with his eyes. Just as she was about to leave, he stretched them as wide open as he could. Laughing lightly, she said,

"I'm sorry, Mr. Johnson I forgot to come back and tell you. I didn't have to choose. Your lady friend was demanding that your personal items be given to her and because she wouldn't calm down, she was made to leave. Sure, he wanted to know why his wife did not come back in, Angela said, "Oh, by the way, your wife left first. She decided she did not want to come back in." His eyes could not hide his disappointment.

Nurse Angela stepped up as close as she could, leaned over and spoke to him in a suggestive manner. She said, "Mr. Johnson, I know you have a daughter with your girlfriend, but you also have a wife of almost thirty years. I can't tell you who or what is most important to you, but I will say this, pray, and ask God to help you.

There were two women here physically fighting today, and please don't take this the wrong way, given the shape you're currently in, and judging by the things I heard come from the tunnels of their hearts and exit through their mouths, trust me, they were not fighting each other over the physical you. For very different reasons, they were fighting for their place of relevance with you. At his nurse's last statement, Mr. Johnson closed his eyes to keep from adding more tears to his already wet face. This was a mess, and he had caused it. Nurse Angela grabbed a soft tissue and wiped his eyes. She told him because he needed to rest, his doctor had prescribed a mild sedative for him through his I.V. to help him sleep. Smiling, she informed him, she was going to be off for the next few days. She winked and told him she was going to pray for him and his situation.

Balling her fist up, she started punching at the air like a boxer. Laughing she said "Just because you can't fight in the natural, don't mean you can't use your heart, mind and spirit to fight. First, you have to sur-render and be honest with God. He already knows everything about everybody. Ask Him to help you. I promise you, He will."

For the first time since suffering his stroke, his eyes smiled. Once his nurse left the room, knowing he only had a few minutes before the sedative would kick in overtaking him, he decided to start where he detoured.

Two years ago, he and Erlene had gotten into the worst argument of their twenty-seven-year marriage. He started it. Having had minor arguments and disagreements over the years, nothing ever rose to the level of threats, specifically the threat to leave. Mr. Johnson remembering what his nurse said about God knowing everything about everybody. Inwardly he had to admit; he had planned the argument and its outcome weeks before it happened.

He had an agenda. Seemingly out of nowhere, nothing she said or did was right, prompting him to respond by giving her the silent treatment. When he did speak to her, it was to complain about everything from her cooking and cleaning to her appearance. Exaggerating her weight gain, she sensed something was going on with him. Erlene, being SMART, saw through his charade and called a spade a spade. Being married to him for as long as she had, she knew her man.

This was not original. However, she was tired of him starting stuff with her for no reason, so she called his bluff. This time he had a reason; her name was Gigi. He and his wife were forty-nine, Gigi was thirty, and smoking hot! He met her at the eye mart. He had gone alone to get his eyes examined. He was not wearing his wedding band. Gigi was the clerk who fitted him for his new eyeglasses. After his exam, she saw embarrassment on his face. Aging, his vision had changed; he had graduated to bifocals.

Sensing he was uncomfortable with his new vision reality, Georganne introduced herself then offered him a comforting compliment. Looking directly into his eyes, she told him the worst thing about him having to wear glasses was, his beautiful "hazelicious" eyes were going to be hidden behind them. His blush invited her next suggestion, contact lens. He left that day but returned two weeks later. In retrospect,

Mr. Johnson now knew what he did not know then, she worked on commission.

When he returned, Georganne invited him to call her by her nickname, Gigi. She convinced him to buy a backup pair of glasses and a transition pair, specifically for night driving. Although he rarely left the house after dark, he bought them because she told him to. She also talked him into purchasing a subscription of disposable contacts by offering to stand over him and help him insert them. By the third time he had gone back to purchase a cleaning kit, he had worked up the nerve to ask her if he could buy her lunch for being so helpful.

This was a few days before his planned argument with his wife, Erlene. The day he started in on her, she was ready. As if she had been waiting all week for it, she met him where he was and went off on him. He had pushed her too far. Grabbing the bag, he had already packed and hidden in the basement, he walked out. At the time, unbeknown to him, days before, Erlene found his to-go bag. She added something important to it and subtracted something of value from it, then put it back where he had hidden it and waited. She did not give him a chance to give her a "We need some time apart speech." When he grabbed his bag and walked out the door, she locked it, set the alarm, and went upstairs to bed. He knew this because he heard the alarm activate and saw the light in their bedroom go out before he had a chance to slam his car door. She had foiled his grandstand speech and departure.

He headed to a friend's house, where he stayed for a few weeks before getting his own apartment. In the meantime, through his assisted 20/20 vision, he was clearly seeing Gigi. That young filly made him believe he was a stallion! It was his turn to be stalked. She gave him signs, fed him lines, and in return, he wined, dined, and then had to sign; his name to their daughter's birth certificate! When Gigi told him she was pregnant, she was happy; he was not. She told him she wanted to have a baby and had been trying for some time, and because they were in an exclusive relationship ((though he was married), she was happy to he was going to be her child's father. She said she loved him, and because she was carrying his baby, she wanted him to divorce his wife.

Dazed for days, the bubble he had been flirting with and floating around in for over a year burst the day Gigi's water broke, and their daughter entered the world. Though she was precious and beautiful, he felt guilty for betraying his wife. Jude Johnson was remembering how two weeks after initially leaving, Erlene had reached out to him a few times; she wanted to talk.

Caught up in chasing Gigi around the track, he wished now he would have called her back. He knew Erlene believed she had done the right thing in letting him leave. He also knew it was not pride that stopped her from reaching out to him after he did not respond. She had given him what he thought he wanted. She knew how hard he had pursued her when they first met. His charm had convinced her to elope with him, against what she believed was her parent's best wishes.

Jude thought his wife was probably thinking he was having a mid-life crisis, and instead of buying the red-hot mustang he talked so much about, he chose to chase a red-hot filly. Short of making sure the bills were paid, and she was taken care of through their joint accounts, he assumed Erlene had just decided to saddle up and ride things out while letting whatever had gotten into his system ride its way out! When he didn't respond to her calls, two weeks turned into months. While he thought he was having a good time, she had shifted to her position of STRONG.

He believed she missed him, and whenever he decided he didn't want to run around the track anymore, he could just trot on up to his old barn open his stall, shake off his riding shoes and resume his old way of living. He was Erlene's first, and only, she was a safe bet, his sure thing. He was willing to bet the farm ten to one; she would take him back. Knowing his wife, he also knew his window of opportunity would eventually close.

Not very original, he made plans to pick a break-up, with no chance to make-up, fight with Gigi. Three days before his planned showdown with her, he called Erlene and left a voicemail message; he wanted to talk to her, he missed her. She texted him and agreed to meet him at a nearby restaurant for dinner. He was a "no show." He never made it out the gate. He stood Erlene up because Gigi tripped him up. Intercepting the text, he sent his wife on when and where to meet him, Gigi found out about his planned rendezvous.

Looking and smelling good, he told her he was going out with his friend. She smiled, kissed him on his cheek, then stuck her foot out, on his way out, and down he went. Hitting the floor hard, he suffered a mild concussion. He didn't know letting her put him on her phone plan meant, his messages became her messages. This was the first time Mr. Johnson met nurse Angela. Having to stay overnight at the hospital, she was his nurse.

He remembered back then lying in his hospital bed thinking; he wished he had gone back and asked his wife for his wedding band after discovering it was not in his bag a few days after he had left. Erlene found it and removed it from the small Velcro pocket inside of his to-go bag. He wished he had gone back home and gotten into bed with his wife that night instead of doing her wrong, then staying gone too long. Ending up in the hospital with a concussion, he remembered feeling disgusted with himself. He also remembered feeling like he deserved to be where he was.

After all, he had already done to his wife; he added to that by standing her up. Sure, she didn't know why; he remembered planning to see her as soon as he got released from the hospital. He was going to buy her some flowers, a new ring and beg her to take him back. Instead, Gigi met him at the hospital the next day; she was there to pick him up and take him home with her. That was the day everything changed.

Because he did not use the protection his wife had purchased and added to his to-go bag for his sleepover that lasted for months, coming around the stretch bearing stretch marks and a nose spread was Gigi. She had an announcement; she was pregnant! The window of opportunity had closed.

Stopping short of the finish line, all he could do was lie down and play dead. He could not bring himself to call Erlene.

Weeks turned into months, and before he knew it, by the time they spoke, the news of Gigi's pregnancy devastated her. What he had done to his wife devastated him. He could feel the effects of the sedative drips working. Laying in a hospital bed for a second time, this time paralyzed from the neck down in the dark; tears rolled wildly down both sides of his face. There was no controlling them, and there was no one present to wipe them away.

The next morning when he woke up, his day nurse was moving around in his room. She noticed the dry tear stains on the sides of his face. Aware he could not speak, rhetorically, she asked if his tears were from pain he had experienced during the night. Looking at her sarcastically, his eyes responded, "What do you think?" The truth was his mind caused his heart to experience significant pain, producing the tears that had dried on his face during the night.

The day nurse ignored him. Since it was clear she could not read his eyes, he rolled them at her. She was not his favorite nurse. Angela would have understood right away what happened and why. His last thought before she started poking and prodding was, "It's going to be a long weekend." Half of the day had gone by before he was told by the head nurse who stopped in to check on him that because of what happened the day before, it was decided by his doctor, he was not to have any visitors until Tuesday and then only one at a time.

That made him feel better; at least he knew why no one had come. After lunch, he started to think about his last thoughts before dozing off the night before. Remembering what nurse Angela said, he resumed his story with the truth. He remembered the deafening silence he heard on the other end of the phone the day he snuck out of Gigi's apartment and went to his friend's house to use his phone and call Erlene. He told her what happened and why he didn't make it to dinner. More importantly, he told her why he wouldn't be making it home.

Gigi was pregnant. If silence could be measured in octaves, what he heard from his wife's end of the phone was a minus one. Hallucinating, he almost thought he heard her laugh. He didn't; the noise he heard was her tears falling softly. Unable to bear them, he told her he was sorry, he loved her, then he hung up. Looking at his friend, he became angry with him. His foolish friend had encouraged and supported him in leaving his wife. Mr. Johnson couldn't see it then but realized while lying in a hospital bed for a second time; his friend was jealous of his relationship with his wife.

He asked himself why he took advice from a man who constantly stepped out on his wife. A man who, after being gone three days with a woman half his age, suffered a mild heart attack. Then instead of the young woman calling the ambulance, she called him a taxi and sent him back home to his wife! Thank God when he arrived, his wife called 911. Not wanting his minor heart attack to turn into a major one, she rode to the hospital with him.

She waited until she got back home alone later that evening to call her attorney. Days later, when he was released from the hospital, she sent a taxi to pick him up. When he got home and opened the door, she was gone and so was all the furniture. He remembered his friend told him his wife had left two notes. The first one was stuck on the inside of the front door. She had also drawn an arrow with red lipstick from the front door to their back yard, leading him to the second note she left for him. It was held down by a single brick. The first note (from the front door) read:

> "You thought I didn't know what you were up to. You left as my husband; she sent you back as a patient, I don't think so! Let me be clear if you had been home in mind, heart, and body with me and had become a patient, I would have taken very good care of you with great patience. Enjoy your memories.
>
> Signed,
> Out of Patience!

Laughing inside, Mr. Johnson thought he felt his cheekbone move. He always felt like his friend's wife had her suspicions and was waiting for her husband to get caught. I guess he wasn't that original either. Mr. Johnson thought:

What a classic case of the phrase "Birds of a feather flock together."

> "Do not be deceived: "Bad company corrupts good
> morals." Become sober minded as you ought and stop
> sinning; for some have no knowledge of God. I speak
> this to your shame."

(1 Corinthians 15:33-34)

With his mind back on his own situation, he started to worry. His wife was beautiful, and over the years, on a few occasions, he had to shake a stick at a fellow or two from staring at her inappropriately. What if wife had decided the best way to get over him was to get under someone new? The "what if's" jumping around in his mind caused a stampede of thoughts, sending his blood pressure up, bringing his evening nurse into his room. She said nothing. She checked his vitals, changed his bedpan, flipped him over, cleaned him haphazardly, and left. All he could do was cry himself to sleep. He couldn't believe what he had done to himself, his wife, and their life. Uneventful, Sunday and Monday came and went. Tuesday morning, he opened his eyes to find nurse Angela smiling at him. He missed her so much; he smiled back. He was able to move his facial muscles. The doctor told him feeling would start to come back slowly; he was grateful.

Leaning over him for a second time, she told him she had prayed for him over the weekend. This made him smile, showing his teeth. To his surprise, he could, so he thought he would try and speak. Severely slurring his words, it was a start. Nurse Angela smiled broadly; she told him it would only be a matter of time before he would be able to speak words clearly.

His return smile had more to do with her being back than his physical progression. His doctor told him he would likely recover; he expected this. What he had not expected was God using his nurse as a helm, steering him to face his truth and his choice for change. As if she had read his mind, she said, "Mr. Johnson, one of the most powerful changes, is a change of mind. It's a beginning that will surely cause directional change.

> Emotions are strong, but a decision is stronger, it can override everything. Just ask the prodigal son; he did not let embarrassment, fear, filth, gossip, or even the thought of hearing "I told you so" stop him from running home, causing his status to change. Because his father loved him deeply, his return was greatly celebrated.

(ref. Luke 15:11-32)

Mr. Johnson, I pray you choose the tool of change!" Just then, the door opened, in walked Gigi. To Angela's surprise, she had not brought their daughter with her to see her father. As if the nurse was not there, Gigi rushed to Jude's bedside, kissed his forehead, looked in his eyes, and asked how he was doing and if there had been any change. She also asked him if he could he talk?

Mr. Johnson shot his nurse a look. Reading his eyes and the wrinkle lines on his forehead, they read, "please don't tell her anything." Nurse Angela chuckled; he didn't have to worry about her updating Gigi. After all, not only did Gigi not ask her anything; she did not speak to her when she entered the room. Angela looked at him and said, "Mr. Johnson, I'll be back. His eyes following her to the door were screaming, "Don't leave!"

Angela winked and said, "I won't be long." Gigi looked at her as if she had missed something. Fortunately for him, Angela returned just in time to not miss the real reason why Gigi was there. Rifling through his pants pockets, she was looking for something.

Too bad, she had disregarded his nurse. Pretty sure she knew, what Gigi was looking for, Angela said nothing. She knew where his money and credit cards were, in the hospital's safe. Gigi catching Angela, looking at her nonchalantly, commented that she was surprised there had been no change in his condition. Angela said nothing. As soon as Gigi left the room, Angela put her hands on her hips, and jokingly scolded Mr. Johnson for pretending there was no change in his condition.

He gave a mild throaty laugh that quickly turned into moans when the door opened again and in walked his wife. She rushed to his beside. Angela was in shock; their eyes were filled with matching idling tears. Erlene turned to her and said, "Hello," then asked, "How is he doing?" Angela didn't look at her patient for approval. Updating Erlene on her husband's condition, she told her he stood a good chance of making a full recovery over time.

She explained he would be there for a few more days, after which he would be transferred to their in-patient care unit to start his rehabilitation journey. Jude smiled as he watched them converse. He could tell Angela was deeply affected by his wife's sincere concern for her estranged husband's condition. Watching and listening to them talk, he could hear by the tone in his nurse's voice; she understood what was unspoken.

The jewel standing in front of her was enough to make any man want to cry and fight their way back from the brink of death, in his case, paralysis. Erlene asked if there was anything she needed to sign or do to ensure he received the best care. Angela smiled as if that was what she was waiting for, someone she trusted with her patient. Choked up a bit, she left abruptly. When she returned from the nurse's station, she handed Erlene a paper to sign; it was his dinner selection.

Mr. Johnson didn't know what she was signing. He only appreciated she was there signing on his behalf. Angela told Erlene she would give them a few minutes.

Backing out the room, Angela caught a clenching glimpse of her patient's wife's affection as she kissed him on his lips. This made her tear up because she hadn't brushed his teeth yet. His wife's actions proved true love was not deterred by bad breath. Moments later, Erlene opened the door looking up and down the hallway for Angela. She was excited! She told Angela her husband squeezed her hand. Angela smiling, said, "that's great."

She told Erlene once he got transferred to their in-patient unit for therapy, gradual movement would be encouraged, leading to strength training for his entire body. Angela really wanted to say, "Please be there for him; he loves and needs you." She didn't say it. Instead, she prayed it. After Angela sealed her prayer with a silent Amen, Erlene hugged her and said, "Thank you for taking such good care of him." Smiling, she told her she would be back in a couple of days. Walking back into her patient's room, he was all smiles. Flickering his fingers, he wanted her to see he could move them.

Laughing, she said, "Relax lover boy, that beauty who just left already told me you were in here getting fresh with her, puckering your lips and holding her hand. He responded with a complete inaudible sentence; this too was progress. Angela could see he was feeling hopeful. He was happy his wife had returned. Turning to him, she told him it was time for him to have his lunch, followed by a nap.

Before leaving she balled her fist up again and told him to continue praying and fighting. He responded by trying to curl his fingers into a fist, signaling he wanted to fight. Angela's last words before leaving were "She's worth fighting for." Mr. Johnson feeling hopeful, rushed inward to talk to himself and God. First, he thanked God for his body that was slowly recovering, then he spoke sweetly about the woman he loved.

He was sorry for not cherishing her, for stepping out on his love and commitment to her, and for not covering her as he had promised God he would. Repentance was walking through his mind and his heart. He knew the unformed words on his tongue coming from the meditations of his heart had reached God's throne. A bright light shining through his window replaced his fear with faith. God's Peace that passes all understanding, steadied places in him that shook without physically moving him.

Erlene did not say much while she was there with him. What she did say, at the very least, confirmed she too had been praying. She told him she had been spending time with her mother, who encouraged her to pray for him, not their marriage. His mother-in-law, like his nurse, were women who embodied unmistakable evidence that they were in a good relationship with God the Father. Erlene's mother told her the enemy of their soul desires to kill, steal, and destroy, but God wills that no man should perish. That is His priority. (ref: John 10:10) and (ref: 2 Peter 3:9)

While he was sure his wife had not minimized his deceitful act against their marriage, her expressed concern was for his soul. She was still attached to him. Therefore, she had a right to pray for his deliverance.

It did not matter how he came out, only that he did. This made him think about his mother. She, too, was a woman of faith. She told him while she carried him, she was drawn to the book of Jude. She believed someday through that book; he would be drawn into a relationship with the Lord, but not before processing through some things. She did her best to encourage his relationship with the Lord. He was six-teen when she died, but he always remembered her telling him, if he ever felt lost, he should read the book she named him after (Jude) with emphasis on verses seventeen through twenty-five and ask God to help him.

It had been years since he had picked up a bible. Remembering the voice of his mother, he promised himself as soon as he was able to, he would read it. After spending some time in thought, he felt himself getting sleepy. Before succumbing to induced sleep, he felt the gentle kiss print his wife left on his lips and heard the words she whispered in his ear.

She told him she had some things to take care of and would be back again soon. An ugly thought popped into his head, causing his heart rate to accelerate. He thought about the response his friend received from his wife when he had left her for another woman for three days. He had been gone for almost two years, and he had fathered a child while he was out gallivanting. His affair was unfair to his wife. Remembering she was RESOURCEFUL he began to wonder what she was planning to do? His heart and head got into a fight. His voice box broke it up by silently screaming, "Help Lord!"

IN THE MEANTIME...

Erlene left the hospital that day. She had quite a few things she needed to do. First, she went to class; then, she went to see her attorney. During her drive home, she thought about how she spent months feeling sorry for herself after her husband left. She thought about Dean Howard and all the talks they had.

She remembered what she said about a championship mare. Erlene loved her husband, and back then, she wanted nothing more than for him to come back home. She knew when he left, it was a mistake, but she also knew if she had tried to make him stay, it would have only been a matter of time before he would try to find a way to leave again. She felt he had developed an itch and would not have stopped until he got it scratched.

Her mind drifted back to the phone call she received about four months after her husband left. It was the ex-wife of Jude's friend. She had left her husband after he suffered a mild heart, resulting from some little blue pills he had taken that were not prescribed by his doctor. Intoxicated, Erlene remembered Jude's friend's wife saying, "People who cheat (men and women), are like dogs tied up in a yard.

After they mark their home territory, they want to go out and mark others." She said, "tied up, they run up and down their yards growling and barking at anyone who walks by, until eventually, they shake themselves loose from their collars and jump the fence." Erlene recalled her saying, "if the fence is too high, a desperate dog will dig a hole under it to get out! Once out, they go around the neighborhood, collecting bones.

Then they bring them back, dig up your beautiful backyard and bury them there." She went on to say, "if you build a brick base around the bottom of the fence thinking you're going to keep them in, Ha! The joke will be on you. Sniffing around in the middle of night, there they go, digging up your yard, looking for them old bones! Howling, whimpering, and reminiscing, they chew on those buried bones."

Changing her tone, she said, "Er, cheating is way more mental than it is physical. Our bodies follow where our minds lead. If that happens to be away from the person we've vowed to love, after the act of cheating is done, our minds and hearts start fighting cause our body done took over and got us jacked up in some mess! Er, that's what happened to your husband. He started hanging out with mine, and before he knew it, he was itching, barking and growling, too.

Girl, trust me, it won't be long before he'll be laid up somewhere howling from hurting" Funny but not funny, Erlene snickered at the thought of her husband's present state. He had been wounded and was lying up in a hospital bed moaning from roaming. Though the voice on the other end of her phone belonged to a woman who was hurting, she couldn't help but remember thinking the old saying was true, "A drunk mind speaks a sober heart." Everything her caller said was true.

Calling her Er, (the nickname her husband had given her) was comforting. It was as though she was advocating on his behalf without knowing it. Erlene remembered the last thing her intoxicated caller said through her tears, "Er, Jude loves you, point-blank. What he is doing is stupid. He got caught up.

Just give him some time, he'll realize it. He's nothing like my husband who's been cheating on me for years. At first, I didn't say anything, because I didn't know what to say. All I knew was, I didn't want him to leave me.

When I ignored his cheating, it got worst, so I raised the fence and laid down some concrete rules. That didn't help. I could tell, when he was talking to me, he was digging around in the dirt, in his mind." She went on to say, "I couldn't compete with his ghost girlfriends. His cheating started to mess with my self-esteem, so to fight back, I started cheating." Hitting the bottom of her drunk, crying, she said, "Er, don't be like me, you're a good woman, I used to be.

Don't let this make you bitter like it made me. You hang in there; Jude is a good dude who made a bad choice. Take care of yourself for me and enjoy your life. You're a winner! If fact, do me a favor, do something you've always wanted to. I've got to go but first, let me tell you what I did the day I left that man." Laughing out loud, she said, "Girl, when the doctor told me what caused my husband's mild heart attack, I kissed him on his forehead in the hospital, then went straight to the pet store.

I bought a bunch of doggy bones and treats. I came home, went out to our backyard, dug some holes, and put those bones and delights in them, then covered them back up with the dirt. Then I left him two notes and a map telling him to enjoy nibbling and licking on his memories." Erlene remembered laughing so hard, it brought her to tears. She also remembered after hanging up, her tears of laughter quickly turned to tears of pain when she realized she had made the right choice by opening their front gate, unleashing her husband, and letting him walk out without his collar (wedding band).

While she understood and respectfully appreciated the analogies made, he was not a dog any more than she was a horse. They were not animals. They were human beings with free wills who vowed before God to love one another, only. God was at the center of their vow, and before making any rash decision, she needed to consult Him. That's when she started seeking the Face of God. What did He have to say about all of this? After spending months in His word and in a support group at her

70

church, she found her footing. To her surprise, she had some different kinds of buried bones of her own she needed to dig up and deal with.

Spending time with her mother, she discovered she had hurt her parents deeply when she and Jude eloped on their graduation day. Her parents had forgiven them and enjoyed loving them in word and deed over the years and were happy when they chose to renew their vows for their twenty-fifth wedding anniversary. This allowed her father to walk her down the aisle and officially give her away, nine months before he passed, away.

Her mother shared their hearts were broken the afternoon of her graduation when she and Jude disappeared afterward, then showed up at her surprised graduation dinner late and with a surprise of her own. Married, her parents chose to focus on the major of her graduating with honors, and the minor of her meeting and marrying someone without their consent. Her mom shared, they would have appreciated the opportunity to have properly met and vetted her college sweetheart, then offer their blessing.

She was their only child. They were blindsided by her first post-graduate decision. They raised her to be an independent thinker; therefore, they decided to cover her and their new son-in-law, in love. For those buried bones, Erlene apologized to her mother from her heart. Back then, she knew deep down inside her parents were hurt by their elopement, but because they said nothing and did just the opposite, embracing them with love over the years, Erlene thought everything was fine.

The way her parents chose to handle it was a demonstration of God's love showing up and working through them. She whispered a prayer asking her father to forgive her and her husband. She realized their action was probably harder on him than her mother. She was sure her mom helped her father process through his initial feelings. She believed her father granted Jude grace because he remembered how he felt when he fell in love with her mother. Everyone thought her mother was crazy to give the man her father used to be a chance.

She realized it was selfish of her not to let her dad meet Jude before she married him. She believed her father would have supported their love. Erlene was her father's pride and joy. She missed him very much. Though she knew, if he had been a living witness to what Jude had done to her (his little princess), he would've had to repent for knocking Jude off his feet. Before Jesus saved her daddy, he was an O.G. (Original Gangster). Her mother was the one who led him to Christ after he chased her around the track until he got dizzy and gave it all up to Jesus. Surrendered, he said yes to the Lord. After some sure signs of him forgetting his old ways and changing to new ones through Christ, her mother said yes to him.

She loved him. Erlene remembered her father telling her he married her mother because she was LOVING, KIND, BEAUTIFUL, FUNNY, SMART, STRONG, RESOURCEFUL, and a FIGHTER. She was exactly like her mother, only by her father's own admission, during their first years of marriage, her mother was challenged to walk in those last four qualities, first. His heart and head had said yes to Jesus, but his body took a minute to catch up. His issue wasn't cheating; he liked engaging in street fights.

Though there was that one time he shared, he had raised his hand to her mother, only to have it be met by what she raised, her grandmother Tamar's wedding gift to them. The women in her family had handed it down for generations. It was her trusted old black iron skillet, a weapon in disguise!

Grandma Tamar was from the country. She gave Erlene's mother the skillet with this advice: "You can crack an egg in it and cook your man something good to eat or flip it over and crack him upside his head good, if he thinks it's you, he gon beat!" Her father told her after his cast came off, so did his boxing gloves. Reminiscing, she was thankful for all the advice and encouragement she had received over the years, even from Jude's friend's ex-wife.

Erlene had resolve she would pray for her and reach out to her someday. RESOURCEFUL, she took her advice to move on with her life and pursue some of her hopes and dreams. When her husband called and told her he wanted to meet for dinner, she was excited. She had missed him and couldn't wait to see him. She also wanted to share what she had been working on in his absence.

Taking classes for months, she was excited. When he stood her up, then knocked her down with the news; he was expecting a baby with Gigi, she almost dropped out of class. Thank God her mother one was there for her. She told her to fight for her life, her husband's life and the souls of all involved, especially the innocent child that would be born into their situation. Erlene decided to stay focus and pursue her dreams.

For her, that meant literally keeping her distance from her husband and his situation but spiritually keeping everyone close in prayer. Her mother told her the enemy seeks to destroy lives here on earth and capture souls for all eternity. She told Erlene, her son-in-law had made a wrong decision with his life, but it should not cost him his soul's eternal rest. She said only Jesus could save that! She began praying regularly with her.

The day Erlene received the call from the hospital informing her, that her husband had been brought in with stroke-like symptoms, she rushed over to be by his side. When she walked into his room and found Gigi leaning over him, that's when the fight started. She forgot where she was, who she was, and Who's she was. She did not stop to think, "WWJD" (What Would Jesus Do)?

Hotter than a firecracker, all Erlene saw was her husband laid up in a hospital bed, and the young woman she felt helped to put him there standing over top of his head, attempting to finish him off. The only thing that brought her back from the brink of insanity was the voice speaking through the nurse when she yelled, "Silence!" It was the voice of the Holy Spirit! Obedient, she stopped, and so did everyone else at the inspired command coming from the small-framed female vessel, God used.

Holy Spirit had arrested the atmosphere. Once outside of room #222, before being drawn into a sequel and possibly literally getting arrested, Erlene decided it was best for her to leave. Walking to her car, she had officially shifted into FIGHTER mode. Remembering her mother's words, she chose to fight the enemy who was after their lives and her husband's soul. She needed to take a minute and get her priorities straight.

She had come too far to forfeit her blessing that had nothing to do with what had just occurred. Looking in the rearview mirror, she laughed; she could see her father's eyes in her reflection. He taught her how to fight when she young. Because her mother disapproved of it, he snuck and taught her a few moves when her mother left the house.

Although she never got into a fight at school, she was glad she paid attention. Gigi's was going to need to put some ice on that pretty-little face of her when she got home. Not proud of her reaction, she knew she needed to repent for her actions. However, at that moment, she felt like a champion boxer who gave her opponent what she deserved: the old one, two, combination punch her daddy used to call "a two-piece snack!"

While sitting in her car thinking about what had just happened, she saw Gigi exit the hospital and get into a red sports car. Stretching her neck, she noticed a guy was driving, and there was a baby strapped in a car seat on the backseat. She wondered why Gigi didn't take her daughter up to see her father. This puzzled Erlene. When they passed her, she noticed the driver was young and very handsome.

She didn't give it much thought until that following Tuesday when she went back to see her husband. That same red car was in the parking lot with the engine running, presumably waiting for Gigi. She knew she was probably upstairs in her husband's room. Not wanting a repeat performance from her visit on the previous Friday, she decided to wait in her car. That decision paid off. After she saw Gigi come out and get in the awaiting vehicle, she went in. After visiting with her husband, she kissed him on the lips and told him she needed to take care of some things, and she would be back soon.

HOSPITAL ROOM#222...

In ways Mr. Johnson could never have imagined, help was on the way. Two days had gone by; he had no visitors. Though he had made a lot of progress with his temporary paralysis slowly subsiding, he was worried. The long road of recovery ahead was looking rather lonely. The kiss his wife left on his lips now had the feel of goodbye. She was not coming back, and he could not blame her. She was his woman, his wife, and it appeared he had traded her in for a girl whose only need for him was his money, not his honey.

He thought how time spent with her always cost him. It was not that way with his wife. She preferred his honey over his money any day. Suddenly being transferred to the in-patient rehabilitation center wasn't so appealing. At least in his room, he had his faithful attentive nurse. He knew she cared about him. He thought about faking his progress, so he wouldn't have to leave, but he knew nurse Angela would have poked or pinched him to expose and verify his true reaction. After his nurse packed up his things, preparing for his transfer to the next building, sitting in his wheelchair like a little child waiting to be picked up from school, sad, he felt like he had lost his dignity. No one was there to go with him.

Angela rubbed his back while waiting for the transport clerk to come and take him to his new home for the next couple of weeks. She told him to keep praying; everything was going to be alright. She asked him if he had a relationship with the Lord. He shook his head, no. He knew the times he had attended church over the years did not add up to him having a relationship with Jesus.

Nurse Angela asked him if he believed God loved him and wanted to help him. He said yes. She asked him if he wanted to accept Jesus Christ as his personal Lord and Savior? He said yes. Closing his door, then their eyes, she prayed with him. He told God he was sorry for what he had done and asked for forgiveness for his sins. He asked Jesus to come into his heart and save him. He wanted to spend the rest of his life for God.

He told God if He helped him to get back on his feet, he would work at being a better man. He added, he understood if his wife did not want to take him back. His desire was to be allowed to sincerely apologize to her and ask her forgiveness. He told God he was wrong for being in a relationship with Gigi. It was not an affair. There was nothing light or loving about that deception. He vowed to break things off with her and work at being a responsible father to their daughter.

Angela wiped her eyes and then his. Looking at him, she said, "Mr. Johnson, God heard your prayer, and not only is he going to heal your body, He, (God) is going to heal your relationships. Silence can sometimes appear to be an enemy to healing and hope. You have repented and asked Jesus to come and live in your heart. I believe God is going to heal your relationship with your wife.

The woman I met and talked to still loves you very much. She might need a little time to remember that, but I believe she will come around in time and "welcome you home." It was four o'clock; it was time. Walking through the door with a smile on her face and out of breath, Erlene said, "Whew! I thought I had missed you." Mr. Johnson looked up at Angela and smiled. His speech was slurred, but she was able to make out what he said, "Thank you for everything, I will never forget you, God bless you." Just then, the transport clerk stepped into the room.

Angela told Erlene there were a couple of papers she needed to sign, releasing him from her unit's care transferring him into in-patient care. Erlene wiped the drool from her husband's mouth and asked the transport clerk to push him out of the room and to please wait for her there. While watching the other side of the closed door, Mr. Johnson was concerned. What were they talking about that he was not allowed to hear?

When laughter erupted, followed by a joyous scream, he exhaled. Then in a flash, his imagination formed a pictured of Gigi getting off the elevator, walking toward him, coming to pick him up. Nervous, he was hoping his wife and his nurse were wrapping things up. He did not want to see that thought manifest. Jude Johnson was ready to go. After the ladies left the room and hugged each other, Angela waved goodbye and promised to stop by to check on him the following week. Once settled into his new room, within minutes, he was wheeled off to therapy. Erlene stayed behind to arrange a few things in his room. When he returned, he rode in mumbling, clearly fussing due to the pain he had endured from being stretched, pushed, and pulled.

Looking up, he was surprised to see his wife was still there. His private room felt cozy; he knew she had added her personal touch to it. He was also surprised to see she had the standard chair in the corner replaced with a reclining sleeper. Did this mean she was planning to stay? Erlene did not stay that night, but she did return two days later and stayed overnight. This was a huge incentive for him.

It was also a scary time for him, as well. Where was Gigi? She had not been to see him. Though he was making significant physical progress, he found himself struggling with mental paralysis. As for Erlene, everything from making decisions about his meals to propping his pillow, she was there for him, not Gigi. Where was she? After the first week, he resigned himself to be happy Erlene was there. He hadn't realized how much he'd missed the balance of her caring ways and organizational skills.

She stepped in and stepped up to care for him after he had stepped out on her. He felt he didn't deserve her love or her help.

Focused, she kept her conversation with him about his recovery efforts. At the beginning of his second week in rehab, nurse Angela came to see him as promised. She stopped by while Erlene was not there. Mr. Johnson was glad; he wanted to ask her a few questions without his wife being present. After they talked about his progress, with his speech still slightly slurred but reasonable, this is what Angela gathered from what he was saying:

He wanted to know if Gigi had come to his old room looking for him. He also wanted to know if his wife had said anything to her about her plans concerning him. Last, but not least, he wanted her to know he had done nothing good to deserve God's grace in having his wife there caring for him. He felt guilty. Angela answering him chose to start with his comment. She told him, God's love, mercy, and grace were extended toward him through his wife.

Next, she confirmed his suspicions, Gigi had not come to the hospital. As for his wife's plans, she told him he needed to ask her himself, but if she had to guess, his wife was probably going to be there for him. She told him not to worry but to trust God and focus his energy on making a full recovery. Mr. Johnson knew what it felt like to be brushed off.

He believed Angela knew more than she was willing to say. He was right. Moments later in walked Erlene. After greeting him with a smile and a kiss, she asked Angela if she would step out of his room into the hallway so she could have a word with her. Mr. Johnson didn't know why he found himself bothered by their secrecy.

Perturbed and a bit suspicious, he felt like a child being reported on by his teacher to his parent. If there was a conspiracy and his nurse was feeding his wife information, and his wife was planning to sign papers to leave him there alone in the care of whomever, he was not going to sit still and let that happen. Rolling himself over to the door, he leaned forward then opened it. Angela and Erlene looked at him with surprise.

He hadn't realized, sheer will had encouraged his upper body strength to wheel him to the door. When the ladies smiled, he relaxed. Nurse Angela praising and teasing him, simultaneously, put her hand on his shoulder and said, "Glory to God! You are going to be walking out of here by the weekend! By the end of the week, he was not walking, but he could stand up. The night before he was to be released, he couldn't sleep. To his knowledge, Gigi had not been there to see him and quite frankly, he didn't know where he was going, once he was released from the hospital. He was almost sure that since Gigi had not come back to check on him, he was not expected or welcomed to return to his last known address, the apartment he shared with Georganne. What happened to her and had his wife, with the power to sign for him, arranged for him to be placed in a rehabilitation home?

Was there a taxi waiting downstairs for him? He was afraid to ask. After signing a few papers, Erlene hugged Angela and handed her what appeared to be a card in a white envelope, then looked at her husband and said, "Let's go home." Riding in the car alongside his wife felt surreal. He didn't know what to say. He could not help himself; he felt like she was setting him up. He could not get comfortable. Between the pain he was feeling from getting situated in the car to his secretion of fear, he was an anxious mess. Pulling up in front of their home, he relaxed when he saw the temporary wheelchair ramp his wife had added for easy access in entering and exiting.

With Erlene's assistance, it took a few minutes for him to stand up, turn around and sit back down in his wheelchair. Happy to be rolled through the doors of his home, he smiled when he saw all their furniture was still there. Some pieces were arranged differently, but after quickly scanning their downstairs everything was there. Rolling him toward the room next to the kitchen, he was surprised. Erlene had converted his office on the first floor into a bedroom, his bedroom.

It was accessible and convenient. The bathroom next to it had a stand-up shower in it. It was a perfect fit for his recovery. Wheeling him into his new room, he still could not help but feel like a shoe was going to dropped or be thrown at him. He waited, nothing happened.

80

Erlene turned on the flat-screen television she had mounted on the wall for him, then helped him into his favorite recliner that had been moved in the room for him.

After complaining about pain, she fixed him some lunch, gave him his medicine, then threw a blanket over him for comfort. His mind was still racing; this was too good to be true. Tired of sweating, he surrendered. Whatever Erlene had planned for him he was going to have to deal with it; he was tired of his mind playing tricks on him. Over the next two months, things had become routine. His physical therapist came twice a week; he was making great progress.

Erlene had set up his computer in his room for work and his amusement. She cooked his meals, made sure he took his meds, helped to bathed him, and propped his pillows. She was kind to him. Still, she made time to do what she needed to do for herself. She left the house for hours on end a few days a week. He didn't ask her where she was going before she left or where she had been when she came back. He felt he didn't have the right to. It bothered him, but because she never brought up Gigi, his daughter, or what he had done, he asked her nothing.

He knew she hadn't forgotten what had happened, but he hadn't stopped to realize his wife had forgiven him. He was about to find that all out. After three months of being at home, his health had improved immensely. Though moving slow, he could stand up, sit down and shower on his own. Erlene laughed a few times from their upstairs bedroom when she heard the refrigerator door open in the middle of the night. He was up getting his own snacks.

He made noise on purpose, hoping she would come downstairs. Instead, she turned off the lights, turned over and went to sleep. One night a fierce storm knocked the power out in their neighborhood.

Jude thought he heard Erlene call his name. Remembering how she hated to be alone during thunderstorms, he grabbed his cane and his pain pills. Standing at the bottom of the steps, he prayed, closed his eyes, and up he went, one step at a time. By the time he had reached the top he was in fiery pain, but he made it.

Passing one closed door after another he finally reached the master bedroom. Opening the door, he found Erlene curled up in the bed. When she turned and saw him standing over her, she almost screamed until she realized it was him. Forgetting his pain, he moved closer to the bed then asked, "May I?" Erlene's answer was in her tears. He slid in the bed slowly and she slid in his arms quickly.

This was the first time he had held his wife in over two years. He started to tear up in the dark. She was already crying. Neither of them said a word. Jude thought about all the nights over the last two years she had slept alone, or had she? Mr. Johnson thought, "he left as her husband, returned as a patient, and yet he was still her warm, familiar blanket." The thunder stopped; the power was still out.

There in the dark, their beating hearts were in competition. One of them was going to have to say something. Mr. Johnson had taken his pain meds. Knowing he would not be able to stay awake long, he had a few things he needed to say to his wife. Though his speech had improved tremendously, and it would be a challenge for him to convey his heart, he had to try. Holding her, as best as he could, stuttering calling her by her cuddle name, he said, "Er, I want to apologize to you for what I did to you, to us.

You did not deserve to be treated the way you were. When we met in college, I fell in love with you the first time I saw you sitting on my row. I knew you were going to be my wife. I waited over three years for you to go out with me. I couldn't understand why you went out with those other jerks, but I knew eventually you would give me a chance.

Once I got to know you, you reminded me of my mother in so many ways. I loved her and missed her so much. I was afraid that once we graduated, I would never see you again. I know I was wrong for convincing you to elope with me, but I thought your parents would not have approved of me, so I manipulated you because I didn't want to lose you, and for that, I am sorry. I made a promise to God and you that I did not keep.

Please forgive me. If you have someone else you want to be with, I understand. I was wrong for getting involved with Gigi, and now I have a child who doesn't deserve to suffer because of my poor decisions. I don't know what you want me to do, but I want you to know I appreciate everything you have done and do for me. I know I would not have made the progress I have if it wasn't for God and you. When I am better, if you want me to move out, I will.

Thank you for who you are and for loving me all those years. You deserved better than some old foolish, broken-down man. Er, if you have met someone, I won't stand in your way. But if you haven't and you can find it in your heart to forgive me and give me, us, another chance, I would never mistreat you again. I would spend the rest of my life doing whatever I could in my power to give you everything you want and deserve."

Jude couldn't see Erlene's smile in the dark. There was something she wanted. Knowing he was not going to stop talking before his will and his words were overpowered by his medicine, she exhaled softly. She had a few things she wanted to say before sleep claimed him.

Turning toward him, she said, "Jude, I forgave you a long time ago, and I never stopped loving you. You are here because I am responsible for keeping my vow if allowed, "in sickness or in health." After gently reaching for his other arm, wrapping it around her, Mrs. Johnson told Mr. Johnson they could talk more about things in the morning. Giving him her final words for the night, she said, "let's just enjoy holding our returned prodigal love tonight."

That was the best night's sleep he had in years. When he woke up the next day, it was noon. Erlene was not lying next to him. With his default still slightly set on panic, he started looking around. He was in his old bedroom. His sight was good, and so was his ears. He could hear his wife singing. His nose was happy too. He could smell a treat, bacon! His wife was cooking breakfast. His body chiming in ruined what was trending.

Aching, it needed more than bacon. He was hurting but not nearly as much as he thought he should be after climbing those stairs the previous night. Just then, Erlene burst through the door with brunch and his medicine. She told him she had canceled his therapy for the day and had declared it a "stay in bed and talk day." They had a lot to talk about. After enjoying their breakfast, Erlene gave her husband his medicine.

Enjoying the pineapple slices his wife had prepared for him made him smile. She remembered how much he loved them. It was little things like that he missed. Remembering what nurse Angela said, he did not want to lose his wife. He remembered what he heard her say the night before, but he was not overwhelmingly convinced things were going to work out in his favor. There was still this issue of Gigi and his daughter.

After doing the dishes, Erlene walked back into their room and got back into bed with him. By the time "The Johnsons" emerged from their boardroom bedroom meeting at 5 p.m. that afternoon, love had covered much ground, answering most of his questions and giving him the shining opportunity to be an answer to his wife's heart's request. Mr. Johnson was grateful his champion FIGHTER wife, fought Gigi.

Bringing her husband up to speed on all that had happened, this is what she told him:

"The day she saw Gigi leave the hospital with a handsome young man and her baby, Erlene followed them. Watching the couple exit the vehicle was not a problem. Watching them share a kiss was. This made her suspicious. Using her contacts in the system she worked for, she went to work investigating.

She discovered her husband was not the baby's father according to the child's birth certificate. When she told her husband, all he could do was shake his head, He remembered signing a document, but because Gigi couldn't find his glasses at the time and he trusted her, he signed where she told him to. After she uncovered that information and some financial discrepancies, she went to see their attorney.

The attorney explained what immediate legal steps she could take to resolve several issues. Erlene told her husband, she decided to take some of their attorney's advice and some of her own. At the advice of her attorney, privy to Mr. Johnson's accounts, Erlene made some changes. Jude realized (without sharing it) that was why Gigi came to see him the second time; she wanted the twenty-seven hundred dollars he had in his wallet when he was admitted.

Gigi had apparently tried to get cash from his bankcards first, and because Erlene changed the passwords to everything, she could not. And when she tried to use his credit cards, they were all declined.

Instead of filing papers in court as suggested by her attorney, Erlene positioned herself then waited.

By the end of the week, she received a call. It was Gigi. She was hot! Screaming obscenities at her, Gigi ended her rant with, "I need money for his child!" Calm, Erlene started her response with: "That's not my husband's child. I have a copy of the birth certificate. I also have copies of his financial records and a few checks that were signed and recently cashed by a young man captured on camera while my husband is laid up in the hospital paralyzed.

I spoke with our attorney and was advised that since the money came from our joint account, I should press charges. Since it was only four hundred and sixty-three dollars, I'm going to let you keep that, but you can't have him or his things. It would be best for you to have his things packed by noon on Friday. One of my husband's friends will be there to pick them up.

Also, I called the car dealership; they will be sending an associate to pick up the sports car that was purchased without me or my husband's signature. And before you say anything, I know where you work. I have no problem letting your supervisor know how you earn your commission by seducing their customers. I don't want you to lose your job, you're going to need it to take care of your daughter."

Coming in the stretch, Erlene said, Georganne, whatever you had with my husband is over. Please do not contact either of us again, if you do, I will move forward with charges. And let me warn you, 'You did not have to deal with me as his estranged wife, but trust me, you do not want to deal with me as his covenant wife. One last thing, I sincerely apologize for jumping on you, for you jumping on my husband. I hope you can forgive me. I am going to pray for you and your daughter.

What you and my husband did was wrong. I have already forgiven him, and I have decided to forgive you. I'm letting you know; God can help you if you ask Him too." Gigi screamed, "Whatever!" then hung up the phone. Still talking to her husband, Erlene told him; she knew her apology was empty, and she was sorry for that; it was going to take her some time to feel sincerely sorry for responding the way she did. Granting Georganne grace by not having her and her accomplice arrested was her literal act of forgiveness.

Well aware, it took two to tango, not excluding her husband, she told him, people who leave their mates and those who deliberately go after other people's mates (especially married) are selfish agents of evil, and if the shoe were on the other foot, they would not appreciate another person interrupting their relationship, even if it was on the rocks.

In most cases, it will only be a matter of time before they find themselves dumped and reduced to a buried bone in the backyard of somebody's mind. As for her husband, it was her prayer that through his confession of faith in Christ and the renewing of his mind, a new concrete foundation would be laid in his mind with Jesus Christ as the Chief Corner Stone.

> "Jesus said to them, "Did you never read in the Scriptures, 'The stone which the builders rejected, This became the chief cornerstone; This came about from the Lord, And it is marvelous in our eyes '?"

(Matthew 21:42)

Resuming the telling of what happened after their phone call, Erlene told him that Gigi packed most of his things, and his friend picked them up as scheduled. Erlene had them stored in the room across from their bedroom. Mr. Johnson had only minutes to privately mourn the daughter he thought was his. He felt like such a fool. Gigi was a gold digger who dug into the wrong pockets. His wife was a FIGHTER.

She didn't have her great-grandma Tamar's skillet, but she had her father's right hook and a shovel that she used to dig up the truth and bury the lies in Christ, never to be resurrected. After Erlene finished answering his questions, Mr. Johnson looked at her and said, "I'm sorry. Thank you honey for fighting for me, for us.

I love you. Erlene took a deep breath preparing to release her request. Looking at her husband, she said, "You asked me if there was someone else? When you left me, initially I was hurt, I thought you'd be gone for just a few days. After two weeks, I called you and left messages. When you did not respond, I became angry. Months later, I received a call from your friend's ex-wife. Although she was intoxicated, she gave me some good advice. She told me her husband cheating on her caused her to go out and cheat on him. She found someone new.

She also told me I should do something for myself, something that made me happy. Love makes me happy, the giving and receiving of it. When you called me and told me you were having a baby with Gigi, I knew I needed to find someone to love and someone to love me." Looking at her husband, she could see a cloud of confusion forming over his countenance. His thought, "Here is the shoe I was waiting for to be thrown at me." Her thought, He looks like he about to have a heart attack!"

Grabbing his hands, she said, " Honey, I did fall in love with someone else. In fact, I've been spending time with two young men, and I love them both." Before her husband could fall out the bed, she ended his suspense. Erlene told him that she had been taking classes because she wanted to adopt two three-year-old twin boys from her daycare. The boys' mother had died, and their father did not come back for them.

He dropped them off at daycare one day with their backpacks stuffed with clothes, a few toys, and a note. He loved them but felt he could not take care of them. In the letter he wrote, he was not coming back for them. Erlene told her husband the boys were immediately taken to CPS (Child Protection Services). She felt bad because they were innocent children who only wanted to be love. Erlene said she did not judge their father; she prayed for him to return or for a family member to step up and take the boys. No one did.

She shared with her husband the boys were eventually moved to foster care. After being in daycare with her all day, when it was time for them to leave, they would cry. To calm them and get them to get in the transport van, she promised them she would be there the next day waiting for them. Erlene told her husband that's when she decided to hire someone to find their father.

Once he was found, she met with him. She told her husband she asked him if she could adopt the boys. He said yes but because of how he left them, they became a ward of the state. She was told she would have to go through the proper channels to get them. However, because he agreed to her adopting them, their attorney told her it would strengthen her case.

Having the opportunity to talk with their father, he told her he loved his boys, but after their mother's death, he felt overwhelmed and was not able to take care of them. He said he wanted to do what was best for them, and that was why he chose to give them up. He wanted them to have a chance to have a good life.

He said his sons liked her, and he knew she was a caring individual who would know where to send them. Crying, he told her he never thought in a million years she would want to take them and that he was grateful. The only thing he asked was if she was granted custody if she would send him pictures from time to time as they grew. Erlene told her husband she agreed, and a far as seeing them someday, they would cross that bridge when they came to it.

She did not want them to replace him. After speaking with their father, she realized he had not left them or given them away; in his own words, "he had given them up," surrendered them to better. She believed God had reserved the twins for them to care for. Looking at her husband with sweet vulnerability, she said, "Honey, only God knew He was working to bring us all together."

Erlene went on to tell her husband she watched them for months, arrive and leave unhappy in the city van. This broke her heart, leading her to pray fervently for them. After praying about it, she decided to take the necessary classes to become their foster parent, with plans to adopt them later.

Lowering her head, Erlene told Jude; the day he called and told her he missed her and wanted to meet her at the restaurant, she was going to tell him what she had been up to. She loved and missed him. She had three reasons to welcome him home with open arms. Her chances of getting the boys sooner would have increased tremendously with the prospect of her husband being back in the home.

When he didn't show up, she had to go and register as a single parent. She was advised that if she wanted to be considered in having the boys placed in her care alone, she had to agree to some extra parenting classes. Raising her head but lowering her voice, she told him the afternoon she received the call he was in the hospital; earlier that morning, she had received a call from the foster care office.

They were considering placing the boys with another family. That news put wood on an already low burning fire. Erlene told her husband, when she walked into his hospital room and saw Gigi leaning over him, that threw gasoline on the fire, causing her to explode, taking her frustration out on Gigi!

She told her husband she was angry with them and if he had not already been lying in bed paralyzed, he might have caught a right hook too! However, seeing him lying there helpless broke her.

She shared she knew she had to accept, he had a daughter with Georganne, but she was his family, too. She was his wife. She wanted him and the boys. She was not going to give up. In fact, listening to her biggest supporter, her mother, by faith, she decided to reset and re-apply as a couple.

Her mother told her she was sure her son-in-law, and according to her, 'her grandbabies,' were coming home. Before Erlene could say another word, Jude kissed her and said, "Yes, sweetheart, yes!" We can adopt them. You fought for me; I want to fight for you and them. Erlene smiled; this was the man she ran from her first three years of college. Letting him catch her in her senior year was the best thing she could have ever done.

She married a prizeman in the Lord. Love and forgiveness were prevailing. She knew her husband loved her and meant what he said about doing anything she wanted. His sincere yes, mattered. He asked her to tell him about the boys, starting with their names. Smiling enthusiastically, she told him their names were Zerah and Perez.

It was her husband who pointed out the nickname he had given her, "Er" was hidden in the boy's names. This made Erlene burst into tears. Her husband always had an eye and insight for things like that. The rest of the day and evening, "The Johnsons" spent time catching up with each other, sharing their love.

SIX MONTH LATER...

Appearing in courtroom #222, Mr. and Mrs. Jude Johnson became the legal parents of two. After the judge finished reading the last line, one by one, they stepped up and signed. They were awarded custody of their new sons Zerah and Perez. Jude Johnson gave each of his sons a certificate with their new middle and last names on it. They were officially Z'Er'ah and P'Er'ez, Jude Johnson.

Walking out of the courthouse together as a family looking up at the sky, Erlene winked at the SON (Jesus) and thanked Him for navigating her through her dark season. She thanked the Lord for reminding her, she and Jude Johnson were one in Him. He did not let her give up in spirit on them. She was grateful she did not let bitterness eat up her soul and cause her to forfeit the blessings God had reserved for her.

Her earthly father would be proud to know she had learned how to box in the spirit too. Jude, about ninety-three percent recovered, saw how happy the boys made his wife. He also saw how happy they were when the judge told them they would be going home with their new parents, them. Walking through the door of their home together, they were greeted by extended family members and a few friends. Erlene's mother had put together a small surprise party.

Mr. Johnson was happily surprised to see nurse, Angela. She was there whistling, cheering, and pointing up at the banner draped across their catwalk. This made him look up. The banner read, "Welcome Home." Looking at Angela, she gave him her signature wink, causing him to blink. In an instance, he remembered her confident response to his uncertainty, the day she prayed with him when he surrendered his life to the Lord.

Recalling, he remembered her saying, "Mr. Johnson, God heard your prayer, and not only is He going to heal your body, He, (God) is going to heal your relationships. Silence can sometimes appear to be an enemy to healing and hope. You have repented and asked Jesus to come and live in your heart. I believe God is going to heal your relationship with your wife. The woman I met and talked to still loves you very much. She might need a little time to remember that, but I believe she will come around in time and "welcome you home."

It was the fulfillment of a prophecy! The banner was for him too! He had been given the second chance he asked God for when he was her patient. Recovered and in relationship with Christ, he was back with his wife, and he was a father again, this time by his choosing, and God's choice for the boys. Following a trail of balloons, Zerah and Perez ran past him toward the back door.

Opening it they shouted and jumped for joy at the sight of their new playground in their backyard. Running outside sampling the swing, and the sliding board, Erlene and Jude stood in the doorway watching and laughing. Quickly turning to her husband, she said, "Honey, thank you for loving me and agreeing to help me love them. I could not do this without you. Digging up the yard and having that playground set placed in it for the boys was a great idea.

He looked down at her through his aged hazel eyes, then gently lifted her right hand like a referee in a boxing match and jokingly said; "In this corner, we have Erlene, my prizefighter, friend, lover, and wife, the only woman I want standing by me, until the end of my life, (until death do we part). Just then the boys rushed by them, on their way upstairs to see their room.

Jude told Erlene, although they had the space, he thought because the boys had already suffered so much loss, he thought it would be best if they shared a room until they got older; Erlene agreed.

As the afternoon started winding down, Erlene's mother gave a touching welcome home speech. She hugged her daughter, son-in-law, and her new grandsons. Not a crier, she cried tears of joy when the boys called her Grammy for the first time. She loved the sound of that. Jude's friend was sitting on the couch next to his ex-wife.

They had come to the party together. Happy to see them together, Erlene pulled her to the side and thanked her. She told her she did what she suggested, and God blessed her with her new sons and the return of her husband. Erlene told her she would be praying for them, then asked her if she could take her to lunch once things settled.

Jude's friend's ex-wife smiling, told Erlene she saw what God had done for them. Jude told Erlene, his friend told him, that when she called and asked if he would go and pick his things up from Gigi's apartment, although he was sure she knew he had helped him (Jude) when he left her, she did not hold it against him.

He said he realized she was a good woman who loved him very much. He told him when he arrived at Gigi's apartment; another man was there with her. Gigi wasted no time replacing him. He also told him, after he dropped his things off and saw all the alterations and preparations Erlene had made for his return, he realized not only did she love him she valued him.

After he left, he called his ex-wife and apologized to her. Happy, he shared she was a good woman too, and he loved her. Dating her exclusively, he told Jude he was willing to do whatever he needed to do, to win her back. Jude told Erlene, that he told his longtime friend, he had to get himself together, or he could not hang out with him. Laughing, he told Erlene, 'he didn't care if his friend thought he was henpecked, just as long as it was his hen pecking him.

He said his friend laughed and said, "I understand man, Happy WIFE, Happy LIFE!" He said his reply was, "We take care of each other over here, Happy SPOUSE Happy HOUSE! That's what love will do."

Abruptly, commanding the atmosphere, a familiar voice could be heard.

"Everyone, may I have your attention?" It was nurse Angela's turn to speak.

First, she thanked God for the opportunity to have met and cared for Mr. Johnson. She told everyone (without going into details) she had watched God in His faithfulness, work another miracle. She turned and looked at Erlene and said, "You, my dear sister, are FIRE! You are an amazing woman of God, wife and now mother, entrusted by God with these precious boys.

They are blessed to be loved by this family. Also, I would like to thank you and Mr. Johnson for allowing God to use you to bless me, too. He knew my need and used you to provide for it. Thank you so much. Jude smiled, he did not understand what she was talking about, but he smiled anyway. He had planned to ask his wife about it later. Later came in the next fifteen minutes, as Mr. and Mrs. Johnson walked Angela to the door. She had to leave for work.

After she kissed Erlene on the cheek, she winked at Mr. Johnson and said, "I'm going to stay in touch since you won't be coming back to see me. Just so you know, I'm a good babysitter too, if you guys ever need me, call me. Smiling broadly, she raised a remote, clicked it, looked back at her former patient, and said, "Thank you again; I could not have gotten it without you."

Waving as she walked toward her new car, still smiling, Mr. Johnson turned to his wife and said, "What in the world is she talking about?" Smiling mischievously, Erlene said, "She's talking about the money we gave her." "What money?" he asked. "The money that was in your wallet the day you were admitted," she replied." Angela had it inventoried and transferred to the hospital's safe immediately. It was close to three thousand dollars. I gave it to her the day you were transferred to rehab. She deserved it. She took good care of you, starting with calling me and telling me you were there for the second time." Waving at her as she drove off, saying her name slowly, the Holy Spirit whispered this revelation in his inner ear, "ANGELA was A, A N G E L, on assignment while he was in the HOSPITAL.

"Let love of the brethren continue. Do not neglect to show HOSPITALITY to strangers, for by this some have entertained ANGELS without knowing it." (Hebrews 13:1-2)

Tearing up, he was happy his wife had blessed her for blessing them. He never said anything about the money. He thought Gigi had gotten it. He forgot who Angela, his nurse (now revealed angel) was, and who he was married to, Erlene; "She was, LOVING, KIND, BEAUTIFUL, FUNNY, SMART, STRONG, RESOURCEFUL and a FIGHTER, all qualities her family would be the recipients of going forward. Raising both hands in praise to God, love was declared "The Winner" in the Johnson's home.

> "but as for me and my house, we will serve the Lord."
> (Joshua 24:15 in part)

LATER THAT EVENING...

After their guest left and the boys had been bathed, tucked into their beds and were fast asleep. Mr. Johnson had a surprise for his wife. Using his computer, he contacted Dean Howard's niece and had her paint a lovely family portrait for his wife. While she was in the shower, he laid it across their bed. After drying her hair, she saw it. Standing with her mouth open in "awe" it was a picture of a farm with miles of green grass and a red barn with an open door.

What melted her heart and caused her tears to flow was the sight of two beautiful adult horses, one brown (male), the other beige (female), and two identical brown colts (twins) standing next to each other grazing. After wiping his wife's tears, Mr. Johnson locked their barn door (bedroom door), and the mare and her stallion, older now, trotted a few laps around their paced track.

This was their family portrait...

In remembrance of his beloved mother, Jude shared this passage of scripture with his sons.

> "But you, beloved, ought to remember the words that
> were spoken beforehand by the apostles of our Lord

Jesus Christ, that they were saying to you, "In the last times there will be mockers, following after their own ungodly lusts." These are the ones who cause divisions, worldly-minded, devoid of the Spirit.

But you, beloved, building yourselves up on your most holy faith, praying in the Holy Spirit, keep yourselves in the love of God, waiting anxiously for the mercy of our Lord Jesus Christ to eternal life. And have mercy on some, who are doubting; save others, snatching them out of the fire; and on some have mercy with fear, hating even the garment polluted by the flesh.

Now to Him who is able to keep you from stumbling, and to make you stand in the presence of His glory blameless with great joy, to the only God our Savior, through Jesus Christ our Lord, be glory, majesty, dominion and authority, before all time and now and forever.

Amen."

(Jude 1:17-25)

#2

THE ONE NIGHT STAND THAT STOOD

Their day in court...

Docket# 8 Case#678...

S itting in the courtroom's mediation room, waiting for her child's father to walk through the door, Bethany looked down at her beautiful baby boy as she cradled him in her arms. Smiling deeply, she was still getting to know and appreciate him. Drowning out the voices around her, she had just enough time to revisit how they got there...

Barring biologics, the real question she had for her sophisticated self after the birth of her son was, why her son's father? Of all the men she could have chosen to father her child, why him? She passed up two senior partners from the firm she worked at, way too many wealthy flirting clients, and a countless number of six figured salary earning male colleagues, all to play slip-n-slide with a drop-dead gorgeous cashier at her local cleaners.

Bethany remembered meeting him for the first time when she picked up her dry cleaning one Friday after work. The previous young woman who worked there; was not there. She assumed the obvious mother-to-be, had finally gone out on maternity leave. Bethany was glad she had. She remembered looking at her while waiting one day and thinking, "Working under these sweltering conditions in this sweatbox, that cashier's baby is going to come out with an attitude for sure!"

If the cleaners had air conditioning, you could not feel it. They did, however, have the nerve to have something you could see and feel. Positioned near the front register was a high-powered industrial fan blowing hot air on the customer while they were waited on, one at a time. It was hell hot in there! Bethany always made sure she had her claim ticket in her hand for pick-up. She wanted to get in and out as quickly as possible.

She made sure not to make eye contact or engage the pregnant cashier in small talk about her big belly. If the cashier had been in her third trimester during the winter months when it was cold outside and warm inside, she would not have mind chatting her up about her pending motherhood. Fanning herself with her hand, as far as she was concerned, that clerk picked the wrong time of year to get pregnant!

Making a mental note to herself while waiting her turn to be helped one afternoon, this is what she dictated, "If I ever decide to get pregnant, I need to conceive in early summer. Instead of being a June bride, I want to conceive my baby in June. This way, during my first trimester I will not be uncomfortable in the dreaded heat of summer. By the time fall and early winter arrives, I will be in my second trimester enjoying the holidays, especially 'Thanksgiving.'

I can gain as much weight as I want to and blame it on my growing baby. Next, Christmas will roll around. I will be singing 'Santa Baby' and still eating as I open all the lovely gifts slipped under my tree for my baby and me! New Year, I should be entering my third trimester. I think I will stay home and celebrate the ball drop on television, while I wait for my literal ball (baby) to drop. Valentine's day, I will probably just relax, prop my feet up, and enjoy a few sweet treats.

Late February, early March, people will be filing for their tax refunds. E-filing, they will receive them and be eager to spend, spend, spend! Planning my event, myself, I will pull off the most fabulous baby shower, enabling me to get everything I will need for my baby. Finally, on schedule, preferably a girl, my mini-me should arrive shortly after that, allowing me the opportunity to repeat my seasonal cycle somewhat comfortably, while I get to know my new baby girl."

The note she dictated to herself turned out to be a draft that drifted into changed. From her desired June date conception and her late winter's calculated delivery date, to the gender of her baby, her choices changed on a dime the day she lost her claim ticket. That was the day the store's new male cashier smiling, took his time to search through the backlog of clothing marked 30 days or more to find her dry cleaning.

It was early May and unusually hot outside. The inside heat from the cleaners was set on "lake of fire" hot! Reappearing, holding up her Gucci suit for her nod confirmation, the sight of the male clerk, challenged her attention. She was in the middle of being hypnotized by the sweat beads on his forehead, dripping down his face in formation. That day she became a human fan. Blowing her flirt on him, she attempted to cool him off.

Removing her designer sunglasses, she thanked him with her smile while batting her smudged proof lashes. Looking directly into her eyes, she attempted to guide his eyes down to the counter, where she was in the process of sliding him a ten-dollar tip. Once she released it, without looking down at the denomination, he politely slid it back toward her and said, "I'm glad I was able to find your suit; I'm sure you look good in it too. How about you let me take you out?"

She looked at him with mild contempt. According to her immediate thought, he obviously did not realize the suit she was picking up cost two hundred dollars. Could he even afford to take her out? Standing behind the counter in front of a cash register wearing a sweat-soaked black t-shirt, he asked her out. Amused, she put her shades back on before responding. Bethany remembered rolling her eyes and thinking from behind her shades, "How dare he ask me out!"

Conceited, she quickly resolved, even with the high-powered fan blowing hot air, changing her hairstyle, and causing her face to sweat, she knew she looked good to him. Though his invitation was met with absurdity in her mind, that did not stop her eyes from checking out his form in the muscle t-shirt and Levi jeans he had on. Gorgeous, he was "sugar pie hunny bun fine" but broke! Straightening her posture, he read her body language. Before she got a chance to reject him verbally, he disappeared between the hanging plastic-covered clothes. Mumbling to herself, she said, "Umh! That was rude." Obliviously to her own rudeness, she rolled her eyes again and headed for the door.

When she opened the door, the ring chime singing, signaled she had left. Before reaching her car, she turned around and looked through the break in the letters on the window. He had reappeared. After making eye contact with her, he quickly dashed out of sight again. Sitting in her air-conditioned vehicle, she was livid and hot. How dare the likes of him not accept her tip, compliment her, ask her out, then withdraw his invitation by turning his back on her and speed-walk away.

This was not over. She was going to home, find something in her closet that needed to be dry cleaned, and go back the next afternoon. Not able to find anything that evening, she smeared a little eye makeup on the inside collar (just in case they could not get it out) of one of her silk blouses and headed back to the cleaners the next day after work. When she walked in this time, the cashier had on a short-sleeved collared shirt, with no sign of sweat. She quickly surmised he must have just started his shift. One thing had not changed; he was still as fine as ever! Getting to the point, she gave him an uppity hello, then extended her blouse to him.

He smiled and greeted her with the same beautiful smile she met yesterday and a perceived, all is forgiven, "Hello." Not really wanting to establish eye contact, she realized what she had come to do was silly. So, instead of being petty, she cleared her throat, pointed to the stain, and asked if the clerk if the cleaners could get it out without ruining the fabric. She told him it was one of her favorite blouses.

He rubbed the fabric gently, looked up at her, smiled, and said, "this soft pink against your skin, I'm sure it looks lovely on you." His eyes were different. Maybe he realized the words he used the last time he asked her out were not flattering. She was sure he was gearing up to ask her out again, this time with politeness. Her yes was ready. She waited. Smiling, he handed her a claim ticket and said, "Have a good day, ma'am."

When the door chimed this time, she turned around to see if he was watching her, he was not. Instead, still standing at the register, he had his head down, obviously reading something. By the time she got in her car, she didn't know how she felt. He called her ma'am! She didn't know which was worst, that or the fact her mind had shot him down the day before, and he didn't try again. She rationed, she was one of their best customers, maybe he realized he could have gotten into trouble for flirting with her. For the next four months, she went to the cleaners at least once a week to either drop off or picked up her dry cleaning.

Collecting or presenting her claim ticket in most cases was done without incident. Sometimes, it seemed like he wanted to ask her something, and other times he was just polite. She wished she hadn't shot him down so quickly the first time he asked. He appeared to be a nice man, one she realized she liked. By the end of August, the young woman who had left to have her baby in May was back. What a difference having her baby and dropping her pregnancy weight was. She looked terrific! Looking down at her hand, she was wearing a beautiful, expensive diamond wedding ring set. Bethany remembered thinking the clerk's rings were what women affectionately refer to among themselves as "Somebody reeeally loves her jewelry!" Commenting about them and asking about her baby, in that order, the female cashier explained she took her rings off because she could not fit them after her second trimester.

Contrary to the steamy environment inside the cleaners, Bethany found herself lingering. Striking up a conversation with the new mother, she asked to see pictures of her baby. She was hoping to get a glimpse of the father. The clerk had a baby boy, he was too cute! Her husband, judging from the pictures she saw, was older than his wife but distinguishingly handsome.

After glancing through the pictures, looking for something or rather someone, one thing was confirmed. In his absence, the male cashier she found herself admitting within she was attracted to; he was not the father.

The clerk told Bethany her name. She had been married for three years. Bethany liked talking to her until she started talking about religion.

This clerk would always find a way to interject something about God's blessings and being a believer in Jesus Christ, therefore cutting her conversation with her short. Laughing to herself, she found herself jokingly saying, "As hot as it was in that cleaners, that woman needed to believe there was a place called heaven, because she was working in hell!

Over the next weeks, when she went to the cleaners, she talked a little and listen a lot, hoping her new friend would mention the male clerk who no longer worked there. She was careful in her query. She wanted to get close enough to the new mother to be able to casually ask about the guy she had replaced, who replaced her, while she was on maternity leave.

Because she did not want to come out directly and ask about him, she spent a lot of money on dry cleaning, unnecessarily. She even re-gifted the clerk a fifty-dollar gift card for her to purchase something for her baby. Covertly working the female cashier, she listened selectively; Bethany had a plan.

While getting to know the clerk, genuinely concerned about her working conditions, she gave her what she thought was a fantastic suggestion to share with the owner—a suggestion that would help her and the store's customer, which included her.

Wanting so much to inquire about the male cashier, her sophisticated pride would not let her. She practiced asking in her mirror at home a few times. She thought she could say, "Hey, by the way, who was the guy that worked here while you were out, and where is he now?" She didn't want to say he was rude because a recorded complaint against him might reflect badly on his resume'.

Then she thought she would try short and sweet; "Hey, where's the other guy?" Not wanting to run the risk of being exposed, she never asked. She told herself she was not that desperate. Her truth in conflict; her heart was desperate; her pride was not. It was time to forget about him and move on. With that thought on board, she decided it was time for her to start dating again. The month of June had come and gone.

Summer was about to leave and make room for Fall's leaves. Not in a relationship, she missed her conception opportunity according to her plan for the year. She thought she had better stop acting so stuck up, or by June of the following year, she would not have a man, giving her the chance to conceive. That following June, still a bit stuck up, she had no prospects for conception of a baby, however, she did conceive, termination.

She, her supervisor, and everyone in her department were let go for something criminal her supervisor had done. Though everyone was deposed, they were not all charged. A baby was the furthest thing from her mind the day she received her notice of termination. She needed a new job and not just any job; she had standards. Home for a few weeks, she finally received the call she had been waiting for. Her supervisor alone was being charged. Though she had not committed his crime, failure to report what she knew he was doing was her crime, punishable by permanent separation from the firm she had worked at for over five years. The firm hired all new personnel. Because of the news coverage it received, she, like many of her colleagues, were blackballed. She applied for several positions in many places immediately after being cleared, but no other firm in town would hire her.

What was she going to do? She had rent and utilities, a car note and insurance to pay. She also had to buy gas and food. And what about her budget for grooming? Her vanity necessities, her hair, nails, lashes, facial and body massages, how was she going to afford them? And how could she forget her monthly cleaner's bill, these things need to be paid. This was not good. What was she going to do?

Remembering her cashier friend rambling on about how Jesus can fix anything, she started to pray. Instead, she told herself, "I can fix this myself, I still look good." Although she, like everyone else in her department were offered a substantial severance package, she determined it would not be enough for very long. Thumbing through her phone contacts, she found herself searching for the numbers of some of the wealthy men she had passed up.

Calling one number after the other, she found it disconnected, or the caller was no longer interested. Since half of her potentials were colleagues, they were in the same predicament she was, they, too, had been dismissed! As time went on during that summer, her trips to the cleaners lessened, then stopped. She was not working; therefore, she had no need for dry cleaning services.

Answering her phone one evening, it was a female colleague from her old firm. Still unemployed, her answer to their predicament was a night out on the town. Her former colleague suggested they dressed up and go out and have some fun. She said they could take their minds off their troubles by dancing and drowning them in champagne bubbles!

That was music to Bethany's ears. Because the last time she checked, "she still looked good." Selecting her soft pink silk blouse and her white linen short swing skirt, with her face lightly made up and smelling summer fresh good, they hit the town. Positioned next to each other, they partied in three different clubs before midnight. Drinking, flirting, and drinking some more, they were celebrating two things; getting fired and not being able to get re-hired.

At the second club they went to, Bethany thought she saw something or rather, someone familiar. Excusing herself while her friend was caught up talking to a man she had just danced with, Bethany left the third club and slipped back into the second one. Looking around, she did not see who she thought she had. Instead, she felt, then heard him as he touched her waist gently from behind and said, "You look good tonight.

Do you wanna dance?" With his hands just above her hips, she had finally gotten that second invitation from his lips. Turning around slowly, already locked into his seductive grip, when the music started, her yes, was in full swing. Her body language speaking communicated with his. Because everything happened so fast, her head stopped spinning when she buried it in the crease in his chest.

Hearing his steady heartbeat opposite of the music's beat caused the rest of her to release her tension and relax in his muscular tenderness as she softly inhaled his perfectly blended exotic musk oil. Remembering what he said to her the day she brought the silk pink blouse she was wearing in, to be cleaned, she whispered up in his ear, "So what do you think about what you see, does this soft pink look LOVELY on me?" He answered by smiling. Through her mild intoxication, she understood his handsome smile was a definite, yes!

From what little she knew and remembered about this man, she chose to magnify three things, make that four; He was fine, hardworking, he still liked her, and his arms was where she needed to be in that moment. Her world had changed in a flash, and with all she had been going through, especially being fired with no prospects of getting hired, this was her silver lining, her needed validation; she was still good looking. Swaying her back and forth through two consecutive songs, she found him to be light on his feet, a perfect dance partner.

She rationed in her impaired mind; there was no way her intoxication was misleading her. They had fire chemistry! Chasing caution into the wind, their dance turned into an all-night romance. By morning, the man at the center of her late-night "ro (man) ce" was gone. Grabbing her phone, she had several messages from the colleague she had left in club number three. She never returned. Quickly texting her, she apologized and told her she was fine and would call her later but didn't.

Bethany sat on the side of her bed. Rubbing her head, she was shocked, she had never done anything like that before. Trying to remember the man she danced with all night was challenging. It was like some superhero had swooped in, rescued her from despair, then disappeared. She wanted to know, who was that "Musk" smelling man? Where was he? She looked around to see if just maybe she had dreamt it all. He left no note as far as she could see, there was no trace of him. That is until she looked down and pick up what he had inadvertently left, confirming she had indeed entertained a stranger.

The pit of her stomach, her lower region, and the onset of a massive headache checked in, one by one. Fully awake, the evidence could now be felt. It was not a dream. Slightly hungover, she laid back down and cried herself to sleep. For the next couple of months, still unemployed, between her tears and her rocky road ice cream, she beat herself up for dropping her guard and behaving desperate and reckless. She told no one about her secret rendezvous.

One day she got a call for an interview. Looking through her closet, she found her favorite interview suit. Because it had been in her closet so long, she decided to have it dry cleaned. For her, there was something about a fresh, clean-smelling suit. The jacket fit fine, but when she tried to zip up the skirt, the zipper stopped halfway. Was she bloated? Quickly trying to remember when she had her last monthly, which didn't come monthly for her like most women, due to her diagnosed irregular cycle, she concluded it must have been all the ice cream she had consumed over the last couple of months.

What else could it be? Confirmed pregnant, she wept. It was November, not June. Bethany knew who the father was, but she did not know where he was. The only thing he left behind was a black belt with some very distinguishing markings she could not make out: that and his apparent DNA. She did not go for the interview.

She did, however, finally call her colleague back, and without sharing her condition, told her about the job vacancy. Her friend applied and got the job. As for her, she was pregnant and alone. Her family lived in another town, and because her previous situation was reported on the local news there, she was not ready to face her family and friends. Adding her current dilemma to the mix, she decided to come up with an excuse not to go home for Thanksgiving and Christmas.

She spent the holidays alone feeding and rubbing her belly while crying. Torturing herself, she watched the holiday "Hallmark" movies. They were sweet and predictable. For two hours, she watched would-be lovers fight their attraction, get together then break up behind a jealous ex or misunderstanding. Then, within the last fifteen minutes, the lovers would find their way back to each other, kiss in the snow, around a Christmas tree or under a mistletoe, and live happily ever after.

Bah Humbug! All this was shown between tons of sponsored commercials. Still, Bethany watched. Her life was not a scripted movie. There were no sponsors, and she had no idea where her leading man was. She decided it was best to keep things quiet until she could come up with a believable story that wouldn't paint her as a loose woman or a fool.

A few days before New Year's, while home waiting on a delivery from her grocery store, the doorbell rang.

Foregoing looking through her peephole, she swung her door open. It was not her food delivery; it was the woman for the cleaners with a delivery of her own. She had clothes in a clear plastic bag draped across her arm. When she saw Bethany's round protruding stomach, she almost dropped them. Her eyes were as big as her smile. Stepping in uninvited, she laid the clothes down on the couch and asked, "May I?"

Bethany nodded, yes. The clerk, laughing, said, "I told my husband there was a reasonable explanation for why you did not come back to get your expensive clothes." Puzzled, Bethany looked at her, causing her to explain. She said, "Judah's Cleaners is one of our family-owned and run businesses. My husband always inventories items that have been there for more than 60 days. He likes to reach out to the owners before donating them at the end of 90 days.

You have been one of our most loyal customers. And since your name and address were on file, and you have not been in the store for a while, I wanted to bring them to you and give them to you free of charge and check on you in the process. I'm glad I did." Bethany sat down and started to cry. Just then, the doorbell rang again. The clerk opened it and accepted the groceries.

She quickly refrigerated the items that needed to be refrigerated and was back by Bethany's side in a matter of minutes. Still crying, for the first time, these were tears of relief, someone other than her doctor, her neighbors, and the delivery people saw her. Finally, there was someone she believed genuinely cared, someone she felt she could tell her unadulterated truth to.

Slightly embarrassed, she forgot the clerk's name but not her spirit of love. This had to be God helping her. She had only whispered her request to Him in prayer, that, along with the identity and whereabouts of her baby's father. This was the beginning of her prayers being answered. Comfortable with her, she told her visitor everything that had happened to her in the last ten months. To garner sympathy, she purposely started with the loss of her job. By the time she was sure "Tamia" (she remembered her name) would not judge her, she told her about her encounter at the cleaners, dating back to the day she walked in, and she (Tamia) wasn't there. Instead, there was a handsome young man with a beautiful smile.

When Bethany was done, Tamia was the one looking stun. Excusing herself, Bethany went to retrieve the belt with the distinguished buckle her baby's father had left behind. Handing it to Tamia, she watched in slow motion as her guest stared at the buckle, closed her eyes, then ran her fingers over it. Immediately Bethany knew, Tamia understood the markings, she did not.

Gently gripping the belt, a tear fell from her eye as she beheld the belt's buckle. Still running her fingers across the markings, she looked Bethany in the face and said, "Based on what you have shared, it would have been okay for you to ask me about him." My husband has a belt like this. I am pretty sure I know the answer. However, the one to your question, has two possible answers: Zerah, or Perez.

They are my husband, Shelah's brothers. They are identical twins, and both managed the store while I was on maternity leave." Bethany was officially having an out of body experience. Not only was she pregnant by a twin; she had flirted with two different men who were kin. The question now, which ones' child was she carrying within!

Reading Bethany's face, Tamia quickly explained. Both brothers had the same belt. The signet buckle was given to them from their father, Judah, who still resided in their homeland. Going back through Bethany's story, she picked out two things to help with her paternity mystery. Speaking, Tamia said, "While they are indeed identical twins, one brother likes to wear t-shirts with his jeans, and the other brother likes to wear short-sleeved collared shirts with his jeans.

You said one brother, in speaking of how you looked in your clothing, said, 'I'm sure you look GOOD in it, too' and the other brother said, 'I'm sure it looks LOVELY on you.' Those were two different responses from two different men." Bethany could not help but laugh. This was not a romantic drama, but it was certainly shaping up to be a comedy! At that point, she did not care if Tamia thought she was crazy.

In her mind, she was on her way to being certifiable! She had bought her ticket, got her hand-stamped, and was well on her way to la-la land with her baby strapped inside of her. But before liftoff, she still needed to know which one had fathered her child? Before Tamia could say another word, Bethany remembered the words whispered in her ear that night, "You look GOOD tonight."

Sure, of the man but not the name, she found herself saying within, where only her baby could hear, "I pray your daddy is not the rude one." She got exactly the opposite of what she asked for. Tamia verified what Bethany in moments had believed.

Perez was her baby's father. Tamia told Bethany that both brothers were out of the country on business and were scheduled to come back in the fall of the following year. What kind of answer was that concerning his whereabouts? Tamia asked if she could leave her baby's father's information with her so she could call or write and tell him.

Tamia said, "I am sure he would want to know." That last statement wrapped up the evening for Bethany; she wanted to be alone. She needed time to think about his rights, her rights, and what was right for her unborn child. Because she believed Tamia's heart was in the right place, she let her pray for her and her baby before she left. Tamia ended her prayer in a plea, "Lord, please help guide her to do what You would have her to do."

The last thing Tamia said after leaving the handwritten information and Bethany's dry cleaning was, "I am so excited! I am going to be an aunt! I am here for you. You are now my family." Closing her door after saying goodnight, Bethany remembered asking the air, "God, why is she trying to put what she wants me to do, on You?"

Easing down onto her plush chair, looking at her big belly, still in a state of crazy, she laughed until her baby kicked her and made what seemed like a full turn in her stomach, adjusting her back into sanity. Sane again, armed with some answers, she started to cry. She was glad Tamia told her why he was gone the morning she woke up. He did not have super-powers, but he did fly. He had taken a business flight out of the country. He was not there in town, being rude, hiding from her.

Picking up his belt, she held it close. This and the memories of his scent, and senses were all he had left her. As if their baby understood her thoughts, she was kicked again, reminding her he also left her someone special. Keeping her word, Tamia called and stopped by often, sometimes bringing her baby with her. Bethany was glad for the company. Her new family member shared her faith with her in word, acts of kindness and love.

She also shared things about Perez with her, hoping to provoke her to write or call and tell him he was going to a father. Bethany wasn't ready. Tamia's patience paid off in one area at a time. Bethany started to ask questions about her faith in Christ, and on Mother's Day, she gave her life to the Lord. She was about to become a mother. That was a game changer.

Tamia's demonstration of love, friendship, and respect won her over. She was there for her, walking with her through her pregnancy. She told no one, not even her husband. When Tamia wasn't there in her home, God's comforting presence was. Though Tamia would be there having lunch with her the day her water broke. Not conceived in June according to her fantasy plan, weighing in at a whopping, 8 pounds and 5 ounces her son came screaming into the world on June 3rd.

She welcomed family and friends who visited with her and her baby while they were in the hospital. She was overjoyed at the birth of her son. Still not comfortable with the way he came about, she found a way (before having him) to share her pregnancy with her family and a few friends. After speaking with Tamia and learning the identity of her son's father, she forged her own edited truth, a melodrama that allowed her to preserve her dignity.

She explained:

> "I met my baby's father on a hot day. Immediately showing his interest, he waited on me. He worked through a lot to find what pleased me. For the next few months, we took things slow. We saw each other often and exchanged items. Devastated by the loss of my job, I took some time to myself. When I reached my lowest, he was there to pick me up.

Whispering the good, while holding me in his arms,
I felt comforted. The escape he provided, I needed. I
said, yes. Soon after, he had to leave the country on
important family business that could not be avoided;
he is an important man. I have his contact information.
I can reach him anytime, day or night. He is the one.
He is missed very much.

He will be surprised when he sees he has a son." Where was the lie?
It was a clever, extracted, shaped, short story. Everyone bought it,
everyone except Tamia. She knew the unedited version, the pieces scattered on the cutting room floor. Still, out of respect for Bethany, she
said nothing to no one.

Tamia visited her and the baby at the hospital, and when she returned
home, she bought her baby over to help her and spend time with her.
One day when she came over, Bethany had received a beautiful bouquet
of flowers. They were from Tamia and her husband thanking her. Her
husband had taken Bethany's suggestion.

He had a wall partition built between the front store's cashier area and
the rear working area. He had two high powered commercial air condi-
tioners installed for the comfort of his wife and their customers. Tamia
told her because of the renovations; they had gained new customers.
Hugging her she told her, she too, appreciated the cool comfort. Both
ladies laughed. Between her mom dropping in from time to time and
Tamia's constant visits, Bethany had more support than she could have
hoped for under the circumstances. Her son was beautiful and healthy,
the center of her new world. His first two months of life went by fast.
The more he grew, the more his little face resembled the faces of his
father and his uncles.

Sleeping one night, she was awakened. Immediately she jumped up and ran to her son's crib. He was fine. Watching him sleep, she realized there was nothing in her closet or jewelry box more precious than the tiny person lying before her. He was priceless, though she had paid a price for going about things the wrong way. And when she least expected it, she had been introduced to God's love and grace by his aunt, Tamia.

This God, who was providing for her and her son in the absence of employment and his father, loved her. Things could have been so different for her. She could have gone to jail, but God! Aware of what her supervisor was doing, as long as she got her paycheck, enabling her to finance her lifestyle, she enabled him by ignoring him. She did not care about his crime at the time. Her lack of integrity cost her everything, leaving her in fear, despair, and perceived desolation.

The night she went out looking for comfort in a bottle and on the dance floor, under the guise of fun, she lost herself in the arms of a man who gave her a son. Watching her son's breathing go up and down and knowing who created it and was sustaining it, keeping it in perfect rhythm, bought soft mommy tears to her eyes. She began to thank God with whispers from her heart.

Praying, using her own words, she prayed; "God, before you brought my son into my life, it was filled with things that didn't breathe. I was empty and lost and didn't know it. Looking at my son helps me truly appreciate the sacrifice You gave in loving the world, so much so that, You, gave Your Only Begotten Son Jesus Christ for my sins and the sin of the whole world. (ref; John 3:16).

Your dear Son Jesus laid down His life for us all, answering sin's punishment of death. In obedience to You, and love for mankind, He gave His life. Conquering death, He rose three days later with ALL POWER in

His Hands, sharing it and eternal life with all who confess with their mouth and believe in their hearts "Jesus is Lord!" (ref; Rom 10: 8-13)

Thank You, Lord, for saving me. I will raise my son to know and love You, Amen."

The quiet of the night answered her. The thing she had been avoiding was once again, front and center, this time with a feathered press. Listening to the voice of reason echoing in her room, she heard, "if their little person could change her life the way he had, she should at least let his father know about the gift he had given her." Honest with herself, she was afraid of being rejected by him, only this time it was not just her. Fear had convinced her he would not care after their "one-night stand."

There! She had finally said it out loud, freeing herself from the grip of self-imposed shame. She had a son now, his needs had to come before hers, and that needed to start with the whole truth. The next morning before the invisible opposing whisperers woke up and had its morning coffee and her ear, she picked up the phone and made the international call.

When she heard Perez's voice, she realized she was wrong to have not made the call before then. When he spoke, his words immediately disarmed the voice of condemnation's missile countdown in her head. Responding with surprise, warmth and great enthusiasm, he kept shouting, "I'm a father! I have a son!"

They talked for fifteen minutes. He had to get back to his meeting but asked if he could Facetime her that evening to see his son. She said yes. After they hung up, Bethany stood over her son's crib; he was sleeping. No tears this time; she was all smiles. She did not expect the phone call to go as well as it did. Her son's father was not only accepting; he was elated! After she talked to God some more, she called Tamia.

Within the hour her son's aunt was there. Hugging, crying, and laughing with her, they celebrated. While Bethany showered, Tamia fed and changed her nephew. After she left, Bethany bathed her son, dressed him in a cute blue outfit, brushed his hair, and waited for his father to call. As promised, daddy Perez called late that afternoon.

He was free for the rest of the evening. All he wanted to do was talk to her and make a virtual connection with his only son. Bethany held their son's face up to the screen. Perez was speechless, and then he wasn't. He was so happy to meet his son. This became their mode of communication day and night for the next week.

Not a prisoner of shame anymore, she told him everything. He was easy to talk to. To her surprise, he told her the day he asked her out, and she laughed; he was embarrassed and devastated because he like her. He told her he had worked up the courage to ask her out. Bethany didn't realize he saw her laughed, for that she was sorry. Perez told her he was the one who called her after her suit had been at the cleaners for 31 days.

The day she came in looking hot and feeling the effects of the heat, she had not lost her claim ticket. She hadn't taken the original one with her when she dropped her suit off. She laughed to herself. Sure, it had to be one of those days when it was hot, and Tamia was working, and all she wanted to do was get out of hell's fire (the cleaners). Perez told her ticket, or no ticket, it was not like her to leave her clothes. He figured she had probably forgotten because she always picked up her dry cleaning.

They both laughed. Bethany did not like the fact that like Tamia, he too saw the high value she had placed on her clothes. Perez told her after she left that day, he needed to keep things professional thereon. She was a customer, and that was their family business. He told her he did not work there much afterward, his twin Zerah did, but when he did work, he was always happy to see her. He told her the night he saw her at the club, his brother had talked him into going out before leaving the next morning. Interrupting him, she said, "Wait, your brother was there too?" He said, "Yes." Bethany started laughing uncontrollably. Once she got her laugh out, she told him she saw his brother that night, first. She said, "Zerah was wearing a green shirt, and your shirt was blue.

I thought I was seeing double, until I danced with you. After you said, 'you look GOOD tonight,' the next thing I knew, you were holding me tight. Now I realize it was Zerah who helped me the next day when I bought my blouse in to be clean. You had no idea that night what I was talking about when I said, "So what do you think about what you see, does this soft pink look LOVELY on me?" You didn't answer; you just smiled. Separated by thousands of miles, she felt his smile before he confirmed it with his words. He said, "My smile was my answer then, and it is my answer now. His comment caused a flutter in her stomach. Just then, their son woke up with his stomach fluttering; he was hungry.

Laughing at their son's timing, she told his father she needed to hang up and take care of his son. Bethany changed and fed their son, then put him down for the night. A few minutes after midnight, her phone rang. It was Perez. She told him his son was asleep. To her surprise, he was calling to talk to her. Bracing herself, she sat at the foot of her bed. He told her the last thing she said about having to take care of their son before hanging up, made him realize, he had not properly thanked her.

Wanting to start by apologizing, he told her he was sorry for the way things happened between them. He knew it was wrong to have stayed the night with her, kiss her on the forehead, then leave without a word. He said, "Leaving, the way I did, knowing how long I was scheduled to be gone, I was sure the next time I saw you, if I ever saw you again, you would probably have been married.

Me, touching my dream turned into a nightmare for you when you woke up the next morning, and I wasn't there. I left abruptly because I had an important flight to catch. I missed that flight and had to wait three hours for the next one. While at the airport I wanted to call, I started to call, but I didn't know what I could possibly say.

I was on my way out of the country on business and would not be back for at least a year. It was selfish of me to have not told you that night, and for that, I am deeply sorry. I was afraid you might have felt what we shared was a mistake. Hearing that made Bethany breathed a sigh of relief; she did not expect an apology from him for something she consented to.

She bore the weight of their night together, alone. Impaired, or not, she made the choice to dance with him all night. Just like when she ignored her supervisor's crimes, the choice was hers and so was the consequence. When she thought she saw him in the second club that night, she went looking for him.

She wanted a chance to see and talk to him, outside of his workplace. She was hoping he would extend another invitation for her to go out with him. Dancing with him she got her wish, she was already out with him. She received his invitation and visitation in a state of intoxication all in the same night.

As awful as she had been toward him, she realized she had feelings for him. She did not know why. She liked to dress nice, turn heads, then turned down the invitations from lookers who likened her to eye candy. She was a dedicated "look but don't touch" kind of girl who did not consider herself easy, but for him, she was.

Did he still like her? It was her turn to speak. Instead of asking that question, she chose to apologize to him. When she finished, their airway was quiet but clear. Waking for his 3 a.m. feeding, their son provided their drama with a much needed, commercial break. Perez asked if she could position the camera so he could watch.

Covering herself, she fed their son, burped him, changed him then put him back down to sleep. Yawning in awe, he told her he could not wait to hold him. They talked a little longer until they were satisfied with their apology exchange. Before hanging up, they agreed to continue talking via phone and Internet.

By day eight, Bethany had learned so much about the man who had fathered her child. Among her discoveries, she was happy to find; he still liked her very much. In the wee hours of the morning, she learned he came from a family of faith. He told her he was a believer in Christ and had a relationship with the Lord.

He explained he walked away from the Lord years ago when his father sent him and his brother to the United States to attend a major university to pursue a degree in business. It made him angry because he had other plans for himself that did not include his family's business. Once he and his twin brother arrived, diligently working with their older brother at his cleaners, he understood why his father sent them there. They needed structure and discipline. Their father had other plans for them.

Once they graduated, he promoted them as overseer of two of his new international businesses. Perez told her he was sent to one country to negotiate and establish a business for his father, and his twin brother was sent to another country to do the same. He told her he agreed to go out with his brother the night they danced because he did not know how long it would be before they saw each other again.

As it turned out, Tamia, respecting her brother-in-law too, had not told her everything. Bethany surprised herself. Though she heard him correctly, she did not respond to the hint of his wealth the way she would have a year ago. Between her growing faith in God and the blessing of her son, her priorities were changing. She was already wealthy in love. The more they talked, the more they learned about one another.

Bethany knew a couple of things for sure the morning her son's father called with a request. He told her he had arranged to fly back to the states in three weeks. He wanted to see his son and her; the order didn't matter. She was excited! He told her he was making plans to transfer some of his assets into a trust fund account for their son. He also wanted to set up an account for her access as well.

His follow up request would test everything they had shared over the last weeks. Bethany could hear the hesitation in his voice. Helping him out, she said, "You know I used to work for a law firm; I understand protocol. Please, go ahead, say what you need to. I trust you." Smiling, he said, "The account I'm setting up for our son has a pending clause requiring proof of paternal verification."

Then he told her what he needed and what courtroom to meet him in, on the date specified. Bethany would not hesitate or run the risk of sending him the wrong message. She trusted him. She knew he had no time to butter her up. What he had to ask of her was hard but necessary. Smiling into the camera, she said, "Yes, Perez, we will be there with bells on."

The smile that made her come back to the cleaners weekly and back to the club that night was staring at her from two different places and two different faces. One was coming from her computer screen, and the other, cooing, was looking up from a crib. She would oblige the court's process. However, she knew he knew, in his heart, her son was his son.

Their Day In Court...

Bethany, Tamia, and her husband, Shelah, were all sitting in the courtroom's mediation room waiting when the door opened, and in walked a man with her son's face. Immediately Bethany knew it was Zerah, not Perez. Although he had a big bright, beautiful smile on his face, Bethany knew that was not the man she had become acquainted with.

Zerah smiling hugged everyone, including her. He told everyone Perez had gone upstairs to pick up some documents and would be coming soon. Looking at Bethany reaching for his nephew, he asked, "May I hold him?" Smiling, she handed him to his uncle, though secretly inside, she was hoping to let his father hold him first. Just then, in walked the smiling face from the man she knew intimately, internationally, and now intentionally.

She was expecting him to want to hold his son first. Instead, he reached for her and held her. His embrace was warm, loving, and long. He knew which one came first, the chicken, then the egg. Kissing her on her cheek, she blushed as Tamia's eyes smiled at her. Speechless, she was happy when he released her and playfully said to his brother, "Can I please hold my son now?"

Zerah said, "Only if you promise to give him back; he is adorable. He looks just like me!" Everyone except Bethany laughed; she blushed privately. Zerah was right; that face had fooled her a time or two. Watching Perez reach for then hold their son so gently made her cry. She did not want them to see her tears, but she could not stop them.

Tamia was immediately by her side, gently rubbing her back. Looking around the small space in the mediation room, Bethany saw family love. Now she understood why Tamia would work under the conditions she had and why her loving husband concerned about her, and his customers made the necessary renovations he did. They loved each other. She also understood why their father, Judah, invested in his son's education.

He understood the power of love and support. Not very close to her own family, Bethany had been independent and on her own since her late teens. She had never experienced the kind of love and lean, surrounding her. Her new family members depended on one another. She was grateful her son was the product of such love.

Not sure what the future held for her and her son's father, she had great confidence in God's love that reigned in her son's father's family. Her son was going to grow up loved and not alone. The knock at the door interrupted her thoughts. It was Perez's family's attorney. He asked Bethany and Perez to step outside the room. Perez handed his son to his smiling brother.

Once outside, everything was explained to Bethany. Her background in law was useful when it came to understanding contractual terms and agreements. Her sealed paternity test documents sent over weeks ago from her baby's doctor's office had been received and verified by the courts.

The only thing they needed to do when called in before the judge, was raise their right hand and swear to their identity. Having a moment alone, Bethany discreetly pulled Perez's belt with his signet buckle from her purse and attempted to hand it to him. Leaning in, he whispered, "Keep it for me; I know it will be safe with you."

DOCKET #8 CASE#678...

Their case was being called. Perez and Bethany approached Judge Deborah's bench and was sworn in. After that, their paternal findings were read for the record. Next both parties were asked if they agreed. They did. After that, the asset transfer was read.

Bethany thought her knees were going to give out when she heard what her son's father had given him, and he was not even six months old. The whole time the Judge was speaking, Perez was smiling and glancing at her in intervals. All Bethany could whisper was, "Thank You, Father." Looking at the Judge, she realized, instead of standing there being sentenced for a corporate conspiracy charge for failing to expose her supervisor, to her left, STOOD a man covering her and her son with the signet of his love.

She felt she did not deserve things to have turned out the way they had for her. God had been GOOD to her, her son, and his father. Tamia was right when she said she was now a part of their family." Leaving court that day with her new family, Bethany was beyond happy. Zerah stayed in town for a few days to spend time with his family to include his new nephew, but Perez had arranged to stay for a few weeks. He wanted to spend time getting to know his son. Perez stayed with his brother and sister-in-law at night and was at Bethany's apartment throughout the day. It was nice watching daddy Perez interact with his son, especially when it came to changing him.

He learned to be quick, or duck, or risk getting a sprinkled shower. The day she fell asleep on her couch and was able to take a full uninterrupted nap, she felt like she had slept for eight hours. Refreshed, she woke up to find her son's father stretched out across her bed with their son lying with his head on his chest; both were sound asleep.

The scene of their previous crime had been redeemed. Enjoying her peep show, she watched the rhythm of their chest go up and down in sync. It was a joy to watch. Her son was cute, and his daddy was fine!

On that note, she turned and left the room. Heading for the kitchen to prepare dinner, she found herself floating. She thought about making it a candlelight dinner, then laughed as she turned her chandelier up setting it on maximum lighting. Things had been going well, and she did not want to go backwards.

They were developing a friendship with respect for one another. She liked how that made her feel. They were in a good place. There was no pressure, until there was. Three days before he was scheduled to leave, after preparing his plate and putting it in the microwave, her heart started to speak. She didn't want him to go. She loved him and didn't know how, or even if she should tell him before he left.

She had misjudged him from day, and night one. Talking to herself, she said, "He is such a gentle caring man. He didn't leave me alone. Well, actually he did, but he came back. He's here now, and I love him." She heard her son gurgling just as he and his father turned the corner into her kitchen. Perez leaned in, kissed her on her cheek then handed her their son. Her sense of smell told her why she received that peck on her cheek.

Laughing, she thought he needed to be changed. Touching the bottom of his disposable diaper, she realized his father had already changed him.

Their little one had just passed gas. After the baby was secure in her arms, with his left hand, he held up a little gold baby bracelet with his family's signet on it for his son. That caused Bethany to release a dam of tears. After he gently wiped her tears, he reached into his right pocket.

Retrieving a small black box from it, he told her God had forgiven them and blessed them with a beautiful son. He told her, he could tell she was still beating herself up, and wanted her to stop because he loved her. Instantly, she knew why he had passed their son to her. Kneeling on one knee, he produced a gorgeous oval "Estelle" diamond engagement ring and asked, "Will you marry me?"

Bethany didn't answer; her mind got caught in the crossfire between the sparkling ring (she knew real diamonds) and the man she had a one-night stand with who STOOD beside her in court. Acknowledging her and her son, he was now kneeling, asking her to be his wife! Immediately she saw fear creeping in his eyes as his smile started to fade.

His face appeared to be questioning if he had made a mistake again in asking? Responding to his countenance then his voice, Bethany said, No! I mean, Yes! Yes! Yes! I will marry you! Recovering his fumbling smile, he slipped her engagement ring on her finger then kissed his fiance' passionately but briefly. Pulling back, they looked at their son simultaneously and burst into laughter.

Without saying a word, they knew what the other was thinking; there was warmth and familiarity in their engagement kiss. After they shared a good laugh, Bethany reminded him, he was only going to be there for a few more days. Without discussing where they were going to live, she asked was he planning for them to go to the justice of the peace before he left.

Perez flashed the smile he had given to his son, the one she had fallen in love with and would follow anywhere. Rubbing his hand across her ring finger, he said, "I waited to have you before the wrong way. I will not ruin my God-given chance to have you the right way. You and our son are the jewels in my crown; your price is far above rubies. I am going to go and finish setting things up to include training my management team.

I will be back in three months for good, only needing to go back quarterly." Looking at her, he smiled and said, "You can accompany me if you would like to." In the meantime, my love, I want you to continue being a great mother to our son and take that time to plan the wedding of your dreams. I want to see you in a beautiful wedding dress walking toward me as I have imagined so many times before.

You pick the day and the time, and your groom will, as you say, 'be there with bells on.'" Of all things to think about at that moment, she thought about the day he slid her ten-dollar tip back across the counter to her without even looking down at it. She had the nerve to feel insulted that he wouldn't take it. She had no idea who he was or what he valued.

She was happy her son's father, her fiancé, and her soon-to-be husband was a man of God. When Bethany told Tamia, she was beside herself with joy! She couldn't prove it, but she had a strong feeling Tamia already knew of her brother-in-law's intentions because he presented her with the perfect, "Somebody reeeally loves her!" engagement ring.

FOUR MONTHS LATER...

Bethany met the man possessing the original beautiful face, that had been passed down to her son through his father, her father-in-law, Judah. The overwhelming joy on his face told her he was happy to meet his new grandson and the woman who had steadied, then stole his youngest son's heart. What he (Judah) could not tame as a father in his son, perfectly aligned itself through the love of his daughter-in-law and beloved grandson.

In front of God, their parents, family members, friends, and most of all their beloved son, in holy matrimony, Perez and Bethany STOOD, and became ONE.

Perez and Bethany vowed to declare...

"He is The Lord, The God of Israel!"

"I will give you the treasures of darkness and hidden wealth of secret places, So, that you may know that it is I, The Lord, the God of Israel, who calls you by your name. For the sake of Jacob My servant, And Israel My chosen one, I have also called you by your name; I have given you a title of honor, though you have not known Me.

I am the Lord, and there is no other; Besides Me, there is no God. I will gird you, though you have not known Me; That men may know from the rising to the setting of the sun that there is no one besides Me. I am the Lord, and there is no other, The One forming light and creating darkness, causing well-being, and creating calamity, I am the Lord who does all these things.

(Isaiah 45:3-7)

Selah!

#3

Loose (Vow) Els

S tanding tall and lean with a soft beige nude-colored dress on that
appeared to blend in perfectly with her long legs, Mrs. Jones, with
her back to her students, started writing on the board. Without turning
around, she pronounced each letter with diction and great clarity as she
wrote them, then spoke them; "a, e, i, o, u and sometimes y." A junior
in college, twenty, soon to be twenty-one and legal, Richard had two
problems, one MAJOR, one MINOR. His dilemma ironically was
settled around the letters, i, u, and always, y. His confession and question ran consecutively, "(I) Richard have a thing for (U) Mrs. Jones and
don't understand (Y) we can't be together." Sitting in class daydreaming
with her back turned to him, he found his focus floating around those
letters again. From his confession to his standing question, he wanted
to know why they could not see each other outside of class? Whatever
the problem was, he needed to find a way around it or straight through
it. Fortunately for him, the MINOR of his two problems was slated to
be eliminated in three weeks, on his twenty-first birthday.

His roommate Jack had made plans for him to celebrate that mile-
stone birthday by hanging out with fellow students at a local restaurant. The restaurant he chose was known for its good food and
Karaoke entertainment. However, Richard wanted to do something

else on his special day. He wanted to confront his MAJOR problem, his Creative Writing Instructor, Mrs. Jones. He wanted to ask her out to dinner. This problem had many heads; the main two were monumental within themselves. She was his teacher, and the school's policy dictated; teachers could not date students. Then there was their age difference. She was almost twice his age, thirty-four years old, to be exact. The first time Richard saw her, it was on a Friday afternoon in the registration office. He was standing in line; she was not. Standing on the same side of the counter, he assumed she was a student who had already been helped or that she was one of the office clerks. Ironically, with her back turned to him then, he heard her laugh before he heard her speak, causing his interest to peak. One of the clerks said something funny, causing her to let out a playful laugh. When she turned around to leave, looking through his glasses, his eyes betrayed him first. Before he knew it, a flash flood warning swept through his body, overpowered his muscles, and shut them down.

Four textbooks and a pile of papers he was carrying became light as feathers then quickly turned into bricks as they went crashing to the floor at the sight of her beauty. Embarrassed, he dropped down quickly to collect them. Although there were three other female students in line, two in front of him and one behind, it was Mrs. Jones who stooped down to help him gather his things. Her actions prompted the young lady standing in line behind him to bend down and help too. Both ladies establishing eye contact chuckled at the weight of the books they recovered on his behalf. Richard cleared his throat and thanked them both. Mrs. Jones looking at the cover of one of the books she picked up, handed it to him, smiled, and said, "You're welcome, I'll see you soon," then headed for the door. The other young lady responded to him by saying, "oh no problem," then she followed her response up with a question.

She asked Richard if he was a new student. Preoccupied with the alluring perfume the first woman was wearing, his mind had followed his nose out the door after her. It took a few seconds before he realized the other young lady who helped him, was asking him a question. Recalibrating his senses, he smiled politely and thanked her again for assisting him. After answering her question, she extended her hand and introduced herself; her name was, Shugar. During their additional ten-minute wait in line, they exchanged brief bios and contact information. Shugar told Richard her friends called her Shug, then invited him to do the same. She shared that she too was a junior. Recognizing two of his books as ones she also had, they compared schedules. They were going to be taking two classes together, "Classical Studies" and "Creative Writing." This was the beginning of their friendship. Before meeting Shugar that day, along with a couple of other things to adjust, Richard had come to the registration office to switch his creative writing class out for a basic writing class. Meeting Shug changed that. The concerns he had about challenges the creative writing class might have held, subsided. He had made a new friend, with the potential of becoming a study buddy to help him through the class. After finalizing his scheduling concerns, turning to leave, he heard Shug whisper, "Wait for me, I'll only be few seconds." Those few seconds gave birth to a new beginning.

With classes scheduled to start that following Monday, Richard decided to go out and have a little fun before the grind of school began. Agreeing to meet his old friends for Karaoke, he invited Shug to accompany him. Introducing his new friend to his old ones went off without a hitch. Shugar was cute and smart and she had a bubbly personality. She became popular off the break because she was as sweet as the sound of her name.

Richard's two oldest college friends Jack, (his roommate) and Carol (their platonic friend), were both seniors. Whispering behind their backs, Carol and Jack shared their thoughts about Richard and Shugar; they made a cute couple and might be attracted to one another. They got part of it right. More than evident, smitten, Shug was attracted to Richard. Not able to get a read on Richard, his feelings (to them) seemed to be a bit of a mystery. Out with her new friends, laughing with them at the amateur singers, singing off-key, Shugar took them and Richard by surprise when she, without warning, got up and moved toward the microphone. Flipping through the song catalog, she chose song #173. Looking around at the crowd, preparing to continue feeding their stomachs and laughter, she locked eyes with the three people sitting at her table. Judging by the looks on their faces, she could see what she was about to do, was going to be a make-or-break friendship moment. Shugar took a deep breath. Once the music started, everyone immediately recognized the upbeat song and the original artist. Snapping their fingers, lending her their support, they were hoping she could sing. If she couldn't, she would get points for picking a great song for them to rock to. Shugar opened her mouth and began singing a song by the famous recording artist Whitney Houston.

> "There's a boy I know, he's the one I dream of
> Looks into my eyes, takes me to the clouds above
> Oh, I lose control, can't seem to get enough
> When I wake from dreaming, tell me is it really love,
> Ooh, how will I know (don't trust your feelings).
> How will I know, if he really loves me, I say a prayer
> with every heartbeat
> How will I know, (love can be deceiving), how will I
> know etc...)"

She had everyone up on their feet, clapping and cheering her on. Richard smiled at the unsuspecting thought that Shugar, soft-spoken and petite in stature, housed such a powerful singing voice. It was a shock to them all. The table her new friends were sitting at became the center of attention. Beaming with pride to the onlookers, Richard, Jack, and Carol were all smiles. There were playing it off as though they had known her for years and was aware of her huge talent. She left their table as Shugar and returned with them all, calling her Shug, because like Shug from the movie, "The Color Purple,": that little woman could sang! The excitement in Richard's eyes said he was glad he had brought her with him, though she was searching his eyes for his personal applauses. He did not disappoint her. In fact, already standing, he hugged her then pulled the chair out for her next to him. Everyone was looking at her. Shug had raised the bar for the following amateur singers who dared to follow her. There were no takers until twenty minutes later. An older intoxicated male got up and attempted to sing a Barry White Classic;

"Cause you just keep telling me this and telling me that
you say once I'm with you, I'll never go back...etc."

His performance quickly reminded everyone where they were "Amateur Night Karaoke," where the only requirements needed were ten percent courage and ninety percent fun. It was not a competition with competent singers but rather the okey-dokey of karaoke. Richard remembered thinking how special Shug was. Not only was she nice and full of life she was his soon-to-be classmate and a great singer. Monday morning came quickly. The creative writing class he shared with Shug was his second class of the day. By the time he'd arrived at their classroom, Shug was already there standing outside the door. Fidgety, like an elementary school girl waiting for her best friend to arrive, she smiled when she saw Richard. Once inside, they were surprised to see it was a full house.

135

There were only a few seats left. Shug looked around, searching for two seats next to each other. Richard, on the other hand, was preoccupied. His nose had immediately recognized a ghostly fragrance in the air; though faint, it could not be mistaken. It was the soft fragrance worn by the woman from the registration office who helped him, and Shug pick up his books and papers. Now he understood why she said, "I'll see you soon." Looking around, she was not there. Quickly he thought, "If this is the second class of the day, she must have been in the first one." Remembering her words indirectly, he realized she hinted, their paths would cross again.

Using his nose like a hound dog, he tried to pinpoint exactly where she may have sat in the previous class. Shug interrupted his search with a fragrance of her own. It was young, fresh, and fruity, clearly, from some inexpensive body wash and spray combo set. Between her and the other women and men settled in their seats who had obviously bathe themselves in body washes and sprays that morning, the clash caused his nose's trail to go cold. Meanwhile, Shug found two seats, one in front of the other. She chose to sit in the one behind him. He was glad; he did not want her to turn around and catch his face and mind in conversation. He was busy trying to figure out the best way to track down the woman his eyes and nose met on Friday. If it meant leaving his first-period class early on the next day or missing it altogether to catch a glimpse of her after her class ended, he was willing to do so.

His second thought was to wait until after class and ask the instructor if the scent of the woman he sought was in the previous class. Yes, he thought, "I'll just ask the instructor if their nose; knows her." Looking up at the board beside the title "Instructor," he saw the name, "Mrs. Tamara Jones." Settling there, he thought that might be the best thing to do, ask Mrs. Jones. Closing his eyes briefly, he felt a tap on his shoulder; it was Shug passing a clipboard with a sign-in sheet attached to it. He was the last one that needed to sign it before handing it to their instructor once she entered the room and requested it. Indistinct chatter could be heard outside the classroom. Richard was sure one of the voices belonged to Mrs. Jones. Closing his eyes again, superficially shutting out the silent energy and chatter going on around him, he decided he would wait in the dark, in his mind for the voices outside the door to trail off before opening his eyes.

Closing his eyes was a mistake. He drifted into sleep fast. His ears missed the alarm he had set for himself. Without warning, the door swung open, and in walked the instructor. His sense of smell stood at attention as the instructor's perfume from Friday ran right up his nose and smacked his brain. Affecting his ears, he could not hear. Looking at her, he could see her mouth moving, but he could not hear her. Everyone in front of him turned around with looks of confusion on their faces. He realized then, whatever the teacher had just said, had something to do with him. Shug nudged him and whispered, "She's asking for the sign-in sheet."

Shaking off what had temporarily immobilized him, he stood up and moved quickly past two people seated in front of him. Just as he was about to hand the clipboard to her, it slipped out of his hand. The clipboard went one way, the sign-in sheet went another way. Because he was directly in front of her when it happened, they bent down together to retrieve the fallen items. He went for the clipboard while she picked up the pen and paper. Smiling, without flirt in her voice, playfully, she said, "I see you like dropping things. I hope this doesn't mean you will be dropping my class." Everyone, close by smiled or let out a light laugh. Richard had provided them all with an icebreaker. Looking back at Shug, who had inside knowledge, he could see she found what their teacher said to be funny, too. Narrowing the conversation lane to the two of them, with definite flirt in his voice, he smiled and said, "No chance of that; I finish what I start." Then he stood up and handed her the sign-in sheet, letting his lingering stare communicate a personal note of "to be continued…"

Taking his seat, he remembered coasting through the class that day, only taking notes on his new favorite subject, her. He paid attention to the details concerning her, the way she walked, talked, and used her hands as an extended form of communication. When she turned to write on the board, that was his moment to store the data he had downloaded while watching her.

Pretending to listen, provided a great cover for his secret mission; getting to know Mrs. Tamara Jones on a personal level. Class for the day was finally over, so was his covert operation. Walking toward the door he heard Mrs. Jones phone ring. He watched her answer it. She said hello, then cradled her phone for privacy, before giving her response. After rambling off some instructions to the person on the other end, she hung up and dashed out the door. There would be no opportunity to speak with her after class. It was okay, his nose had found the woman he was smelling for. He just needed to go home and place his thoughts on a mental vision board. He needed to step back and figure out exactly what had happened that day, then make plans for the next. Shug was standing outside the classroom waiting for him. When came out, she clowned him about dropping the clipboard and the remarks made by their instructor. Teasing, she told him how funny she thought it was, he had dropped something in front of their teacher a second time, not knowing who she was the first time. What she cited in laughter as a coincidence, He secretly claimed as fate. Her next words sent him into a complete tailspin. Commenting, she said, "Mrs. Jones is very pretty, I bet her husband really loves her." Every part of his being froze. What! How could he have missed the letter "r," in her title which now stood for, "STOP!"

Mrs. Jones was married!

Oblivious to his reaction to the revelation she had just blurted out, Shug continued talking. Unknowingly, she was talking to herself. The rest of the day was a blur; he knew he had to let go of any hopes or plans of pursuing Mrs. Jones. By the end of the week, he had moved on in action but not in thought. That Friday night he, and his friends (to include Shug) found themselves back at their new favorite spot. First up, the Barry White wannabe singer. He was at the microphone, harassing people with his untrained, ratchet voice. Shug had no plans to sing that evening, that is until Jack, Richard's old friend, and her now declared new one made public his private observation concerning his roommate. Jack suggested Shug sing a song for Richard, who, according to him, had not been acting like his usual happy self. He asked if she would sing a song to cheer him up. Leaping at the chance to make him smile, Shug asked Richard if he had a request. Smiling slightly at his private thought, his brain started singing a few lines from rapper Nelly's song, "Dilemma."

> "No matter what I do, all I think about is you, even when I'm with my Boo, you know I'm crazy over you...etc."

It was a good thing the microphone was not hooked up to his mind. Scrambling, not sure what to suggest, he told Shug to pick something for him. Walking toward the small stage area, applauses broke out from people who were there the first time she sang. Familiar with her voice, they grew louder. Excited, they knew they were in for a treat. After making her selection, looking in the direction of her table, she said, "I was asked to sing a song to cheer up one of our friends, who seems to be down in the dumps about something; I hope this song encourages you and lifts your spirit." Because it was an old Ray Charles song, many did not catch on until after she sang a few bars;

> "You are so beautiful to me, can't you see. You're every-
> thing I hope for; you're everything I need. You are so
> beautiful to me, etc..."

Repeating those verses a few times in her beautiful singing voice brought a calm to the atmosphere. Just as she was finishing up, one by one, the restaurant-goers stood up to applaud Shug and her rendition of this legendary song. Looking over at Richard, she took a mental snapshot of his handsome smile that appeared out of nowhere. She felt responsible for generating it. What she didn't know was, she was not the reason for it. As she was ending the song, softly, "You are so beau-tiful to me," one of the people who stood up to clap, catching Richard's eye, was Mrs. Jones! She was the reason for his smile. Shug was singing his thoughts and feelings for her, and seemly out of nowhere, there she was. He could not help himself, and he did not know why. Seated at the table with her was an older gentleman who clapped but did not stand. Immediately, he felt a twinge of jealousy, followed by shame. He was wrong, and he knew it.

As Shug stepped down into the sea of applause, Richard and the others watched as Mrs. Jones met her and whisked her off, obviously taking her to meet her date. Stretching their necks, they watched as Shug shook the older man's hand then sat down to talk, presumably with Mr. and Mrs. Jones. Richard desperately wanted to know what they were talking about, and because he kept looking over at them, he had to let the others at his table know why. He explained that Mrs. Jones was his and Shug's instructor. He did not tell them the other part, about Mrs. Jones being "so beautiful to him." About ten minutes later, escorted by her instructor, Shug came back to their table. Mrs. Jones said a general hello to everyone and complimented her student Shugar on her singing in front of her peers. Richard felt terrible. Shug sang that beautiful song for him, and in re-directing, he made it about Mrs. Jones. Not sure if he needed to remind her that he too was one her students, he chose to say nothing, allowing her to introduce herself to everyone as their instructor if she recognized him. Smiling, she looked at Richard and asked if he sang too? She remembered him. Laughing lightly, he shook his head from side to side and said, "Trust me, you don't want to hear me sing." She reminded him they were at Karaoke, then suggested that he try. Before he could reply, jokingly, she said, "Are you afraid you will drop the mic?"

Laughing, he answered, "I'm not afraid. I will if you will." It was her turn to blush sheepishly. She responded by saying, "Me, oh no!" Richard wasn't sure, but he thought he detected something in her voice. Laughter broke out around the table as everyone besides Shug (before being asked) offered their version of, "No, not me, I can't sing!" Looking back over her shoulder, Mrs. Jones told everyone it was good talking with them, but she needed to get back to her table. Richard did not want her to leave. She did anyway. Wishing everyone a good evening, she waved and walked back to her table.

Leaving, Richard noticed she was wearing a different perfume; his nose quickly filed it under, HER. He was torn. On the one hand, he was elated to have had a surprise encounter with HER, with no chance of having something more, while on the other hand, there was Shug, a beautiful songbird, who was available, liked him, and wanted him. Since Mrs. Jones was married, he knew he needed to work hard at shifting his affections. The choice, though not overwhelming, was evident. Slowing, turning to look at Shug differently (putting action behind his decision), he leaned in close, hoping to activate a delayed connection with her. He was looking for a spark. It happened; there was a MAJOR connection! However, it would not be the one he had talked himself into, minutes before receiving new information. Before he could speak empty words to Shug, sitting next to him in the form of an announcement, she told everyone why her teacher asked her to come to her table. If she knew what Richard had decided about their future minutes before she spoke, she might have chosen not to share the information; she did. Not only would it not work in her favor, it would also change Richard's choice pursuit. Here he was preparing to initiate a closer relationship with her, when out of her mouth came a shocking, game-changing piece to the puzzle he was preparing to shift, then shelf. Mrs. Tamara Jones was not married! As it turned out, the older gentleman at the table with her was Reverend Jones, her father. She was widowed not once but twice. Continuing, Shug said, "Mrs. Jones told me her father wanted to go out to dinner. He wanted to dine someplace that had music, so she chose this karaoke restaurant because she wanted to see her father smile and laugh a little. She was sure here; he could do both."

Shug rambling on said, "Mrs. Jones said, she heard about the karaoke restaurant from some other students and teachers and thought it would be a great idea to check the place out with her date, her aging father." She said Mrs. Jones came up to her and told her the song she sang was her father and deceased mother's wedding song, and since she sang it so beautifully, she asked her if she did not mind coming over so her father could meet her. Shug went on to say, upon being introduced to the Reverend, he told her how much hearing her sing that song blessed him, bringing back precious memories of his dear wife. He thanked her for her gift in song and told her she should let the Lord use the voice He had given to her. Everything Shug said, after sharing Mrs. Jones's marital status, Richard did not hear. Mrs. Jones was a widow; his heart kept echoing it over, and over again. Shug noticing a slight shift in Richard's posture as he moved back from her, asked if there was something, he wanted to say to her. Richard's heart and mind were in conflict. His heart was still processing the news that Mrs. Jones was not married, while his mind's last thought was to pursue Shug.

Not sure what to say, his mouth speaking his mind's last thought, released this response, "You are so beautiful to me." Oh no! What had he done? Words he wanted to say to Mrs. (not married) Jones, he said them to Shug. It was too late; they could not be retrieved; she had already digested them. Smiling, Shug said, "I chose that song because that's how I feel about you too." According to what he had just blurted out, Richard told Shug in a few words; he likes her as well. He was one man on two roads. With one foot planted on each, he was heading in two different directions with this surety; sooner or later, his feet would meet at the intersection of "Choose One."

After Richard's confession that night, Shug's excitement could not be contained. It showed up everywhere he was, starting with her request for him to drop her off at her dorm that night. He agreed, hoping he could use the opportunity to tell her; he liked her as a friend. However, once he pulled up in front of her dorm and got out to open her door, stepping out, she stood by, signaling she wanted him to walk her to her dorm's door. Jack, co-signing, quickly moved to the front passenger's seat and changed the radio station. Richard, not sure what to do about her request, looked to Jack for bailout help. Instead, Jack smiled and shooed him on. Once at her door, she grabbed both of his hands and said, "I've liked you ever since the first moment I saw your beautiful face, the day me and Mrs. Jones helped you pick up your things. I hope I don't scare you when I say, I would love to have a baby that looks just like you someday." Judging by the look on his face, she had done just that.

He could smell the imaginary rubber burning from his dress shoes; he was ready to run. Laughing heartily, Shug attempted to smooth over her last statement by passing it off as a joke. Gently punching at him, she told him to lighten up. Richard gave her half of a smile; this was not funny to him, not funny at all. This was one time he appreciated living up to what his family and friends always said about him being a man of few words. Attempting to lighten up, he thought about what she said and could not help but blushed at her genuine compliment. After all, it wasn't every day a woman told him she thought he was handsome and would like to have a little carbon copy of him. Laughing lightly while backing up, he said goodnight, then quickly turned to leave. Walking back to his car, thinking, he felt bad. A kiss on her cheek was out of the question, even though he believed she expected at least that from him.

Approaching his car, he could see Jack in the front passenger seat laughing. Guessing Jack's laughter resulted from his suspicions of things escalating between him and Shug without his consent, Richard peeved a bit, got in and without saying a word, turned the key in the ignition, and sped off. Once Jack stopped laughing, he looked at Richard, who wasn't laughing. Getting serious, he started pointing out some of Shug's finest qualities, starting with how fine she was. Hearing Jack fire off one great thing after another about her, looking straight ahead at the road, his private thought was, "She really is any man's dream girl, and I'm the one she wants, me, and apparently my baby!

Jack is right. Besides what chance could I ever have at becoming a contender for the heart of Mrs. Tamara Jones." Pulling up to their apartment, Jack asked Richard point-blank, "What is your problem with her?" Richard shrugged his shoulder and decided not to tell Jack why there was static on his part concerning Shug. Because Jack's verbal resume' concerning her was compelling, it made Richard think. Looking away from Richard and out his window, he continued to line up and lay out what he thought made her special; "Man, she's beautiful, smart, funny, and talented."

He finished his observation and defense of her resting his case with, "Man, if I were you, I would date her." Everything his friend and room-mate said about her was true. Still, something was missing, and at that moment, he did not know what it was. His thoughts kept drifting back to Tamara. The following week was no different; thoughts of her stayed on his mind. So much so, the admiring glances Shug threw his way; he hardly took notice. Distracted, caught up, he barely paid attention in his classes, especially his creative writing class. Richard was not sure, but it seemed as if his instructor (Mrs. Jones) was a bit distracted too.

By the end of the week, he felt he needed to say something to her to test what he thought might be in the air between them. He chose that following Friday for two reasons; one, Shug had already told him she would not be in class that day, and two, the next day (Saturday) was his birthday. If he, was wrong about his suspicions, he would need the weekend to recover. Checking his watch every five minutes, he became increasingly aware of one thing; his window of opportunity was closing. With only five minutes left before it would be time to leave her pres-ence, Richard's anxiety was through the roof. To add more pressure to his rising panic, Mrs. Jones announced that for personal reasons, she would be out for the next two months." She told them they would be getting a substitute teacher and would be receiving their assignments from him. Smiling slightly, she told them she would be checking in and she expected them to complete all the work they would be given. Richard's mental anxiety and physical sweating had timed out. It was all his fault. He had prepared nothing to say to her.

Two months was a long time. He was going to have to wait. Walking past her, unconsciously, he found his nose drawing a huge whiff to last him for a while. Just as he turned to give his eyes an equal opportunity, he saw her bend down. She had accidentally dropped the pile of papers she was holding. Without thinking, he sprang into action. Within seconds he had collected all the papers she had dropped before she had a chance to. Impressed, with her hands on her hips and a look of gratitude on her face, she smiled and said, "Thank you, now we are even." Looking up at her, not thinking once or twice, he said, "No, I still owe you one. Is it possible for me to make it up to you by buying you a cup of coffee?" Mild shock appeared on her face; Richard saw it register. There was a brief pause that seemed like a long one before she answered by saying, "Thank you but..." his selective hearing kicked in, shutting out the rest of her words, not allowing him to hear the end of her sentence. From where he was kneeling, shifting to recovery mode, he wished for a sinkhole. It would have been okay if the floor opened up and swallowed him whole. After standing and handing her the papers, she smiled. His hearing turned back up in time to hear her say, "So I guess I will see you guys at karaoke tonight." She went on to say, "By the way, I did not see Shugar in class today, is she okay?" Richard responded by saying, "She told a few of us (purposely distancing himself from Shug), she wasn't feeling well yesterday."

Mrs. Jones replied by saying, "Awwh, I hope she feels better. I hope she comes tonight. I would love to hear her sing again." Playing it off, Richard said, "If I talk to her (again, distancing himself from her), I will tell her." Tamara smiled, then said, "I may not be able to have coffee with you, but I can definitely hear you sing while I have my dinner." Laughing, Richard said in a playful tone, "I told you, I will if you will." Looking around and seeing the classroom was empty, they scrambled to leave each other's presence. Richard quickly walking to the door was excited; his insides were about to burst. He wished he had allowed himself to hear the rest of what she said. It didn't matter; he was going to see her that evening.

Elated, he felt as if God was granting him undeserved favor. He would not have to wait two months before seeing her again. His radar's needle had moved from thought to belief; he was sure there was something between them. That thought was sharply interrupted by his ringing phone. It was Shug. He wasn't sure if he should answer it, then he remembered Mrs. Jones's request, she wanted to hear her sing again. Answering his phone, Shug immediately asked about the classroom work she'd missed and if there were any homework assignments from either of them. Lost for words; he didn't know, he hadn't paid attention in class and he wasn't paying attention then. He did not ask her how she was feeling. Intuitively, she noted it. He did tell her Mrs. Jones asked about her and was planning to come to the restaurant that night.

Speaking nonchalantly, he told her Mrs. Jones was hoping to hear her sing. Shug told him she hadn't planned on coming that evening. Richard nearly flipped inside out from her response. He needed her to come. Volunteering her health status (because he did not ask), she told him, although her cold was practically gone, she was still a little nasally and thought she should stay home and rest. She also shared she needed to study for an exam. Desperate, Richard pleaded, "Please come Shug, do it for me. It can be your birthday present to me." With a smile that could be heard through her mildly hoarse voice on the phone, she said, "Okay man, I'll do it for you, but you'll have to pick me up and drop me off at home after I sing."

Blinded by his agenda, wanting things to be perfect, he said, "Yes, I promise. I will pick you up at seven." Richard did not keep part of his promise. When Shug stepped out of her dormitory, she was dressed to impress. High stepping in cowboy boots, she was smokin hot! Her face appeared to be professionally made up. She had let her hair down and it was bouncing with every step she took. She had on a cowgirl blouse and a brown suede mini skirt. Richard had no choice but to compliment her. Pulling the lever in his brain, his eyes popped out, automatically causing his mouth to open. All he could say was, "Wow! You look great!"

Shug expected more, at least a hug. She accepted what his voice offered. Making an excuse for him, she reasoned, she was still getting over a cold and might be slightly contagious. The ride to the restaurant was unusually quiet; she could tell Richard was preoccupied. It concerned her a bit, but she felt as soon as she sang for him, like before, his mood would change. Once inside the restaurant, Richard's senses scanning, went looking for Mrs. Jones. His eyes found her sitting at a table with another female teacher he recognized. On purpose, Richard pulled out a chair for Shug next to Jack, away from him. As soon as the announcement was made for amateur singers to step up to the microphone to sing, Shug looked at Richard, winked, and said, "Wish me luck!" Strutting to the mic in her cowboy boots and short skirt outfit, all would hear they were a match for her song selection. Shocking everyone, she started to sing, "Man! I feel like a woman!" Shug tore into country singer Shania Twain's song with unmistakable star power. Her performance had everyone up on their feet, clapping. The women feeling sassy were swaying from side to side, including Mrs. Jones and her teacher friend. Before the song was over, Mrs. Jones walked over to Richard's table and leaned in close to his ear. Because of the background noise, she whispered above the music, "She's an amazing singer."

Richard turned. With her so close to him, he looked into her eyes as if he were Shugar's agent and said, "Yes, she's great!" Redirecting his undivided attention to the woman standing close to him, he thought she was gorgeous. Dressed down in jeans and a t-shirt, she was showing off her mature curves. Her face was lightly made up, highlighting her natural beauty. Her smell, the thing he had come to appreciate about her, set his nose ablaze, intimately mesmerizing his mind. Under his breath singing along with Shug, changing the lyrics to the song, he found his nose singing, "Man! She smells like a woman!"

Coming up from behind Mrs. Jones, her teacher friend tapped her on the shoulder then mouthed something to her face. Whatever it was produced a mild horrid look of concern from Tamara; it turns out the other teacher had an emergency and needed to leave right away. Mrs. Jones turned to the group and told them she wanted to stay and ask Shugar to sing another song, but because she rode with her friend, who needed to leave, she had to go too. Jack shrugged his shoulders and said, okay. Richard spoke up and said, "Stay; we'll be sure you get home." Jack shot Richard a "Who will?" look.

Jack had known him for over two years; he was finally beginning to figure out what was going on. Richard's facial expression, telling it all would later be confirmed by his mouth. Just then, the other teacher interjecting said, "Tamara stay, have a good time, I'll call you later," then turned and left without giving her a chance to object. Tamara smiling, chose to sit between Jack and their mutual friend Carol. Shug finally made her way back to their table after being stopped several times to accept compliments from her adoring karaoke fans. What she walked into made her feel uneasy.

Everyone at their table praised for her outfit that fit the song she had just sung. Honing directly in on Mrs. Jones, she immediately went into apology mode. First, she apologized for missing class, then for the coarseness in her voice. Jack jumping in, said, "You sounded great! In fact, it added some twang to your country sound." Everyone burst into laughter. Mrs. Jones told her it was alright; Richard had informed her earlier that she was not feeling well. Shug did not remember him sharing that fact. Jack paying attention, was listening to every detail.

Mrs. Jones told Shugar she had a fantastic voice, and she thought she was good enough to sing professionally.

Shug thanked her, then asked if she sang. Tamara told her she used to sing many years ago in the choir at her father's church. She told her she missed singing and wanted to thank her for reminding her how much she loved it. This caused Shugar to blush. Leaning in, Mrs. Jones asked her if she would sing a song for her. First Richard, the man she liked, and now her teacher was requesting her to engage her gift on their behalf. Jack, Carol, and Richard watched closely as the two ladies talked between themselves. Shug emerged from their girl huddle with a smile on her face and headed back to the microphone.

Speaking into it, she told the crowd while the DJ worked to locate her next song, she wanted everyone to join her in singing happy birthday to their friend who would be celebrating his birthday the following day. Following her lead, everyone helped her sing happy birthday to Richard, including a smiling Mrs. Tamara Jones. Once the DJ located her request, she gave her teacher a thumbs up. Speaking into the microphone she said, "Guys, I want you to travel back in time with me for this one." Looking directly at Mrs. Jones smiling, she said, "This one is for you." Slowly swaying to the music's intro, she began to sing;

> "Tonight you're mine, completely, you give your love so sweetly, Tonight the light of love is in your eyes, will you love me tomorrow...etc
>
> I'd like to know that your love is a love I can be sure of, so tell me now and I won't ask again, will you still love me tomorrow?"

Mrs. Jones snapping her fingers, rocking from side to side, closed her eyes as the old sultry sixties, song by "The Shirelles" moved her. Unfiltered, the lyrics passing through Shugar's young soul, escaped through her lips. Being a song recorded before she was born, using the teleprompter, she did an outstanding job in keeping time, matching the lyrics with the music. From the restaurant's stage, observing Richard's reaction to Mrs. Jone's actions caused her to have her very own chain reaction. The sweet smile that came to life on his face, the one she had been working so hard to bring out since the first day they met, had been hiding, waiting for this moment.

This other woman was indirectly using her and the lyrics to that song to send Richard a message. Mrs. Jones, not her, possessed the key that unlocked his intimate smile. Signaling the DJ to play a second song she had considered singing, ever since she had sensed Richard's feelings for her were not mutual, she felt it was now appropriate to do so. Closing her eyes, she blasted through Deniece William's song, "Silly."

> "Silly of me to think that I could ever have for my guy, how I love you
>
> Silly of me to go around and brag about the love I found, I say you are the best, well I can't tell the rest.
>
> And foolish of me to tell them all that every night and day you call when you care less, your just a lover out to score and I know that I should be looking for more, what could it be in you I see,
>
> Oh, oh, oh, love oh love, stop making a fool of me..etc"

Feeling silly and embarrassed, shifting gears with the microphone as her stick, she offered Richard a warning through the lyrics of her next song selection. Fast-tracking it, she stepped her game up with a Motown oldie from "Diana Ross" and "The Supremes." Shaking her hips as the old folks say, she was "sanging."

> "Baby, baby, I'm aware of where you go, each time you leave my door, I watch you walk down the street, knowing your other love you'll meet, this before you run to her, leaving me alone and hurt, think it o, o, ver, (after I've been good to you), think it o, o, ver, (after i've been sweet to you).
>
> STOP! In the name of love, before you break my heart...etc"

It was too late; her heart was already showing signs of cracking. She returned to their table, where everyone, oblivious to her subliminal message by way of her song selections, was raving over her phenomenal back-to-back performances. Through a forced smile, she thanked them. She was minutes away from bursting into tears; she needed to leave. Upset, she wanted to go home and cry in private. Fragile in heart, Shug hoped her tears did not pop out during her ride home with Richard.

She did not want him to see her cry. Her wish would be granted; Richard would not see her cry, Jack would. By the time she said good-night to the fans who stopped by her table, she turned to look for Richard. According to Jack, he had gone to the men's bathroom ten minutes ago. Was he hiding from her? Jack walked over, touched her arm gently and told her he was leaving. He offered to drive her home.

At that moment, any remaining doubt she had about what she witnessed from the stage was removed and replaced with the sure thought, Richard had used her.

When he said, "Please come Shug, do it for me. It can be your birthday present to me." The truth was, he did it for her, the other woman, Tamara Jones. Leaving, Shug wrapped a scarf around her neck and whispered goodnight to the ladies left at the table, Carol and Mrs. Jones. She did not bother to ask them to tell Richard goodnight for her. Richard returned minutes after Jack and Shug left. As if he had been spying, he did not seem a bit surprised that they were no longer there. After two more songs by others and a few laughs, Carol announced she was ready to leave. Mrs. Jones nodded in agreement; she was ready to leave as well.

Richard told them to wait by the door while he went to pay their table's bill. Stepping outside, walking toward the parking lot, everyone was smiling, that is until Carol said abruptly, "Well, goodnight." then darted for her car parked next to Richard's. After she jumped in, she started the engine, waved, then pulled off. Looking at Richard with her lips slightly parted, his teacher said, "I thought we were all riding together." Richard opened his front passenger door for her and said, "I told you I would get you home, and I am going to do just that." Tamara, protesting, said, "No, you said 'we' will get you home. I can't ride alone with you, you're my student, and the school has strict rules and policies about things like this." Grinning, Richard said, "Look around, there's no one here to tell on you. And if it will make you feel better, I have a hat and sunglasses in my glove compartment. If you put them on, no one will recognize you." Tamara looking around, heard laughter; someone was coming. Quickly, she jumped in his car and scooted down in the seat; she did not want to be seen. After turning on his radio, he asked her where she lived. Heading in the direction of her home, they began to talk. The closer they got to her house, the more comfortable they became with sharing in small talk.

By the time they were about to approach her exit (the one that would take her away from him for a couple of months,) being close to her, caught up in her personal ambiance and cradled by her soft exotic perfume, Richard found the courage he needed to take a leap in faith. Looking straight ahead, he asked, "If she wanted to get coffee?" Turning to look at him with caution in her eyes, she started repeating what she had said to him earlier that day. Before she could finish her sentence, interrupting, he said, "The breakfast spot is twenty-five miles away from here?" It was now or never; if she said "no," he would respect her wishes and take her home.

Ten miles into their continued drive, Richard was falling fast and hard for Tamara. In his head, he was preparing his line of questions for her. Eased, strategically among them would be the question as to why she had not dropped the 'r' in her title of Mrs?" Considering she was a widow, he wanted to know. One question he did not have to ask, was if she liked him; that answer was becoming increasingly clear. When they arrived, he peeked his head in the door of the twenty-four-hour diner, like he was Tamara's personal secret service agent. With her standing close behind him, she laughed when he turned and whispered, "The coast is clear."

Holding the door open for her, he laughed then stepped to the side, letting his royal highness enter first. Three cups of coffee later, sitting in their comfortable booth in the back corner, Richard and Tamara exchanged quite a bit of information through smiles and laughter.

There were a few serious moments of conversation. For Tamara, she briefly explained, without being asked, why she still carried Mrs, as her title. She had married her first husband when she was eighteen. She loved him very much. She shared he had a rare heart disease and died a few years after they were married. Lowering her head said she married again a few years later, and within a couple of years, her second husband passed. She did not share the details of his cause of death. Even though her marital status had changed without her consent, not once but twice, she decided on paper, she would change her title when she was ready. Richard understood her need for disguise. Emotionally she was not ready and did not want to appear to any male suitors; she was available.

Next, she shared why she was taking the next two months off; it was not for a vacation. Her father, the Reverend, was terminally ill; she wanted to stay home and help take care of him. This Richard understood too. Having two serious points of sharing himself, he shared that though his parents were wealthy, in his opinion, they were too religious. He told Tamara he believed in God but needed to be his own man and not do what was expected of him to do; follow in his father's footsteps. His father wanted him to be a minister; he wanted to be a writer. He made her smile with sentiment when he told her he worked to put himself through school in pursuit of his dream. Tamara looked like she wanted to say something but declined to speak. Next, without warning, he told her he was not trying to scare her, but he needed to tell her how much he admired her and the way she carried herself. Blushing, she thanked him for the honey drips of compliments he poured over her.

Chuckling, she said, "You're sweet, and I have to admit, while it's nice to hear these wonderful things, I am your teacher, and I am four-teen years older than you. In a different time and place, this probably would have been okay." Looking her in her eyes, he cleared his throat and responded by saying, "You won't be my teacher forever." Then he looked down at his watch and said, "In exactly twenty-nine minutes, there will be a thirteen-year age difference between us, and as for a different time and place, we are here right now for a reason. Tamara appreciated the way Richard smoothed over their age difference. The next twenty-eight minutes went by rather quickly. Looking down at her dainty wristwatch, Tamara started the count down, "Five, four, three, two, one, 'Happy Birthday'!" Speechless, it was his turn to blush from her celebratory acknowledgment of him.

This was the best unexpected birthday present ever! Signaling for their waitress, Tamara asked if they had any cake and ice cream; she explained it was her friend's birthday. Reappearing moments later, their waitress presented them with a piece of cake and told them it was the last one left. She had placed one single lit candle in the middle of it. She also placed two separate bowls of vanilla ice cream in front of them. Tamara smiling, thanked her, then told Richard to make a wish. He looked at her, closed his big-dreamy eyes, and in a hush, blew out the candle. Sharing his cake with her, the giddy little girl in her asked him what he had wished for. The newly twenty-one-year-old young man laughing lightly, said, "I can't tell you. I need my wish to come." Because of how he looked at her, she knew whatever it was; it had something to do with her. Glowing, her cheeks responded by turning rosy. Nervous, she looked down at her watch for an out. It was time to go. Though it had been refreshing to be in Richard's company, it was after midnight. That was not the main reason why she needed to leave. Richard's suspected wish was on the verge of coming true.

Her heart conspiring with her head whispered within, "Happy Birthday to you; I think I am falling for you too." Before leaving, Richard thanked their waitresses and gave her a twenty-dollar tip. The ride back to town and then Tamara's home went by quickly. Time seemed to have evaporated as they breathed in each other's essence in the small space between them. If he had gotten pulled over by the police, he would have been charged with being D.U.I.(Driving Under the Influence) and found guilty of love.

He was floating on a cloud while his accomplice (Tamara) had butterflies of her own floating around in her stomach. Exiting the highway with only two miles left before reaching her home, steering his vehicle with his left hand, gentle confidence encouraged him to reached over and put his right hand on top of Tamara's left hand. She responded by turning her hand ever so slightly. Opening it, she accepted his silent invitation to hold hands. No words were spoken as they rode the last two miles in silent "sweet-n- low" exchanges of human electricity. Pulling up in front of the home she shared with her father, Richard was not surprised to find it to be big and beautiful.

Well lit, he could see the colorful flowers that surrounded it and their perfectly manicured lawn. This time it was Tamara who sat in silent protest; she was not ready to leave. As much as Richard wanted her to stay, his concern moved to her father. Although his date told him her father had a live-in nurse, he did not want to be guilty of keeping the Reverend's daughter out too late. Before Tamara's eloquent presence could change his mind, he got out and hurried around to the passenger side of his car. Opening the door, he extended his hand to help her from his vehicle. Slowly walking her to her door, the crickets could be heard doing their thing. They were singing their midnight love song. When they reached her front door, Tamara spoke first.

Softly exhaling, she said, "Thank you for the drive and the coffee, I needed that, and again, Happy Birthday Richard, I hope you enjoy the rest of your day." Smiling, he inhaled her exhale because she had said his name so sweetly. Responding, he said, "Thank you, Tamara, for the pleasure of your company and if you really want me to enjoy the rest of my day, be a part of it by calling me later to wish me happy birthday again." Tamara sighed; before she could tell him for the third time what she could not do and why, he placed a piece of paper in the palm of the hand she let him hold. His touch had already paved the way. Backing away from her slowly, he smiled and whispered, "Goodnight, Tamara." I hope to hear from you soon. Once inside his car, he waited for her to enter her residence and closed the door. After the lights came on inside, he drove off. On his ride home, all he could think about was her and how full his heart was. The closer he got to his apartment, Shug's face appeared in his mind.

He realized he needed to be honest with her and let her know how he felt. He cared for her but not the way he believed she wanted him to. It was too late, according to his roommate; she already knew. When he walked through the door, he was met with Jack's disgust. Jack told him; Shug cried all the way to her dorm and then again in his arms once she got inside. He told Richard he took her out for coffee to let her talk about how she felt. Jack told his roommate and friend she did not want him to know how she felt. She wanted to forget about him. Instantly Richard understood exactly how vulnerable her heart must have been. Unlike him with Tamara, he had a chance to prepare himself for the possibility of rejection, Shug was blindsided by his. Time and chance that night took them to two different coffee houses in different directions. His rendezvous was met with returned attraction. Richard sat down and tried to explain to Jack how he felt about Tamara. Jack shook his head. He told Richard he did not understand. Without being disrespectful, he pointed out the difference in the ages of the women. Then sarcastically asked his friend to, "Make it make sense?" What he did not know about Richard was that he had always been attracted to older women. He stopped apologizing for it back in high school. He was always thought of as an old soul, wise and mature beyond his years. Younger women were attracted to him for those reasons, while older women were intrigued by him for those very same reasons.

The choice was always his to make. Dating up and down the scale, he had dated a few young ladies his age but found himself attracted to and more comfortable with women older than him. It was not a fetish; it was merely his preference. Shugar was a cute young lady, funny, smart, talented, and sweet. As for Tamara, in his opinion, she was a classic. Naturally flavored, she was beautiful, intelligent, reserved in humor, and fine like aged wine. Summing her up in two words, she was, "Soft and Seasoned."

As promised, he found himself at the intersection of "Choose One." Shugar or Tamara, which one did he want? He chose the road that led to Tamara. Jack seeing the look in Richard's eyes as he described his thoughts and feeling concerning Tamara, commenting with subtle sarcasm, said, "Well my friend, looks like you got bit by a cougar." Richard looked at his friend of two years and said, "Call it what you want; I'm in love. Catching only a few winks, Richard rose early. Up all day, he waited for Tamara to call. Later, Jack and Carol talked him into going to karaoke for a little while; after all, it was his birthday. No one told him Shug would be there. Richard sat up straight when he heard her amplified voice; she was singing Gloria Gaynor's "kick em to the curb" anthem song;

> "I will survive for as long as I know how to love I know
> I'll stay alive, I've got all my life to live, I've got all my
> love to give.
>
> Go on now go, walk out the door, just turn around
> now cause you're not welcomed anymore, etc..."

Shug was on the warpath! He was sorry he had inadvertently hurt her. Even though Jack was not supposed to tell him how she felt, he knew he needed to talk to her. However, it was not going to be that night, not while she had that weapon (microphone) in her hand. He did not want her too embarrassed him by putting a name and face to her revenge song list. He decided to leave before she finished her set. Back at home simmering in disappointment, Richard thought about doing some homework to clear his mind. Instead, he opted to listen to music to relax; it had been a long day. Shug was upset with him, and Tamara had not called him. Hitting the play button, releasing his playlist, he settled back in his recliner. First up, "The Isley Brother's singing"

> "Drifting on a memory, ain't no place I'd rather be, than
> with you, loving you etc..."

Drifted he did. By the time he woke up, it was after 11 p.m., Jack was not home, and Tamara had not called. If she had changed her mind about him, he would have to accept it; however, it would not change his feelings for her or his mind about Shug, for who he still owed an apology. It was his turn to feel what she must have felt, accept he was not angry with Tamara for not calling him. He did not regret the time spent with her. He thought, "It is better to have loved and lost than to have never loved at all." Tamara left him with a lasting birthday present, the memory and scent of her presence. Just as he was about to call it a night, his phone rang. The caller i.d. read, "Tamara Jones"; it was her! Not wanting to appear anxious, he picked up on the last ring. Controlling his breathing, he said, "Hello." Tamara's smile could be heard through her words. She told him she was calling to wish him a happy birthday, again, per his request.

Laughing lightly, she told him to look at the time, he did. It had almost been twenty-four hours since they'd sat down and had coffee together. They both laughed then exchanged information about their day. Richard, trying to impress Tamara told her he had thought about doing some homework when she called. Jokingly she said, "Judging by the last paper you turned in for my class, I would say that's a very good idea." They both laughed, then quickly ran out of words. When silent breathing took the place of words, they knew it was time to hang up. Before hanging up, Richard's desperation could be counted on to speak. Wanting to continue communicating with her, he started his last possible words to her for a while with, "I understand your need to be home with your father, but if there is anything I can do or help you with, even if it's just to talk, I'm here for you." Two months was a long time not to see her, let alone hear her voice.

As much as he wanted her to know he needed her, he would not add his own need for her to her already emotionally challenging equation. His offer was met with silence for several seconds. When Tamara did answer, it was to sincerely say, "Thank you, I appreciate your kindness." All he could add to that was, "I mean it, goodnight Tamara." After she said good-night and hung up her phone, he whispered, "I love you" into his receiver. That following Monday morning was his real first day of school. Knowing Tamara was not on campus, he was able to focus on his schoolwork; he was behind in all his classes.

He now had three goals; pass all his classes, apologize to Shug, and wait for Tamara. Thursday afternoon, the opportunity for number two pre-sented itself. Richard caught Shug after class; she had been avoiding him like the plague. He asked if they could have lunch together. To his surprise, she said yes. What he thought would be awkward was not. He started by telling her how beautiful she was.

Without sharing his feelings for Tamara, he told her the following: he was sorry for his misleading actions, he cared about her, and he valued her and their friendship. He was honest, straightforward, and sincere; Shugar appreciated it. Time seemed to have been healing her wounded heart, except it wasn't time; it was Jack. Richard found this out three weeks later. Jack had been acting different, not to mention he had been coming in late without any explanation as to his whereabouts. Easing into a booth at karaoke without anyone knowing he was there one night, he witnessed Jack, who couldn't hold a note, joined Shug (at her request) on stage to sing Diana Ross and Lionel Richie's version of "Endless Love."

Taking the mic, Jack turned to Shug and made this confession, "From the moment my eyes first saw you, you captured my heart " Spying, from where he sat, Richard could see Shugar's sweet blush; she and Jack had a MAJOR connection. Jack singing first started their love song;

> "My love, there's only you in life, the only thing that's bright"

And then Shug sang Diana's part;

> "My first love, you're every breath that I take, your every step I make."

Then they both sang together;

> And I, I want to share all my love with you, no one else will do...etc"

Recalling the night Jack said, "Man, if I were you, I would date her." He got his wish "to be him." Richard was thrilled his friends had gotten together. They were both good people; they deserved each other. This made him come face to face with how much he missed his love, Tamara. It had been over a month since they had last spoken. Suddenly, his exposed heart turned on him. It became difficult to hear Jack and Shug sing about their endless love for one another. Raw feelings of jealousy poked him in the gut, taunting him because of what his friends had found and could openly sing about on stage. To add insult to his injured heart, his gut singing, whispered, "Silly of you to think that you."" What was once a promising start of love involving Tamara, had seemingly fallen off the grid. He needed to leave.

Just as he slipped in un-noticed, he slipped out in the same manner. Richard found himself driving down the highway heading toward the scene of the crime of his heartbreak, the diner. Thinking about the love his friends had found while blasting an old song on the radio made him think about the love he had found and lost. His heart started singing along with "The Moment's" and their rendition of "Love On A Two Way Street":

> "I found love on a two way street and lost it on a lonely
> highway. True love will never die, so I've been told etc..."

Caught up in the lyrics to the song, he was startled by his phone when it rang through his car's stereo system, interrupting his croon. The first shock quickly dissipated when the second one was realized; it was her. Tamara was calling. The phone rang for the third time. What was he waiting for? Before he could say hello, he could hear her tears. She was calling because she needed to talk. Richard, in a bold move, ask if he could come to her. That was the right call because she said yes. Whipping his car around almost on two wheels, he was on his way to her. Not giving her a chance to change her mind, he quickly told her he would see her soon and politely hung up.

He punched selection #7 then settled back in the driver's seat. Listening to Oletha Adam's strong, intense vocal rendition of "Get Here" piping through his stereo caused his foot to respond by adding pressure to his gas pedal;

"You can reach me railway, you can reach me by trailways, you can reach me on an airplane, you can reach me with your mind.

You can reach me by caravan cross the desert like an Arab man, I don't care how you get here just get here if you can.

There are hills and mountains between us, always something to get over, if I had my way, surely you would be closer, I need you closer".

Speeding down the highway, he was on his way to Tamara's unspoken request to "Get Here." When he arrived, she let him in. Once he saw her face, he could see she had been crying for some time. She did not try to conceal the pain coming from her heart.

Her father was dying, and so was a part of her. To Richard's surprise, without speaking, she led him to her father's room. Standing by his bedside, the former training his parents had instilled in him came rushing up from his heart and spirit as he gently reached for her father's hand and prayed a deep abiding prayer to God on his behalf. Seemingly gaining his last rites strength, her father rose up slightly. Looking Richard in his eyes, he offered him a faint smile, as if he had been waiting on him to come and relieve him.

There was a silent spiritual exchange held in the looks and the holding of their hands and hearts. Unaware, Tamara was witnessing a changing of the guards for her heart. She stepped back as she sensed something happening between the two men. With days left to live, not aware or concerned with Richard's age, somewhere in her father's spirit, the blessing of God allowing him to meet the man that had brought a smile to his daughter's face and heart (when she thought he wasn't looking), gave him much comfort.

With so little time left, he met and embraced the man God sent, who held his daughter's happiness and God's promise of marriage and motherhood for her. Watching his daughter go through the "TRIALS and TRIBULATIONS" she had endured over the years, from losing her mother to having to bury not one, but two husbands was hard for him to watch. He thought she had given up on letting love find and claim her again. The day he heard his daughter singing around the house again was a personal joy for him in his last days.

He knew without her saying it; she was falling in love, this time with a man of God. Just as he was preparing to go and live in the presence of the Lord, Richard's presence and prayer were his parting gifts. God had kept His promise to her father before calling him to his eternal rest. His daughter's heart would be left in loving, capable hands, hands though briefly, he has personally held. Verified in spirit, he knew the man he met on his death bed, loved God, and his beloved daughter. Because he could sense Richard would be there for her, he could finally see the runway. It was time for him to leave. His bedroom had become a spiritual airport. Preparing to depart his daughter's life, he was grateful to have had the opportunity to (in passing) engage Richard, her arriving future. Her eagle on assignment had landed...

Richard helped Tamara with her father's final arrangements. Jack, Shugar, and Carol were present at the funeral. Tamara asked Shugar if she would sing. Honoring Tamara's father's request from the night he heard her sing at karaoke, "to let the Lord use the voice He had given her," opening her mouth, she sang the old hymn, "Amazing Grace," from her soul;

"Amazing grace how sweet the sound that saved a wretched like me, I once was lost but now I'm found was blind but now I see...etc"

Richard sat, then stood by Tamara. He was there for her every step of the way, keeping the unspoken promise he had made her father. It was his shoulder she cried on. His arms held hers through it all. After her father had been laid to rest, just as she had playfully predicted in their beginning, Richard dropped her class. On that note, she met his challenge of, "I will if you will." Following his lead, she dropped out of school too, she resigned.

Tamara's father's death caused a maturing Richard to reach out and revive his relationship with his parents, especially his father. He was a type of prodigal son, returning home. Breathing life back into their relationship, he apologized to his parents. After which, he asked for his father's help. He told his dad he was right all along about God's call on his life, then thanked him for continuing to love and pray for him unconditionally. Richard shared with his father how God's Hand had always been on him and his life. Praying with his earthly father, in his own few words speaking, Richard prayed, "God, please forgive me for walking away from you. Father, I understand the importance of allowing the Holy Spirit to guide me in my life. Thank you, Lord, for watching over me and not letting me miss my blessing. Lord, I am ready to accept Your call for me to ministry."

After thanking God for the safe return of his son in spirit, Richard's father asked, "Son, what happened?" Joyfully, Richard replied, "Father, it is not what happened, but rather who happened?"

With love in his eyes, he answered his father by saying, "The who is my fiancee', Ms. Tamara Jones, my good thing, my blessing from The Lord."

"He who finds a wife finds a good thing And obtains favor from the Lord."

(Proverbs 18:22)

FOUR YEARS LATER...

Happily married three and a half years, Richard, Tamara, and their twin boys, Zerah and Perez, continued to live in the home left to the couple by Tamara's father. Renovation were made to include their very own state of the art game room, featuring karaoke. Jack, his wife Shugar, and their little carbon copy son, Jack Jr., were frequent guests at their home and church, where they were introduced to Jesus Christ. Not fully persuaded in Christ yet, Richard, because of his own experiences, knew how important it was not to judge their friends but to love and pray for them, all while lifting up the name of Jesus, letting the Lord draw them to Himself as He has promised in scripture He would:

"And if I, I am lifted up from the earth, will draw all men into Myself." (John 12:32)

Richard and Tamara's love would be right there for them and their twins' playmate, baby Jack. In the end Tamara was happy she said yes to Richard, and Shugar was grateful Richard said no to her; otherwise, she would have missed the opportunity to love and be adored by her "Endless Love," Jack. Overseeing, God had worked everything out.

Tamara fulfilling her father's secret dying wish, returned to the choir as the Assistant Director. Richard preparing to graduate from divinity school, served as a minister in training in her father's church. With much love, help, and guidance from his father, a pending degree in theology, and a bending degree of prayer in "knee-ology," Richard embraced God's call to ministry. God had been good to him, protecting, leading, and guiding him.

He was especially thankful to God for leading him directly to his beloved wife, Tamara. He believed she was the one God had created and fashioned for him the moment he laid eyes on her. Her voice was like sweet music in his ears, while her scent teased his sense of smell. The first time he touched her hand, sparks flew, and when he kissed her lips, their souls were connected forever. Their love conquered the MAJOR and the MINOR of it all.

Riding down the highway on their way to their favorite date night spot, the diner, listening to their pre-recorded music track, Richard, laughing out loud reminded her for the twentieth time how he serenaded her on their honeymoon night, singing, "Daryl and Oat's"; "Sara Smile." Tamara smiling on cue prompted him to sing it again. Using his wife's name, he sang:

> "Baby hair with woman's eye, I can feel you watching in
> the night come along with me and I am waiting for the
> sunrise, when you feel cold, I'll warm you, and when you
> feel you can't go on I'll come and hold you.
>
> It's you and me forever, Tamara smile, oh won't you smile
> awhile for me, Tamara,"

Letting her left hand travel over the middle console, Richard opened his right hand to receive it. Laughing, she said, "Do you remember picking me up to carry me across the threshold, and because you had a knack for dropping things, I said, "Please don't drop me." They both laughed. Continuing she said, "And what about when you held the boys for the first time? I asked you the same thing." They broke into shared laughter again, followed by their comfortable place of silence where time, place, nor age mattered, only their God-ordained love. Tamara reach over and changed the cd. Looking straight ahead, she started reciting her (vow) els, "a, e, i, o, u and sometimes y. "(I) Tamara, have a thing for (U) Richard and here's the reason (Y)." Turning up the volume in their mobile karaoke, holding her husband's hand, closing her eyes, she began (as the old folks used to say) sanging along with Etta James;

"At last, my love has come along, my lonely days are over, and life's like a song...etc"

"I found a dream, that I could speak to, a dream that I can call my own

I found a thrill to press my cheek to a thrill that I have never known etc..."

Pulling up in front of the diner, Richard joined in for the grand finale, singing with his fine as wine, prime RIB (wife);

"Cause (U), "R" mine, AT LAST"...

"So, the Lord God caused a deep sleep to fall upon the man, and he slept; then He took one of his RIBS and closed up the flesh at that place. The Lord God fashioned into a woman the RIB which He had taken from the man and brought her to the man. The man said, "This is now bone of my bones, and flesh of my flesh; She shall be called 'Woman' Because she was taken out of Man."

(Genesis 2:21-23)

#4

SMILING FACES

Standing over his wife of thirty years casket, "The Director" cried sorrowful tears as he stared at his wife's lifeless body, cold to the touch. He was left standing alone after it was announced, "those who wish to have one last look, please come." Those who did walk by glanced into the casket then returned to their seats. Not him; he needed more time. Looking down at his sleeping bride, he needed her to wake up.

He wanted one last chance to look at her smile through his eyes and tell her how much he loved her. He needed her to hear from his lips; she was a good wife, mother, and friend. As if waiting would cause her to wake up, he put his feet in parked and stood there. When that did not seem to work, he wet her face with the tears that fell from his eyes as he leaned down to kiss her rose-colored lips of clay for the last time.

This was not a dream or a fairytale; she was not going to wake up. Out of respect for the dearly departed and her husband, the preacher, who was also their pastor, asked those seated to close their eyes and bow their heads in silence. This request was made to give "The Director" a few more semi-private moments to engage his wife's shell and his memories.

Blinking through his tears, he remembered the first time he saw her. She was standing in line behind him at the post office. Mentally pre-occupied, he was not aware of the clerk signaling for him to come to his station until she gently tapped him on the shoulder and pointed at the awaiting clerk. Looking over his shoulder at her, responding, her smile caused him to do a double-take before heading to the clerk's station. He remembered waiting outside the post office for her after he had mailed his package.

For him, it was love at first and second sight! He knew he wanted her to be his wife and the mother of his children. After eight months of dating, he asked her father's permission to marry her. Her father said yes, and so did she. He had married the girl of his dreams, signed, sealed, and delivered. Their first five years together were full of love and discovery. The years that followed were the employment building years.

Because he wanted his wife to stay home and take care of the children, he was sure they would have someday, he worked hard at preparing and securing his family's wealth and comfort. Around their tenth year of marriage, their nest started to stir. It was not the chirping of little baby birds, but questions, silent then public ones.

Why hadn't his wife conceived? To offset the noise, his wife filled her days volunteering and perfecting her homemaking skills. The predictability of their routine life was perfect, and then it wasn't. Climbing the corporate ladder turned out to be a blessing and a curse for "The Director."

Each rung on the ladder came with more money, power, and appeal, three things other women taking notice of wanted. Suddenly, there was distraction and unwanted attention coming from women everywhere, especially in the workplace. Colleagues and clients made subtle passes that were often missed by him but not his faithful secretary of four years, Pearl. After the women were gone from his presence, Pearl would mimic for her boss their flirty behavior, then point out how it all went over his head.

Afterward, they would share laughter over it. This trusted secretary had been assigned to him when he received his second promotion. With each advancement came the option to choose a new secretary, he did not. Instead, latched on and invested; when he moved up, so did Pearl. Over the years, she had become more than a secretary; she had become a friend, not just to him but to his loving wife.

Pearl was younger than her boss and his wife. Living miles away from her family, they became her adopted family. In the beginning, their relationship was comfortable; his wife trusted her explicitly. When she called for him at the office, she was always immediately put through.

Days her husband wasn't feeling well and came to work anyway; Pearl would call his wife and ask her to encourage him to go home, assuring her she had everything at the office under control. She was an asset in business and a trust friend. Pearl had been invited to their home several times for dinner during the holidays. She, along with a male companion, even accompanied them on a ski trip. His wife liked her very much. Covertly, Pearl was her eyes and ears in the workplace. Though his wife trusted him, she did not trust other women, only her. Privy to personal information surrounding him and his wife, his trusted secretary guarded it. That too, they appreciated.

Before he knew it, his wife and secretary had become gal pals. Together, they went to lunch, dinner, the movies, spas, and on occasions, shopping sprees. This was great! The two women he trusted the most got along well. He did not want to admit it, but his secretary had become somewhat of a wife sitter.

Pearl didn't mind; she admired them as a couple and often teased him about how much he spoiled his wife. As time went on, his increased responsibilities at work lessened his ability to remember a few things in his personal life. This became evident when he, not his trusted secretary, forgot his tenth wedding anniversary.

Springing into action on his behalf, she sent his wife flowers and made dinner reservations for the couple at an exquisite new restaurant his wife had been dropping hints she wanted to dine at. While he was on a conference call with a client, Pearl whispered for him to sign two documents she had already proofread, then by way of sign language, she made a request for him give her his credit card.

Without questioning her, he promptly handed it over to her as he had done so many times before. Grabbing her coat, she dashed out the door. Two hours later, she returned with a small blue "Tiffany" bag.

The Director remembered being on a conference call with a different client by the time she'd returned. Once off the phone, she reminded him it was his anniversary. The ghastly look on The Director's face was instantly erased after she told him not to worry; she had sent his wife flowers, made dinner reservations for him and his wife, and bought her something from her favorite jewelry store to commemorate their special day.

It was almost four o'clock; their dinner reservations were for six. He remembered thanking her with a lifesaving hug and giving her (with pay) the rest of the afternoon and next day off, which happened to be a Friday. The following Monday was a holiday, which meant she would have a very long weekend to enjoy before returning to work that next Tuesday.

She, in turn, hugged him lengthy, kissed him on his cheek (something she had never done before), and told him he was the best boss ever. She smiled gratefully and told him she had big plans for the weekend, and the extra time off would fit into her plans nicely.

After she left his office, he quickly picked up the phone, called his wife, and told her about their dinner plans. He told her he was on his way home and asked if she could be dressed and ready to go by the time he got there. Stopping by his secretary's desk, he picked up the little blue bag marked "Tiffany" and hurried out the door.

Once home, he ran through the shower like a carwash, then jumped into the clothes his wife had laid out for him. After he dabbed on some cologne, he kissed his wife on the cheek, and they headed out for the evening. The car ride was unusually quiet; he could not figure out why. Had he missed something?

He remembered thinking to himself, "I wished her a "Happy Anniversary", accompanied by a kiss when I got home, and before we walked out of the house." I know she got the flowers that were sent because I saw them in the vase on the table."

They were on their way to a new restaurant to celebrate, and he had a gift for her in his coat pocket. Still, there was something in the air between them. Though dinner was nice, a nagging strained feeling could be felt. He remembered thinking once he presented her with her gift, all traces of the unknown tension would disappear.

He was glad dessert was about to be served. He had planned to give his gift to her after dessert and before her signature, end of dinner cup of coffee. She picked over her dessert and did not want coffee that night. She said she was not feeling well and wanted to go home. Because he didn't want the car ride home to be like the one going to the restaurant, he decided to reach in his pocket and pull out her surprise.

His wife's eyes lit up when she saw the little blue bag. Once he removed the two small suede blue boxes from inside of it, she smiled. He remembered whispering, "Happy Anniversary, my love," then handed the boxes across the table to her. Smiling confidently, he prepared himself to be praised for the thoughtful purchase. Once his wife opened the boxes, the anticipated high "Oh Wow!" on her face registered in the low range of "Oh, okay." He knew his wife; something was vastly wrong with the gifts presented to her. Immediately it dawned on him; he did not know what his secretary (on his behalf) had bought for his wife. He did not ask her, nor had he looked in the bag for himself.

This was bad; he was speechless. This was not a deal or a merger. She was not his client; she was his wife. He could not do damage control because he did not know what was in the boxes. Hesitantly he asked her if she liked them, hoping she would give him a clue as to what the items were. "She said nothing at first, then under a smirky grin (without giving him a clue of the contents), she quickly rattled off, "Thank you, honey, they're nice."

For the first time, the confidence he had placed in his secretary came into question. Before pushing himself closer to the edge of his wife's mental ledge, he asked her to let him see the boxes. She gently slid them back across the table to him. Slowly opening the boxes one after the other, like they were lost treasure chests, his mind reacted with an, "Hmm."

Although his mind now understood his wife's reaction, his mouth contradicting his thoughts, voiced something different. "Honey, if you don't like them, I will take them back and get you something else." He was careful not to say he had not personally picked them out. The ride home was worst, then the ride there.

Disconnect was in the air, and because his wife never said what was ailing her at the restaurant, only that "she did not feel well," he was sure by the time they got to their bedroom, her ailment was going to surely be defined as a headache and he did not have to guess what that meant. Anniversary or not, it was going to be lights out, and an unspoken "don't touch me!" Something was very wrong.

His wife's unspoken headache lasted throughout the holiday weekend. Several times he started to call his secretary and ask her why she chose to purchase the items she had on his behalf? Each time he decided against it, remembering she had told him she had made big plans for the weekend. He did not want to disturb her. He chose to wait until she returned the following week.

With Monday off, Tuesday could not come soon enough. As it turned out, he would have to wait a little longer. It was his secretary's turn to have an ache. Aching all over, she had come down with the flu. Calling in, she spoke with their office receptionist, Hannah. Pearl told her she had taken ill and would be out of the office for the next few days with plans to return that Friday. Not wanting to speak to the Director herself, she asked Hannah if she would forward the message to him for her.

Hannah had worked there longer than them both. She told her Pearl she would forward her message. Hannah prayed for her over the phone then told her she would fill in for her while she was out. She suggested that she take the time to fully recover before returning. Hannah also informed her that the company had already reached out to the temporary agency they partnered with and a replacement was on the way.

Hannah told her the shift in responsibilities had already taken place, and she was not to worry. To further put Pearl's mind at ease, she explained, the temp would be handling her receptionist assignment, and she would temporarily be handling her secretarial duties for "The Director." Coughing, Pearl said, "Thank you, I will see you next week."

Hannah sat at Pearl's desk for the next two weeks. Her work performance was beyond exceptional; she did twice the work in half the time. She was older, motherly, and surprisingly, quite efficient. Impressed, the Director made a mental note to ensure she be offered a promotion. He was sure he could get her assigned to one of his colleagues who might be looking for a great secretary if she wanted the job.

He remembered thinking, if it were not for Pearl's loyalty to him and his wife, he would have considered keeping Hannah as his secretary and finding Pearl a new boss, even if it meant ensuring they both received offers they could not refuse. Hannah was just that good. He also found himself remembering how she brought a certain unexplainable peace to their corner of the building. His fond thoughts of her were escalated, the second Tuesday of her work week with him, when his wife called to speak with him. Before hanging up, she asked if he would transfer her back to Hannah; she wanted to talk to her. Cracking his door open, eavesdropping, he overheard Hannah say, in a Ms. Doubtfire kind of voice, "My dear prayer changes things." He was curious, what did his wife need prayer to change that he did not know about?

And if she needed something, why hadn't she asked him first? Quieting his thoughts, leaning in further, he heard Hannah say, "Yes, six-thirty, I will see you then." Now he was rattled. Where was his wife meeting her, and why? He couldn't ask her because then she would have known he had been listening in on her conversation.

He was going to have to wait until he got home and ask his wife. By the time he walked through his front door, his wife was not there. Her car was in the driveway, but she was not there. Just as he was about to dial her number, in search of her, he received a text from her stating she had gone to church and would be back around eight. His dinner was in the oven, set on warm, and his drink was on the side door in the refrigerator.

She signed her message with a red heart and the words, "I love you." Church? What was wrong? His wife had not been to church in years. In the early years of their marriage, she went all the time. He had gone with her a few times but eventually, studying long hours and working, with little time to rest, he stopped. Not long after he stopped, she stopped.

As far as he was concerned, he had worked hard to earn all he possessed. It was him, not God, that provided for them. He did not think it was cynical of him to feel that way. He believed there was a God; he was just unwilling to give said God credit for the hard work he had put in, netting him his wealth and success. Pulling his dinner from the oven, settling down to eat, it crossed his mind to put his hands together and pray.

Looking around at their beautiful home, then staring at his hands, pride inflating his chest, reminded him, that although his wife's paintbrush imagination and interior decorating skills staged their beautiful picture-perfect home; it was his hands that provided the canvas. The right side of his brain warned him that was a dangerous way to think. He chose to ignore it.

Quietly, between small bites of food, his brain reminded him he did not control his breathing or regulate his heartbeat. He was also reminded that though he and his wife were diagnosed by their doctors as physically healthy, conception had managed to evade them. He remembered calculating and thinking after their seventh year of marriage and his second promotion; it was time to start a family. It was not that simple. On the contrary, things got complicated.

The next years were "trying ones," he almost lost his wife. Late in their tenth year of marriage on a cold fall night over a candlelight dinner, the God who held his breath and regulated his heartbeat changed his life forever. Opening his eyes, the Director realized he had been standing over his wife's lifeless body for the last five minutes.

He had been speed dating through the mental pages of their life together as everyone sat quietly, waiting on him. It was time to close the casket. His adult sons stepped up. Positioning themselves, one on each side, they escorted their father back to his seat. The Director sat through the remainder of his wife's service, cradled by his memories.

Advancing to the gravesite (her final resting place), he had previously made arrangements with the cemetery personnel to sit alone with his wife's casket before having it lowered into the ground. The cemetery clerk told him to take all the time he needed. He did.

After everyone, including their children and their families, paid their last respects and left, he sat in the seat closes to the head of her casket. With his face buried in his hands, he wept. Since there was no one around, he cried freely.

Removing tissue from his jacket, he wiped his eyes, blew his nose, and cleared his throat. He was ready to talk to his wife about those "for better or worst trying years" when he almost lost her...

Opening his mouth, he said...

"Sweetheart, the day Pearl called off work because she had come down with the flu, subsequently taking the next two weeks off, then without warning resigning, was a shock to us all. What we later found out was even more shocking. It was discovered she was pregnant. I was very happy for her until I found out who the father-to-be was and how he came-to-be.

It was me. After the initial shock wore off and you and I stopped blaming each other for how it happened, I never truly apologized to you for letting this happen to us. You see, when I first saw you as a young woman, you took my breath away. I knew I wanted to love you, and only you for the rest of my days.

I wanted to give you everything. I went to work early and came home late. I studied day and night to climb the corporate ladder quickly so that I could give you all the things your heart could ever possibly desire. Once I achieved a steady footing, I provided a house for you that you very lovingly turned into a home.

I lavished you with gifts and took you on trips around the world. I opened a limitless account for you and told you to go 'shop until you dropped' which sometimes you did." The Director smiled to himself at the thought of those precious memories. Still smiling in memory, he remembered finding bags hidden in the back in their closet, under their bed, and in the laundry room.

The day he found two new pantsuits hidden in the garage, he remembered sitting his wife down and telling her she did not need to hide any of her purchases from him. She confessed, she realized, she had become a shopaholic! That was the day he gave her an allowance to help her curb her spending. He told her once her allowance was gone, it was gone until the next deposit.

Returning to his confession, he said, "My love, over the years, I started to notice that since you had become friends with Pearl, your spending habits changed. All those playdates together with her, I thought, were good for you." Dropping his head, a fresh round of tears fell from his eyes; he wept bitterly as he thought about how it was later discovered, his wife was spending her allowance all in one place. She was checking out monthly at the same cash register, Pearl.

In short, over the years, as the friendship between his wife and his secretary grew, so did his wife's confidence and dependency on her. Pearl had become like a little sister to his wife, he spoiled his wife, and she spoiled Pearl, just like any big sister would. They did a lot of things together in the name of sisterhood. He would not be there the day Pearl caught his wife crying.

His secretary was asked by him to stop by his home on her way to work to pick up a file he had left that morning. When Pearl walked up to ring the doorbell, she noticed the door was slightly ajar. Preparing to knock, she quickly changed her mind when she heard a woman's voice crying. Panic caused her to push the door open and run in.

The Director remembered his wife telling him, "the crying voice Pearl found was mine." Her private daily communion of tears and disappointment had been interrupted. His wife said, Pearl rushed to her side and sat down beside her, then quickly wrapped her arms around her and held her as she wept. Pearl did not ask any questions.

His wife told him because she (Pearl) did not pry, once her eyes were dry, she decided to answer the unspoken question of, "Why?" As a result of her answer, over the next few months, Pearl had gathered some vital information. After sharing her findings with his wife (only), Pearl finally convinced her to visit a fertility doctor.

His wife desperately wanted to have a baby. Pearl went with her for moral support, offering to assist her with whatever she needed. His wife's crisis became his secretary's emergency. He started to cry again as he revisited the fact that he missed all the warning signs. Pearl began taking longer lunch breaks, leaving early, or calling off from work altogether. He dismissed it as man troubles. Either she was managing her on-again, off-again relationship, or she was taking care of personal business, she did not feel comfortable sharing with him. At any rate, he would respect the privacy she had a right to.

However, he noticed her taking more than her usual number of private calls, two of which resulted in her abruptly leaving in the middle of meetings. Then there were the sudden moves she made, quickly minimizing her computer screen when he approached her desk. At home, he noticed his wife acting in like mannered ways when she was on her computer.

He dismissed it as girlfriend stuff. Pearl had been there for his wife, and he thought his wife was trying to return the favor. Determining their behavior to be normal, he dismissed any notions of worry. He would not pry into their sister relationship. Shaking his head from side to side, speaking to the light wind brushing over him, he said, "My love, I was wrong, I didn't know."

Those words caused that same light wind blowing to turn the page in his confession...

This was a dark chapter he rarely accessed. It was not easy for him to acknowledge, out of desperation, he had made a bad decision. Blinded by his love for his wife and her happiness, during those same trying years while Pearl kept his wife busy with their friendship, he knew deep down inside she wanted something more than anything else he had already given her.

He wanted it too. He wanted a baby. Pearl sensing his frustration of not yet becoming a father, started to drop hints. Eventually, she drew him into a conversation. She planted seeds of information concerning fertility and surrogacy. He found himself listening. Initially, he laughed at the idea of having a baby any other way than what was considered traditional.

The more he thought about it in traffic, at the gym, when he drove by schools and parks, what he once thought was funny, started to slowly gain his attention. Still, he was sure he did not want to father a child that way. He loved his wife, and if it meant living out the rest of their lives together without having children, that was what he was prepared to do. He thought about bringing up adopting a baby for his wife but quickly realized how that sounded.

It would have been exactly as it sounded, a baby for his wife, not him. A child was not a purse, dress, or a pair of shoes, and if he was going to seriously consider bringing a new life, bartered, or borrowed into their lives, their home, he wanted to be emotionally available to help.

Just when he thought he had made peace with his decision, while looking for something in his wife's vanity drawer, he found a small black book with dates and entries. The entries abbreviated were marked "neg." It took him a few minutes to figure out what he was looking at. It was a pregnancy log. Plopping down on the side of their bed, he was overcome with emotions.

He had prided himself on being a good husband who kept his promise to her father to love, honor, protect, and provide for her.

To the best of his ability, he believed he had. Closing his eyes, he caught a visual of piles of imaginary boxes of pregnancy tests she must have purchased over the years. For every negative entry, he imagined she had processed through them alone, that is, until she confided in Pearl.

That was what the ladies had been closed mouth about. He wondered why his wife did not bring it up to him. Then it dawned on him; she probably thought he would never agree to that kind of procedure. She was wrong; he loved her. The Director stood up and moved closer to his wife's casket; touching it, he said, "Sweetheart, I have to tell you something.

After everything came out in the open, I neglected to tell you this truth. That afternoon while you were out, I found your book. I was relieved. Based on my findings, I did not just decide to inquire about surrogacy; I found myself vigorously pursuing that option, not only for you (putting his head down) I did it for me, too. I wanted a son. The mistake I made was keeping my feelings from you.

Selfishly, I told myself it was better to surprise you later than to tell you and run the risk of you talking me out of it. I convinced myself, this was me taking care of you, except truth be told, I wanted to ensure that I would have a legacy (seed) in the earth in the form of a son. We had become divided by one common denominator, Pearl. Unbeknownst to you, I too confided in her.

In expressing my interest, excited, she arranged everything for me with the doctors. She suggested, then, encouraged the position of me keeping my seed extraction and storage from you, my wife. She said because you were an only child, and she was like a sister to you; she should be the surrogate for us.

I drew the line there. I told her I would have to discuss that with you when we were ready to select someone to carry our child. I told her I appreciated her offer and would keep it in mind, though I never would have considered her. I was happy; I had finally positioned myself to give you the ultimate gift, one that would complete us and be an extension of our love. I did not know betrayal would be the price.

The secretary I trusted for many years groomed me for her plan. I remember the day in a split second; I signed on the dotted line while on an important call. Blindly, I signed the documents she shoved in front of me as I had done many times before. I felt there was no need to read them. My confidence in her was not challenged. I did not read the fine print.

Our attorney said the contract was awful but lawful, and unfortunately, if challenged, Pearl would prevail. The night of our tenth anniversary at dinner when you pushed the gift boxes back across the table for me to look inside, when I open the first one and saw that it was a necklace with a single mother pearl, I didn't understand.

What appeared to be beautiful to me represented something or rather someone that was becoming ugly to you. However, when I opened the second box, the one that contained the ruby bracelet with baby-related charms (a bib, bottle, booty, and a tiny silver baby), I saw a mild panic rise from your heart and settle on your face. And because we were keeping secrets from one another, we did not know how those gifts affected the other.

I thought she was trying to encourage you with the hope that you would soon achieve the charms on the bracelet. I would never have selected those insensitive items for you. Later, you shared, to my surprise, you viewed the bracelet as a subliminal taunt and tease from her, of what, without her help, you could not achieve.

The pearl necklace, for obvious reasons was viewed as an irritation. Accordingly, you said those gifts were the spiritual equivalency of shackles for your wrist and a chokehold chain for your neck. You knew instinctively; I had not picked them out for you.

You also knew the flowers and dinner reservations was not my doing as well. I felt terrible for what Pearl had done. The truth is, I forgot our tenth anniversary, and for that, I am still very sorry. According to you, things started to change between you and her months before that anniversary.

You said you had been giving her money for research. Once you decided to take over the research yourself, that did not sit well with her. She felt you no longer needed her. You said you started praying and asking God to help guide you, starting with you wanting to tell me everything. She wanted you to tell me nothing.

God heard your prayer and sent the office receptionist Hannah to intervene. Hannah was known around the office cooler, endearingly as "Praying Hannah." By the time God brought her into our lives, months of damage and deception had already been conceived. I was thankful she agreed to stay on as my secretary when Pearl decided without warning, she would not be returning. I was grateful to God for using Hannah to help us through the birth of that deception and beyond.

God stepped into our situation through her. She led you back to church and introduced you to Jesus Christ. She taught you how to pray for yourself and me. Hannah understood what we did not; she saw in the spirit what we initially could not. In sharing with us that the corporation was her family's business; she said, "The Lord" assigned her to that post years ago.

Strategically placed there, she saw things in the atmosphere others did not. Covering our office with prayer was her God-ordained assignment. When you shared with me what she shared with you, I was floored. She told you, sitting at the receptionist's desk over the years, she had witnessed a lot of people come and go.

Putting through thousands of calls, she was privy to a lot of information. Hannah answered some of the burning questions we had. 'When did Pearl's heart toward us change? Where did she come from? What did she want, and why? Answering, she said, "Pearl not having family in the area, out loneliness and desperation, inserted herself into our lives."

Hannah told you that it was not the first time she (Pearl) was known to have done that. According to her recollection, her first two supervisors' wives caught on quickly and gave their husbands ultimatums concerning Pearl. Terminate her or transfer her!

Hannah said, by the time I had gotten my second promotion, she had become less aggressive in her approach, and because she was good at her job, the company saw no reason to terminate her. She also told you that because it was evident to all, I loved my wife, given the rumors about

Pearl being a woman on the prowl, I was the best person to supervise her, so she was transferred and assigned to me. Hannah said she remembered the day her spiritual antenna went up. She had taken a call from the resort, confirming reservations for four, when we invited Pearl and her guest along with us on our ski trip. She told you, the gentleman that accompanied Pearl was not her significant other as she led us to believe. He was a co-worker from the mailroom.

She had asked him, via the inner office phone to go with her as her date because she wanted to experience vacation life with us in an intimate setting. She added; Pearl paid him to go. Hannah also told you, from that day on, she began to watch and pray for us. She said she could see, the more comfortable I became with my secretary, the closer she got to me. However, her real target was you because you had all the things she wanted. She wanted our home, my money, and my love. She wanted your life.

Pearl's heart never turned from you because she was never for you. Both of us trusted her with everything, especially our secrets.

Hannah said, "Pearl came up from the rear, supported us by working in the middle, only to position herself to lead."

Hannah went on to say, "When rumors started to circulate that Pearl was seen using my credit card, the red flag was waving!" After that she observed Pearl surfing the internet for information about surrogacy; that caused her to step up her prayers for our marriage.

She said she waited for the Lord to tell her when to call you," And when Pearl did not return to work after her first week, the Holy Spirit impressed it upon her to contact you."

She had been thinking about you and wanted to know if it was alright for her to pray for you. You wept while she prayed. She said the Holy Spirit led her to invite you to church with her. You went and within a couple of weeks, praying with her turned into you praying for us. She said, the day you invited her to our home to share your heart's actions with her, she shared the enemy's plan for the demise of our marriage with you.

My beloved, do you remember telling me that Hannah told you the meaning of her name before sharing this story:

"Hannah in Hebrew means "Grace." Hannah was a woman from the bible, who was married to a certain man named Elkanah. He loved her very much. Elkanah also had another wife; she was his wife of convenience; her name was Peninnah. Although Elkanah loved Hannah, she was sad and broken-hearted because she was barren. On the other hand, his wife of convenience had several sons and daughters.

Although Penninah had his children, she did not have his love. And because of it, she set out every day to make Hannah jealous. She taunted her day and night with her quiver of children. Miserable, Hannah cried and prayed. She would not eat; she wanted a son. Her husband told her he loved her more than ten sons and begged her to eat. Still, she would not. Instead, she went to the house of the Lord to see the Priest. She went to make her request known of the Lord. Praying from her soul, voicelessly moving her lips, she was thought to be drunk by Eli the Priest, she was not. Through many tears, she poured out her heart's request for a son. She promised the Lord if He gave her a son, she would give him back to Him to serve in the "House of the Lord."

Moved by her tears, the Priest told her to go home and eat; her petition would be granted. Hannah went back home. Happy, she loved her husband. It was a good night for them both. God opening her womb, promptly shut Peninnah's mouth! God gave her a son. As promised, after Hannah weaned him from her breast, she took him to live with the Priest.

> Her son entered the "House of the Lord" and was trained by the Hand of God who declared, 'And I will raise Me up a Faithful Priest, that shall do according to that which is in My Heart and in My Mind: and I will build him a sure house, and he shall walk before Mine Anointed forever.' (1 Samuel 2:35)

Her son became the great 'Prophet Samuel' of the bible. Because of Hannah's faithfulness, God blessed her with four more children."

You told me as she was nearing the end of her story, she gently reached for your hands and told you that because of Hannah's commitment in prayer and her belief in the Lord, not only did God hear her prayer and bless her with the son she returned to Him, He gave her four more children, totaling five, God's number for 'Grace.' (Ref: 1 Samuel Chapters 1 and 2).

My darling, you told me you wept in Hannah's arms as you cried and prayed. Moving your lips, you prayed your heart's desire. You told me after she let you cry it all out, shifting, she grabbed your hands. Seizing your attention again, she said, "There is something I want you to know about Peninnah; she was Hannah's thorn. We know from this story, Elkanah's two wives lived in the same house (shell).

We know Peninnah had several children that she used as friction to tease and irritate Hannah." Squeezing your hands, looking into your puffy eyes, she said, "I have just described, 'Pearl.' She shocked you in telling you, Penninah in Hebrew means, 'Pearl,' and then she commenced to giving you these scientific facts.

"Natural pearls are formed in the bed of a mollusks (mantle) oyster shell. Grains slips in, friction occurs, therefore causing irritation. If the shell is lined with nacre (polish), eventually it will produce a mother pearl, like the one on the necklace that was picked out for you by your husband's secretary, 'Pearl'.

She told you that the enemy likes to mark his territory. You said you reacted by squeezing Hannah's hands, a squeeze that could not be mistaken; you were angry. When you shared this with me, reflecting on our anniversary dinner, I understood why you said the sight of the necklace immediately irritated you and the ruby bracelet unnerved you. Again, for that, I am deeply sorry.

You told me, shaking your head, that you asked Hannah why she thought Pearl would do such a thing. Hannah told you Pearl was not wise. In referring to scripture she quoted;

"Pearl necklaces and ruby bracelets-why bother? None
of this is even a down payment on Wisdom!"

(ref; Job 28:18 in part MSG)

Hannah told you she did not believe Pearl set out to take your place initially. She felt somewhere along the way; the enemy planted a seed of jealousy in her heart that festered into envy. Because it was not uprooted, it sprouted into undercover covetousness, therefore hatching her carefully laid plan.

Weeks later you told Hannah that it had been documented in the court papers, an early DNA report determined, Pearl was pregnant with twin boys. And then you told her you did not care; you were going to leave me and my unborn, ill-gotten surrogate sons of a Pearl!

You said it was through fighting tears of her own that Hannah implored you not to let the enemy win. She told you not to leave me but to fight in the spirit for us all. She encouraged you to fight for my soul's salvation, our marriage, and our sons. Hannah told you she would pray with you and walk with you through the sure to come, "dark season", the beginning of our "trying years." Gripping your shaking hands, Hannah said, "Like it or not, Pearl 'aka' Penninah is pregnant with you and your husband's sons. Your husband's former secretary used you and deceived him. He unknowingly signed the primary custodial rights of his stored seed over to her. You need to answer the enemy's deception with forgiveness and a fight in God's love through Christ Jesus. She told you, ignoring the situation was not an option because what you ignore, you empower. And for the sake of the innocent lives and souls of our sons and Pearl, who was carrying our sons, you had to pray.

You shared, after wrestling with yourself, you still decided to leave me, but only for a few days. You decided not to 'sit' in the situation that made you sick to your stomach; you needed time alone. Grabbing the surrogate contract, you checked yourself into a hotel, not a psych ward. There you said you cried, prayed, and prepared yourself to fight, only you were not sure what you wanted to fight or who your opponent was.

Were you going to fight me for a divorce, or join forces with me and fight for our marriage and the rights to our sons? You said you told the Lord you were not leaving until He spoke to you and told you what to do.

You trusted Hannah, but you needed to hear the Lord's Voice for yourself. On the third day, you showered and told yourself, although you were not hungry, you needed to eat. The tears you drank over those three days was not enough.

Opening the draw in your hotel room looking for the room service menu, you were surprised to see a Bible neatly tucked away in it. You told me this made you chuckled as you thought to yourself, 'Most hotels quietly stop placing Bibles in their rooms because it was a deterrent for immoral activity, and that was bad for business.'

You said your laughter was replaced with reverential stillness, as for the first time, you heard the Voice of the Lord. The Holy Spirit impressed it upon you to pick up the Word of God and read it. Opening the Bible, you went where you were directed. Initially browsing for the story Hannah had shared with you about Elkanah, his two wives, Eli and Samuel, the Lord led you to another story in the book of Genesis.

A story surrounding some other fascinating characters, Judah, Tamar, Er, Onan, Shelah, Zerah, and Perez. Their story, like ours was filled with twist and turns, resulting from deception and desire that led to trickery then subsequent victory.

After being defrauded, in the end, Tamar got what was promised to her, to the Glory of God! His faithfulness prevailed. In reading their story, you said God engaged your understanding and compassion.

The Director sat back down as tears of appreciation fell gracefully from his eyes...

Speaking softly, he said, "My dear, you told me after you read that story, you stretched your body across the bed as God began to impart deep revelation into your spirit concerning the meaning of what you had just read. You said you saw yourself in their story. Like Tamar, desperately wanting to have a baby, you jumped at the chance to have one by surrogacy." Recalling this memory prompted "The Director" to respond with words of his own.

Speaking out loud, he said, "Though you did not send me into the arms of another woman, finding evidence (his wife's little black book) of what you so desperately wanted laying around spoke to the husband in me. I promised your father when he gave me your hand in marriage that I would do everything in my power to make you happy. I believed I fell short."

Standing up, the Director took one giant step toward his wife's casket. Leaning over it, he threw his arms across it and wept. When he was able to speak again, this is what he said;

"Thank you for coming back home to me. When you called and said you were on your way, I prepared a candlelight dinner for us. I wanted to properly apologize to you for leaving you uncovered and allowing Pearl to charm, then harm you in the worst way. Instead, you walked through the door and told me about your encounter with "The Lord" and what He had instructed you to do. It was my turn to have my 'come to Jesus moment.' That night, I gave my heart to "The Lord."

I became a believer in Jesus Christ. You said the Lord showed you the innocence of our unborn sons through Judah and Tamar's story. And because of my stored (not spilled) seed, He (God) was going to bless me, to influence my sons and generations scheduled to come forth from them. You said the Lord beckoned you to come up higher and accept His plan for our sons and not to focus on the vessel they were coming through but rather the vessels He had chosen to entrust them to; me and you.

He told you our sons would be raised together. You told me, in going over the surrogate custodial papers, there was a clause in fine print that stated, "If multiple births occurred, in the event of a challenge,

the babies were to be divided equally between the surrogate and the biological father if he chose to stake a claim. It further stated if there was an odd number of babies (more than two), Pearl would receive the odd numbered baby or babies.

Pearl was carrying twins, which meant we were entitled to one son each, with Pearl automatically receiving the firstborn of the twins. Digging further, you also discovered, if I elected to, I had been granted the right to name my sons. You asked if for you, I would invoke my right and, in honor of Tamar, name our firstborn son Zerah and our second-born son Perez.

That was an easy, yes! Afterward, you told me the reason you left was that God had drawn you away to speak with you. He wanted to make your acquaintance and confirm His blessing. When our sons were born, so was our resilience. By God's love, grace, and mercy, we forgave Pearl. Our focus was set on building a fortress of love around us all. Initially, co-parenting with Pearl, there were a few very trying moments, but as we grew in God, faith, and His Word, we were reminded, all things were possible through Him,

> "But Jesus looked at them and said to them, "With men
> this is impossible, but with God all things are possible."

(Matt 19:26)

And when we felt weak or angry, and regret tried to revisit us, we called on the name of Jesus; and the Lord renewed our strength.

"I can do all things through Christ who strengthens me.
(Philippians 4:13)

When the boys turned three, and Zerah wanted to come and live with us, because we did not hold a grudge against Pearl but chose to co-parent in love through Christ, putting the boys' needs first, she signed the papers giving us full custody of Zerah! But you already knew that would happen.

God made you a promise in your heart the day they were born when Zerah, as you like to say, 'stuck his hand out first, reached for us, then pulled it back.' God told you His plan. He taught you how to trust and wait on Him and the timing of His promise. I, on the other hand, was deeply touched by God's kindness toward me. He had recovered my seed.

You never regarded Zerah and Perez as your stepsons. We raised our sons to love God and each other. The day you said, "These are my babies, our gifts from God. I am their mother, chosen by God, and I love them with my whole heart " I fell deeper in love with you.

"Behold, children are a gift of the Lord, the fruit of the womb is a reward.

(Psalms 127:3)

God taught me how to love and cover my family in Him properly. With His help, we did not give up on our love or our family. Hannah did not leave us either. And because of her love and true godly friendship, she became grandma "Nana Hannah" to our sons. Remaining close in our lives, she helped to bridge a gap between us all, and for that, I will be forever grateful to her.

Losing your mother at a young age, you felt God had blessed you with the love of a mother through her. She loved you as if you were her very own daughter. She helped us raise our sons in the Lord, and in return, the love they had for her filled her heart daily with great joy." Laughing lightly, The Director said, "I remember the day we asked her if she would be our son's godmother.

After she cried tears of sheer joy, she found me her own trusted replacement secretary then gave me her two-week notice. She said, "God had answered her prayer and changed her assignment to caring for our family full-time, in spirit."

She went on to say, it was her good pleasure to labor in love and prayer for us, and because God had placed our family in her life and her heart, she was no longer barren." She was an angel on assignment from "The Lord." I remember her last words to us before she passed, away. She cautioned us to always remember this scripture;

> "As for you, you meant evil against me, but God meant
> it for good in order to bring about this present result,
> to preserve many people alive."

(Gen 50:20)

She wanted us to understand; what God means to come about; no matter the chosen ways or means by man, His plans will stand. And we can rest confidently in Him and His chosen end, knowing this one thing; someone else's perceived foiled plan can be GOD'S DIVINE PLAN.

"The Lord foils the plans of the nations; He thwarts the purposes of the peoples. But the PLANS of the Lord stand firm forever, the purposes of His heart through all generations. Blessed is the nation whose God is the Lord, the people He chose for His inheritance." (Psalms 33:10)

She told us to keep God first and He will go before us in all things. And now you, my dear, have joined her in the presence of The Lord. (ref 2 Corinth 5:8)

I will miss your tender heart, your loving smile and faithful spirit. You are the love of my life, my best friend, my only wife, and now you have fallen asleep in our Lord and Savior, Jesus Christ. I will be forever grateful to God for allowing me to become one with you. "Signed, Sealed and Delivered," you were a complete package, my dream come true.

Placing his hands on his wife's casket, leaning down, he planted a warm kiss on it and whispered, "I'll be back tomorrow, my love. Sleep well, my darling; death has separated our bodies but never our love."

Loving you always and forever, until we meet again around the throne,

your devoted husband,
"The Director"

#5

Paternity Court

Hello, my name is Patrice. Let me tell you how I ended up in court SIX times in TWO years with the same man...

THE BRIEF...

There I was, on the PCCS (Paternity, Custody, Child Support) level of the courthouse for the FOURTH time, only this time I was there as the plaintiff!

Docket 7, case #1348; the courtroom clerk was calling for me...

Thirty-six weeks pregnant, with my head held down in perceived shame and my stomach poked out ready to place blame, I waddled up to the front of the courtroom. I was pregnant, frustrated, and almost near tears from the literal and emotional weight of everything that had happened to me. I raised my head up just in time to see the look on the judge's face. Appearing to sympathize with me, she quickly shot the defendant's attorney a look of contempt.

"Judge Deborah," inquiring, asked the attorney; why her client was not present? Giving an unacceptable reason for her client's absence, caused the judge to remove her eyeglasses. Adjusting herself on her bench before speaking, Judge Deborah told the attorney she was not satisfied with the excuse provided. After conferring with the clerk, the judge advised the defendant's attorney to have her client respond by noon the next day for an emergency DNA test for medical purposes.

That day, Judge Deborah had also planned to include a ruling on my newly filed request for child support as well. Because my baby's father did not show up, a different date was set for the support hearing. Looking sternly at the attorney from her bench, the judge said, "As for the second matter (child support) your client has two weeks from today to appear before me. He is to be here at 9:00 a.m. sharp. Not another excuse! Looking from me to the attorney, obviously appalled by it all, the judge said, "Counselor, let me reiterate; this medical matter is urgent!

Tell your client, if he is not in my courtroom by noon tomorrow to submit to a blood test, I will issue a bench warrant for his arrest, with contempt charges attached to it. Do I make myself clear?" The attorney responded by saying, "Yes, Your Honor." As for me, tears I thought were going to fall and embarrass me instantly dried up. Help had arrived.

I left the courtroom happy she had ordered my baby's father to come the next day to submit to the blood test. Though it was close to my due date, I was satisfied. In two weeks, I would get another chance to amend my complaint before squeezing my baby out. I was wrong. Per the judge's order, my baby's father responded the next day for the blood test. He also responded two weeks later for the child support hearing. He showed up for court; I did not. I could not. I was busy giving birth the morning of our hearing.

Once the judge was advised why I did not make it to court, a new date was set. This time the date was pushed out to six months later, seemingly fulfilling a prophecy. This worked out for my baby's father. He was given more time to respond to my complaint differently because I was different. In the meantime, there was someone I needed to find, apologize to, and make amends. Let me tell you why:

THE ACTUAL STORY...

The SECOND time I found myself on the PCCS (Paternity, Custody, Child Support) level of the courthouse was well over a year ago. What started as me being there as a supportive spectator quickly turned into me becoming party to an incident that nearly got me arrested! I was there with my boyfriend of five years. During our time together, we had been through everything that could cause a couple to break up.

And several times, we did just that; break up. We never stayed apart long because he always came back to me; he was mine. We had weathered every conceivable storm, except that one, conception. Another young lady had conceived his baby. However, before I found out about the concealed conception, my boyfriend of five years, finally taking our commitment to the next level, proposed to me. He did so, standing and without a ring. He told me he couldn't afford to get one at the time but wanted us to be engaged. Leaning in, he kissed me and said, "If you put it on your credit card, I will make the payments." The next day we went to the jewelry store in the mall. Once we picked out my ring, he left and headed for the food court while I pay for it. I saw the way the salesclerk looked at me.

If she could have gotten away with it, she would have called me a fool to my face or lied and said my credit card was declined. I didn't care; I had my future on my mind. After the charge went through, she explained the terms of the agreement, then handed me the bag and my receipt. I blocked out her covert disdain and headed for the food court to find my unofficial fiancé'. Riding up the escalator, I was so happy. As soon as I spotted him, my feelings started to de-escalate; he was smiling while talking to another woman.

As soon as he saw me, he ended the conversation abruptly and quickly walked towards me. Reading his face, it said, "Don't start with me," so I didn't. We were going to be engaged soon. I wanted to leave the mall the way we had arrived, in good spirits. I handed him the bag; he gave me back the receipt. I told him we would discuss a payment schedule later. He nodded his head, then dropped the jewelry bag inside his shoe bag. He had bought himself some tennis shoes while I was charging my ring. Holding hands, we walked to my car. He told me he had a special way he wanted to re-propose to me before slipping the engagement ring I had purchased on my finger.

A few days went by; he made no mention of any special plans for an engagement, re-enactment. Wondering why it was taking him so long to ask me again, this time with a ring, I asked him. This caused a huge argument. We didn't speak for three days. Five years with him and this was the closes I had gotten to becoming his wife. Two more days went by; I started to worry. I wasn't angry; I was worried. It turns out; I had a reason to be. The word on the street was, he had been arrested! Immediately, I thought he had gotten into a fight. I was shocked to find he was detained because the court deemed him a risk for flight!

When I found out why he was arrested, I nearly lost my mind. He had been picked up on an outstanding warrant for failure to pay child support! I thought there had to be a case of mistaken identity. As it turned out, the person who was mistaken was me. I did not know my almost fiance's true, identity. This was my FIRST time in court with him. Stunned, I sat in the courtroom as "Judge Deborah" read the results from the DNA test he submitted to. The test determined him to be 99.9 percent the father of a child whose mother was not in court that day. He was given three months to come up with a lump sum of arrears (money) owed for back child support.

He was to obtain a cashier check and make it out to the court on behalf of the son he had fathered. I was present, but numb. The judge released him and gave him a court date set for three months later. He met me in the back of the courtroom, attempting to look like he was the victim. Physically I was there, but emotionally, I was "Finding Nemo" lost. A baby? How? When? More importantly, with who? Speechless, I didn't know what to say, or ask. During our five-minute walk to the car garage, neither of us said a word. He had a whole baby he could not deny fathering. I was owed an explanation, which I refused to ask for. My gut was screaming, "That's it! This is the last straw!" Out loud, I said nothing. I was not a weak woman; I was a woman in love with a man who obviously knew nothing about love.

To break the ice, my feelings speaking for me asked, "Do you love her?" Betraying myself, I couldn't believe that was my first question. However, if his answer was yes, our relationship was going to be over by default. If his answer was no, there was room to negotiate. He answered, no. For the next thirty minutes, we sat in our familiar conference room, my car. My hearing was on mute as he spun his lies like a spider on steroids. It didn't matter; somewhere within our human weblink, we had crossed the point of no return.

My common-sense compass was broken; I didn't know where we were or where we were going. I just knew I needed to stop and change directions. Life to him was fun and games. Nothing seemed to matter. He was irresponsible, careless, and unphased. I realized I did not know him at all. We were young adults, acting like children playing with each other like we were dolls. He was my "RAGGEDY ANDY," and I was his "RAGGEDY ANN." We were attached at the hip. Lost in my own thoughts, I said nothing during the ride home.

About a mile from his house, he started to tell me the details of his paternity story. He said he ran into the young lady two years ago and saw her off and on. According to him, he met her when we broke up for three months. After we got back together and broke up repeatedly, he dated her in between our breakups. When we were off, they were on and vice versa. He told me there was never any overlapping. He was not Houdini; therefore, that was not possible. He had, however, without my knowledge, fathered a child.

Angry, I thought, "He needs to stop talking and just enjoyed this ride home." Once I pulled in front of his mother's house, I kept the engine running, signaling I was done talking and listening. I had nothing more to say. Hindsight twenty-twenty, I should have made him give me back the ring I had charged to my account before leaving.

There's love, and then there's addiction. Fueled by the familiar, we sometimes define addiction as love. Initially, an unsuspecting victim, somewhere along the way, I became a willing participant to the pain and deception he offered, changing my status from victim to volunteer. That day, when he got out of my car, I pulled off without saying goodbye; I believed I was done. Instead of driving off into the sunset, I drove off into an onset. For the next couple of weeks, he called me around the clock, at home, and work. My phone rang constantly until finally, I turned it off.

Eventually, he stopped calling. You would have thought I was grateful; I wasn't. My relief from the silence was short-lived. Fear and desperation started to stalk me. I was running from ghosts that weren't chasing me. Determined not to go back to him, one Wednesday night, I let myself be talked into going to Bible study with my sister. She said Jesus could help me. I had nothing left to lose, so I went.

Before I walked in, I made a silent agreement with myself. I was not going up for prayer, I was not looking for a church home, I was not going to turn and talk to my neighbor, and I was only giving five dollars as my offering. Most importantly, I was fine; I did not need to be saved. I liked everything about my life, everything except for my cheating ex-fiancé's ways. I did, however, ask God to fix that situation, since I was in His house.

I wanted Him to answer my prayer from where I was sitting. That night the minister's powerful message of healing, flying from the pulpit was taught and caught. I received it with great joy! Unfortunately, I forgot what he said as soon as my head hit my stony pillow that night. My thoughts immediately drifted back to my ex. Lovesick, my stomach started to ache. I started choking. I couldn't sleep. During church that night, I felt a strong draw to go up for prayer. Not a liar like my ex, I kept my word. I did not go up for prayer. I realized too late; I should have.

> "Similarly these are the ones on whom seed was sown on the rocky places, who, when they hear the word, immediately receive it with joy; and they have no firm root in themselves, but are only temporary; then, when affliction or persecution arises because of the word, immediately they fall away.
>
> And others are the ones on whom seed was sown among the thorns; these are the ones who have heard the word, but the worries of the world, and the deceitfulness of

205

riches, and the desires for other things enter in and choke the word, and it becomes unfruitful."

(Mark 4:16-19)

My inner voice started talking. Last I had checked, there were no calls or messages from my now known ex. The onset had moved to stage two. Trying to remember the powerful message I had heard a few hours ago, I was met with static and interference in my brain. The enemy of my mind and heart started taunting me. As soon as I closed my eyes, my mind suffered a head-on collision.

Pictures and audio of his voice from the conversation we had during our car ride appeared. Enhanced were the words he used in describing his relationship with the other woman, the mother of his child. He said, "when we were off, they were on." So, since we were off, did that mean they were back on? My phone had been on for a couple of days, and there were no calls from him. I found myself in the dark asking, "Where is he?"

And just like that, the switch happened. I found myself reaching for my volunteer badge and pinning it to my chest. I felt like all those years with him were an investment. Let my friends tell it; I should have flushed my relationship with him down the drain long ago, with liquid Drano as a chaser, therefore, unclogging my life. Curiosity joining my mental party asked questions I did not have answers to. "Who was the woman he had a child with, and why was she really taking him to court?

Does she love him, want him? What does she look like? Does his son look like him or her?"

According to the judge's disclosure, their son was a little over a year old. Was she taking him to court because she was done, or had she won? "And now that we are off for good, does that mean they're on for good? Did I hand him over to her without a fight?" Those questions chased sleep away from me that night.

By morning, my eyes were bloodshot red. "Thinkin drinkin," I was hungover from questioning myself all night. Sitting at the breakfast table, dazed from being sleep deprived, my sister handed me a piece of mail; it was open. It was the first payment request for the ring I had paid for but did not have. I pushed my cereal bowl to the side, ran to my room, jumped into my sweatsuit, and then my car. I broke speed limits on my way to his house. I had a legitimate reason to be there at 8:37 a.m. that Saturday morning.

I didn't want a payment; I wanted my ring. Deep down inside, I just wanted to see him, talk to him. I also wanted to make sure he hadn't pawned my ring to get the money he needed for his court-ordered child support. Or worst, I wanted to make sure he hadn't tried to smooth things over with his baby's momma by given her my ring! At any rate, I was going to talk to him. I mustered up the courage to knock on the door, only to be told he wasn't home. Where was he? Slowly walking back to my car, I went from being angry to afraid. Sitting in my car, I decided to wait. I tried to remind myself I was only there to get my ring. Nothing could have been further from the truth. Just as I was about to give up and leave, a car pulled up alongside mine. He was being dropped off by one of his friends.

He got out of his friend's car and hopped into mine. We started to talk. The bags under my eyes gave my position away, that and my line of questioning. Worn down from worry, he made his move. Performing his well-known magic trick, "Poof!" the tables had turned. He was officially the victim. Seated in my passenger seat with no wheel but a spin, he became the driver.

Speaking, he started with how many times he had called me, and I didn't answer, not the fact he had fathered a child he hadn't told me about. According to him, his feelings were hurt. He loved me and wanted to apologize and explain. On the fence swaying back and forth as to whether or not I would take him back, I at least wanted to hear his fairytale explanation.

There were too many unanswered questions, and if I wanted to hear a fraction of the truth, I had to succumb to his accusation, breezed through apology, and settle for his redacted explanation. By noon, I was off the fence and in his arms. We were back on again. I still didn't get what I came for, my ring. Instead, he gave me a fifty-dollar payment and a renewed promise; he had something special planned for me.

As for his baby's momma, listening this time, he told me in detail, she was somebody he knew from high school. She had a crush on him back then and always wanted to date him. They bumped into each other during one of our breakups when he was so broken up behind losing me. According to him, this other woman found out and threw herself at him to help him get over me. He said, when I stop answering my phone, he thought I had met someone new and moved on, so he started spending time with her.

He said when they were intimate, they always used protection except for the one time they didn't, but even then, according to him, he discarded his seed. He went on to say; she mentioned something about wanting a baby. He said a few months later, after we had gotten back together, she called and told him she was pregnant. She also told him she knew he loved me, and because of that, she wanted nothing from him.

He said that made him think the baby wasn't his and was shocked when the warrant squad came to his house and arrested him. Sitting, listening to his tale, trailing off, I thought, "I am a smart, good-looking woman with a good heart and an Associate Degree.

What am I doing here in this space with him, when there are plenty of other fish in the sea?" That was a good question. Unfortunately, I wasn't willing to take my tackle box and go fish for someone new. He was mine, no one else would do.

I didn't believe him, but I didn't want to be without him. When all was said and done, he still wanted me, and I realized I never stop wanting him. He reassured me he did not want to be with the mother of his son. Those declarations were the keys that started the engine of our relationship back up with a warning. I told myself that this was his next to last chance with me. Verbally, I warned him, that if he ever did anything like that again, whether the switch in our relationship was on or off, I would leave him for real, and for good!

After establishing that verbal clause, sealing it with a kiss, the conversation switched to damage control. I told him I would help him do whatever he needed me to do to support him in being a part of his son's life, but I meant what I said; if he did it again, I would leave and never come back. Breaking our verbal agreement; he did it again. Somehow, I was not surprised by his actions. However, what I was genuinely surprised about was who he did it too; me.

MY TURN...

We had been getting along so well. A week before he was due back in court, he took me to the movies, dinner, and the park, where he finally got down on one knee and popped the question. I was so happy! He finally placed the ring I was making payments on, on my finger.

A payment was due, but since he was due back in court the following week with the full amount of the arrears, I made the ring payment for him. As if that wasn't enough, the next day he called me and told me he had a problem. He did not have all the money he needed for his court-ordered payment.

My title had finally changed. I was his fiancee'. I liked the sound of that. Inadvertently, I inherited the role of the financier. What affected him now affected me. With that being said, I took what he gave me, withdrew the rest from my savings account, and got a cashier's check. That payment would catch him up, keeping him from being locked up, per the judge's order. He had started a new job, and I was very proud of him. Together we were on the way to planning our future.

My contribution was my investment. As far as I was concerned, we were handling our first financial transaction as an official couple. I was looking forward to going to court with him. I wanted to stand by his side as his fiancee' and show my support for his child support. As if it was some special event, I bought a new outfit and got my hair and nails done. I was ready to show his baby's mother I had won. At home, in my mirror, I practiced holding my head up and walking alongside my imaginary man. Caught up in the realm of my imagination, I thought, even if his fairytale was a lie, when his baby's momma saw me, she was going to see the gold-plated truth on my left hand, wrapped around my ring finger. I hoped she had planned to bring their son. I wanted to see him and allow him the opportunity to see me, his soon-to-be stepmother.

Two days before my fiance's court date, he called to tell me he had taken the payment down to the court's cashier's office, so he would not have to take off work for the hearing. Because he paid it early, he did not have to appear before the judge. He was happy; I was disappointed. Where I should have been pleased, he was showing some sense of responsibility by not asking for time off his new job, I wasn't. I didn't tell him I was looking forward to seeing his baby's momma and being seen by her. It was okay because my chance would come again several months later.

SAME SCENARIO...

We argued—this time about when he was going to marry me. We weren't speaking, he stopped calling because once again, he had gotten arrested for unpaid child support. Things were much different this time; I was not worried. In fact, I slept like a baby because I was carrying one, his. I was three months pregnant.

And just like before, he needed help from his fiancee's financials. It wasn't much, but still, he needed my help to stay out of jail. If he could have gotten it from his momma or someone else, he would have because this time, the judge stipulated, she wanted my fiance' to appear in court along with the plaintiff (his baby's momma) in thirty days. I had the money, which meant I had to pay to finally see her.

She would be there, but so would I. I was getting a do-over, only this time, I bought a cute body dress to show off my baby bump. Between that and my engagement ring, whoever this woman was, she was going to get the message, he was mine. When his court date arrived, I took off work to go with him. This was my SECOND time in court, the time I spoke about earlier in my story when I almost got arrested.

THIS IS WHAT HAPPENED...

In the car on our way to court, we argued over my shoe choice; I wore stilettos. I wore them because they made my leg muscles look strong and gave my flat behind a much-needed boost. My breast, a bit swollen from pregnancy were propped up, and my mommy-to-be baby bump was on display, ready to shine. I had to walk arm-in-arm with my fiance' to the courthouse to keep from falling. When we reached the PCCS level of the building, and the elevator doors opened, I let his arm go. Stepping out of the elevator, I took off walking like I had practiced at home.

My heels were clicking so loud the people (though not many), sitting down outside the individual courtrooms, lifted their heads to see who was coming down the halls of justice sounding so confident. Looking into a few of their faces, they assumed I was the plaintiff; I was not. I was the fiancee' and mother-to-be of the defendant.

The closer we got to the courtroom his case was scheduled to be heard in, there appeared to be no one sitting outside waiting. As soon as we sat down, one of us immediately stood back up, me. Nervous, I went to peek my head inside the courtroom. Visually sweeping the courtroom like a spy, I only saw one person seated near the front. It was a guy, presumably the courtroom clerk, so I sat back down.

Earlier, when I stepped out of the elevator, I ignored my bladder's meter; it was on full. I needed to go to the bathroom then but chose to make my grand entrance instead. Since it was about thirty minutes left before court was scheduled to begin, I decided to take it slow and make my way back down the hall to the bathroom.

By the time I'd returned, walking toward my fiance' with ease, I could see a young woman sitting next to him; they were talking. The closer I got to them my face became flushed because her face was beautiful. She was his type. Was she his son's mother? She was not. She was his court-appointed attorney from the FIRST time I was there with him. After looking closely, I remembered her; she had changed her hairstyle. This time he introduced me to her. I smiled when he said, "This is my fiancee." She looked me up and down and said, "nice to meet you," then continued talking to him. She did not wait for me to respond. That made me step in close.

Whatever she had to say to him could be said in front of me. I wanted her to know we were a couple, and there were no secrets between us; well, besides that one. Listening, I heard her say because he was working, the judge would likely be imposing a wage assignment (garnishment) to his paycheck because he kept falling behind in his court-ordered support. She asked if he had brought the cashier's check mandated. Pointing at me forced her to talk to me. She asked for the check. Smiling with sarcasm, I handed it to her. She took it, then headed back into the courtroom.

Ten minutes later, she reappeared. His case was about to be called. She needed him to come inside the courtroom. We stood up, and once again, one of us sat back down, me. It was a closed hearing. It didn't matter that I was his fiancee' and financier; I was not allowed to go with him or see in the courtroom. I snapped my fingers. I had missed his baby's momma! It was clear she had arrived while I was in the bathroom. My initial regret was not getting the chance to see her and my fiance's interaction when she got there. I wanted to see their body language exchange.

Ugh! I was peeved at me for having to go pee! It cost me the opportunity to judge her looks and her runway walk against mine. I also wanted her to see that I was there to support my man.

My bladder was empty. All I had to do now was sit and wait. I would catch a glimpse of her coming out. About thirty minutes later, my fiance' stormed out with a shackled look of anger on his face and in his demeanor. His attorney drifted out behind him. She looked at him, then me. Her smirky grin said, "He brought this on himself," my facial response was, "You're right."

Neither of us shared our voiceless conversation with him. Once he calmed down, she handed him some papers. He looked at me angrily and said, "Let's go!" then turned and started walking away without me. I didn't move. I had not done all that had to leave without seeing the woman who had given birth to his baby and induced the anger that had besieged him in that moment. He took a few strides then stopped with his back to me as he read the documents given to him.

He did not realize I wasn't behind him. When he did, he turned and yelled, "Come on!" Just then, the courtroom door opened slowly. In a split second, my attention was split in two different directions. Everything happened so fast. Glancing in a flash at the door, the guy I saw earlier was exiting the courtroom. When I realized it wasn't her, I quickly turned, looked at my fiance' from a short distance, and yelled, "Wait a minute!" My mind was made up, I was not leaving until the woman who could potentially be a problem for the rest of our lives came out of the courtroom.

I wanted to see her face to face! It was too late. I was looking at the back of her head! It was the person I assumed was the courtroom clerk. My eyes traveled up, then down her sleek, finely contoured body. She had on a skirt suit with legs for days. Her calf muscles were real. She had a sexy boy cut, haircut, and in the places where her skin was exposed, she appeared to be African American. We were Caucasian!

My fiance' rolled his eyes like a girl as she was walked toward him at a safe enough distance to pass by. Wait! What? Still, I could not move. Just as she was about to pass him with her head held high, exuding real confidence, I saw his lips move. He was saying something to her. Whatever it was made her stop and turned to him. Breaking free from the shock chains holding me, I scurried from the spot I was in. Reshaping their conversation space, it became a triangle. I wanted to make my presence and point known. Listening and looking at her, mentally I started to compare myself to her.

She was beautiful; I was too. Her skin was a deep even-toned mocha brown; mine (in that moment) was white with blotches of pink. Her makeup was light and seemed to be professionally applied. Mine was heavy and done in five minutes by me. She was dress conservatively; I had on a body dress. She spoke with authority when she talked to him; I didn't speak at all. Her post-pregnancy body looked like it had undoubtedly been whipped into shape by an active gym membership. As for me, with my baby growing inside of me, I was in the beginning stages of being stretched.

Her hair was jet black, cropped, and cut close. Mine was a reddish-brown, long, and curly. I ended my comparison where I started; the elephant in our triangle's eye, and it was not my protruding belly. She was Black; we were White! Watching the two of them exchange words civilly caused singes of his cooling anger to attack, then overthrow me. Where had his fire from five minutes ago gone? They acted as if I, the literal elephant (metaphorically), was not standing there. I was not prejudiced; I was pregnant, territorial, and terrified!

His baby mama could have been any woman of any race in that moment. My problem: the reality of the other woman was there in real-time. Because I was talking to myself and not listening to them, angry with him, deflecting, I took it out on her. Jumping in with my words, I attacked her by saying, "Don't yell at him!" The two of them turned and gave me a puzzling look. No one was yelling. His baby mama snickering, leaned back on her long legs and calmly said, "I don't know who you are, but this does not concern you." That was my cue.

Justified, I yelled, "This does concern me!" She looked at me and put her hands on her hips and said, "I'm talking to my son's father." I pointed to the ring on my finger, poked my stomach out, and said, "I'm his fiancée! We are getting married and having a baby of our own. Whatever you have to say to him concerns me, especially since you took advantage of him when we broke up and got yourself pregnant.

You didn't want him; you just wanted a baby. You said you didn't want anything from him, and now that he doesn't want you, you're trying to get back at him by digging in his pockets!" My fiancé and his son's mother looked at me in mild shock. I looked at him, wondering why he was looking at me like those were lies? I only repeated what he told me.

Oops! I forgot to remember what he told me concerning his baby's mama was not admissible. It was "he said, she said" gossip. And because it was "he" (my fiance') who said it; at best, it was sprinkled with the truth. Clapping her hands together, she burst into laughter. I knew instantly her response to my rant was appropriate. I had exposed him, offended her, and embarrassed myself. Laughing, she said, "Girl, listen, I'm not sure what he told you, but that's not what happened." Then she shot him a look that caused him to look away, silently confirming her last statement.

Already looking like a fool, my mouth opened up, backed me up, and had me sounding off like one! Using a legal term, I had looked up, I said, "This is nothing more than an 'Admission Against Interest.' He is your son's father, but he is not interested in being with you! Before I could catch myself, the volume in my voice shot up, and I yelled, "The past doesn't matter! I'm his future, and you need to move on!" There we were in living color, acting out the lyrics from the famous song "The Boy Is Mine," sung by two young female R&B legends, Brandy and Monica.

Our production was a hot mess! Angry, with nowhere to go but low, I yelled, "We're not going to let you, or your son interfere with our lives!" Mentioning her son was a fatal mistake. That was the death of her diplomacy. She turned into a fire, breathing mama bear! The next thing I knew, my fiance' was standing between us, holding me back. I screamed obscenities at her until two courthouse marshals quickly converged on us. Viewing them as my backup, I jumped from behind my fiance' with bravery and said, "I don't care if I am pregnant, I will whip your..." I never got to finish my empty threat. She squared her shoulders back, and with great dignity, said, "Do not ever fix your mouth to disrespect me or my child again!

You're making all of this noise and all the same mistakes I did. You're pregnant, engaged, and enraged; been there, done that. I had the t-shirt, but I traded it in." Both of you need to get over me, getting over him, and get on with your lives." Speaking from evidential experience, she said, "Sweetheart, I've been where you are." That comment earned my full attention.

Pointing at the walls around us, she said, "Pat, that's your name, right?" Before I could answer, she continued: "I suggest you do yourself a favor. Take a good look around and familiarize yourself with this place; you'll be back here this time next year as the plaintiff!" After she made that startling prediction, she turned and walked toward the elevator. Between her and I, she was the winner of a different contest, "self-respect."

For the first time, I got a glimpse of self-love and what the courage to walk away looked like. Following in her footsteps, shifting in my heart, I walked away from my fiance' but not before doing what she had admonished me to do. Looking around, I found my imagination searching to see if those walls had recorded the profound sound of her words, words that had the feel of poetic prophecy.

Angry and hurt, I decided I was not going to wait until the following year to go back. The next morning, I found myself sitting outside the same courtroom, waiting for my case to be called. This was my THIRD time at the courthouse. I was there to file for child support. Looking around, I felt a cold invisible breeze. Closing my eyes, I heard a familiar echo bouncing off the walls; "Pat, that's your name, right. I suggest you do yourself a favor. Take a good look around, familiarize yourself with this place; you'll be back here next year as the plaintiff!"

It was the voice of my now estranged baby's father's, oldest child's mother. She was right! Her timing was wrong. It was the next day. Still, she predicted my future based on her past. It was as though she was standing over top of me, speaking in a haunting whisper. Looking up over the doorpost, I saw the words "Paternity Court." Inside my heart, I heard, "Pat's-turn- in court."

I should have listened to her instead of being arrogant. I took my anger out on her for no reason. My behavior was unacceptable. I chose to act in ignorance the day before, ranting against a situation I did not have all the facts to. And though I believe she would have truthfully answered any questions I might have had, I chose to insult, then threaten her. My allegiance blinded me to my fiancé. Reliving it in my mind, I wanted to get up and run out of the courthouse. Before I could, my case was called.

"Docket 7, case #1348..." I filed the necessary papers then walked into the next months of my life.

Scene: Hospital Room

After missing my child support court date, six days later, there I was, sitting in a wheelchair waiting to be escorted out of the hospital into my future. Looking at my son resting in my arms, surprisingly, my thoughts drifted to my son's brother's mother, and that awful day in court. Reflecting, I now understood her poise and what was behind her walk away, the day she walked away from us. Her priority was the welfare of her son.

Whatever had or hadn't happened between her and her son's biological father didn't matter; she was over it and him. If he had decided to be a ghost in her son's life, his cash was real and necessary. She was there in court to collect the monetary support she needed; that was it.

Besides leaving me with a haunting promise and my face dragging across the floor, she dropped invisible nuggets of courage like bread-crumbs on her way out of court that day. In spirit, I picked them up, put them in my mouth, and swallowed them. Stored in my heart, like time-release capsules, in intervals, release happened. It started during the ride home with my fiancé. We got into a deal-breaking argument.

I unleashed on him in a way he had never seen or heard from me before. Things changed between us that day.

He had lied to me about his relationship with her. Caught off guard, I completely humiliated myself. I did not care about her race, her truth, or his smoking gun lies. Pregnant, angry, and on the brink of losing my mind, I honed-in on three things I was in possession of; my ring, my choice to marry him, and the baby I was carrying. After that argument, I still had two out of the three.

I gave him back my title as "fiancee'" and all the stress that came with it. I told him I didn't trust him, and I did not want to marry a liar. He said I was too emotional, and if I didn't believe him, why should he marry me? He was right. He called my bluff, and I called his, and just like that, we canceled each other! The next day I took off work again and went back down to the courthouse to file for child support. That was my THIRD time there.

After filing, I went home and cried for a week. I was determined not to call him or accept any calls from him. Oddly enough, I was bothered but not moved. The ghost that used to chase me were reduced to voiceless spooks in the night. Rubbing my belly while thanking God for the person growing inside of me, chased them away. To help me redirect my focus, my sister purchased the book "What to Expect When You're Expecting." Shifting my energy and focus, I was excited about becoming a new mother. I wanted to do my part in helping the development and delivery of a healthy baby and since avoiding stress was on page one, it was done. I changed my phone number and avoided my baby's father. I was thankful for a good job with great healthcare benefits for me and my unborn child, benefits I would need in my third trimester. Early one morning, I received a call from my doctor; he wanted me to come in right away for some tests. They thought my child might be carrying a gene that concerned them. They needed to test me and my baby's father's blood. I did not want to talk to my ex-fiance', so I prayed and asked God to show me what to do.

After praying, I called and left him an urgent message. He called back right away. When I told him what was going on, he accused me of cheating on him and wanting a blood test to confirm he was the father. I hung up on him and started to cry out to God. I said, "God if You're real, please help me! I am sorry for anything I've done wrong. Our baby does not deserve to be punished for our choices. I heard the minister say you are a very present help in the time of trouble.

I need You, Lord! Just then, my doctor called. I explained what happened to him. He told me he would fill out the necessary paperwork to expedite a court order for a blood sample from my baby's father. I called and left him another message, requesting only that he meet me at court the next day. The following morning, I was there; he was not. This was my FOURTH time in court. His attorney was present. She said her client was not able to come because he was working. That excuse did not sit well with the judge. My baby's father was ordered to respond the next day for testing. At that time, he was advised to return in two weeks for our child support hearing. Paternity was established as well as the sex of our child. His reveal party came that afternoon in the form of a phone call, followed by a confirmation letter from my doctor.

It was a boy, and he was the father! When my doctor re-ran the test concerning the gene in question, it turned out to be a non-factor. I believe God turned it! I prayed so much while I waited. God answering my prayer on behalf of my unborn child got my attention. Grateful, prayer became my place of serenity. The more I talked to God, the more peaceful my rest and thoughts of an unknown future became.

The following week while praying, my sister came into my room. She had a piece of mail in her hand. It was my first payment letter from the jewelry store. Handing it to me, she said she was trying to explain the day I ran out and drove to my ex's house that because our names were close in spelling, Patricia (hers), Patrice (mine), she accidentally opened it. She said she knew I was in trouble when I snatched it from her, read it, dropped it, then ran to my room, got dressed, then left.

I put my head down. I remembered brushing her off to go and confront my ex that Saturday morning. Responding in love, she sat down on my bed beside me. Putting her arm around me, she prayed for me. Afterward, she told me she had peeked in on me one evening when I was on my knees, praying; I had fallen asleep. That moved her to go to her room and interceded in prayer for me. Hearing her concern brought me to tears. In between them, I told her what I had been too embarrassed and ashamed to tell her before. She did not judge me or my situation. Instead, she told me God loved us all; me, my son, his father, the other mother, and their son.

God sent her to me at the right time. Ready to receive, I listened with my heart. She said, "Sis, God sees and knows what we are made of. He created us in His image and put the desire for love in us all. She said, He, too, desires to be loved. He wants to be the first place we come to in our search for love. Only He can quench our innate thirst for it by filling us with His unconditional love. GOD, by definition, is LOVE.

> "Beloved, let us love one another, for love is from God;
> and everyone who loves is born of God and knows
> God. The one who does not love does not know God,
> for God is love. (1 John 4:7-8)

She said, "In the acquaintance of His love is where we learn how to love others. When we see them the way God sees them, equipped, we can choose to extend mercy, grant grace, and cover them in love."

Then she went on to say, "I know you think you love your son's father and that he loves you, but the truth is, neither one of you know what true love is if you don't know God." She said, "Sis, strong feelings of affection or addiction are often misconstrued as love. The truth about love can be found in the Bible. 1 Corinthians, chapter 13 (the love chapter) tells us what love is and is not." She told me to read it, then pray and ask God to lead me."

Gently rubbing my stomach, she said, "The baby growing inside of you will enter this world with many natural traits, some from you, some from his father. How he is shaped will be determined by his parents and his perspective village. Other forces with strange voices will attempt to lend their hand at shaping him, but that's where praying, interceding on his behalf, and living a godly life before him as much as possible becomes crucial. God knows we are not perfect beings.

Sometimes in our actions, we waver and faltered. And sometimes we just flat out get it wrong, but God's love and compassion run deep and wide, never-ending, we can find hope in Him.

> "The Lord's loving-kindness indeed never cease, For His compassions never fail. They are new every morning; Great is Your faithfulness. "The Lord is my portion," says my soul, "Therefore I have hope in Him."

(Lamentations 3:22-24)

As believers, we have an advocate with the Father through Jesus Christ. His love for us encouraged His sacrifice. He gave His life to restore mankind's relationship with the Father. While sin caused the separation, Christ's sacrifice corrected it; connecting us back to a place of sacred relationship and fellowship with the Father."

Therefore, the gift of salvation has been extended to all who will freely receive it. She continued by saying, "There is nothing God's Eyes have not seen, or His Ears have not heard. Only His love and power can turn RAGGEDY into RIGHTEOUS and UGLY into HOLY, causing men and women to lay their vices at the Feet of Jesus." Looking through my tears, she told me she loved me and assured me God had heard my prayers. She asked me if I wanted to give God a chance to show me His love and power through Christ. I said, "Yes." That afternoon, I repented and gave my heart, to the Lord.

How amazing was this? Here was my sixteen-year-old little sister embodied with wisdom beyond her years, leading me into a saving faith in Jesus Christ. This was God; he heard my prayer in my seat that Wednesday night at bible study when I refused to get up. He knew my heart and the situation I was sitting in. He came when I invited Him in. Behind the scenes, He (God) was fixing the problem, starting with me. My baby sister was the vessel He chose to use, to rescue me from my familiar.

> "The Lord is close to the brokenhearted; he rescues those whose spirits are crushed. The righteous person faces many troubles, but the Lord comes to the rescue each time." (Psalms 34:18-19)

After giving my heart to the Lord, I started attending church with my sister. A new babe in Christ, preparing to have a baby, I joined her church and went up for prayer every chance I could. I asked the congregation to pray for the health and safe delivery of my baby. I also asked them to pray for my son's father. Excited, I could hardly wait for my little one to arrive.

After my son's father received the letter letting him know our baby was fine, he called my sister and asked her to give me a message. He was happy to know our son was okay. He also told her to tell me he loved me. While he shared his appreciation that our son had been misdiagnosed, I believed in my heart it was not a misdiagnosis; it was a miracle, a DISMISSED diagnosis by the power of prayer!

I was changing; I no longer desired to be drawn in sin's entanglements. My prayer was, "Holy Spirit, I want to cooperate with You, help me to do my part in my transformation." Spiritually aware I was a babe in Christ, while sucking up the milk of the word of God, our baby was born.

> "So, get rid of all evil behavior. Be done with all deceit, hypocrisy, jealousy, and all unkind speech. Like newborn babies, you must crave pure spiritual milk so that you will grow into a full experience of salvation. Cry out for this nourishment, now that you have had a taste of the Lord's kindness."

(1 Peter 2:1-3 NLT)

Born healthy, he weighed seven pounds and two ounces. Immediately after he was born, he had to be taken away from me. I was told, I had developed an extremely high fever. Heavily sedated, I could not care for him the first three days of his life. My family stepped in to help. While in the throes of fever, I thought about the THIRD time I went to court, the day after my ex and I broke up, the day I filed for child support.

I also thought about the FOURTH time I went. It was for two reasons. The first reason was to sign the emergency DNA test, and the second, was to DISMISS my claim for child support. I wanted to drop the request. The reason why was because when I initially filed, I did so because I was angry and on the warpath.

I filed for support at that time because I knew how much my son's father hated going to court. I wanted to punish him. I charged him guilty of lying and leaving me. I was also angry with him for sticking me with the cost of an engagement ring that I returned and only received a fraction of what I had paid for it. He had hurt me, and I wanted him to pay. However, after talking to my sister and giving my life to the Lord, when Jesus came to live in my heart, I became aware of my motives. They were wrong. Rooted in pride, I set myself up for a fall.

"Pride goes before destruction, and a haughty spirit before a fall. (Prov16:18)

I'm not saying if it became necessary to re-apply, I wouldn't; I'm saying I didn't have the right to deprive him of the opportunity to choose to do the right thing for our son on his own, first. Even though he had demonstrated the need to be forced to pay child support, as in the case with his firstborn son, I needed to do things the right way for the right reasons. Becoming a born-again believer in Christ and carrying my son changed me. When my doctor thought our son was in crisis, I was distraught; I prayed and believed God. He alone made everything alright. As for my baby, the more he grew inside of me, the more dependent I became on God. Reading God's word, especially, "I Corinthians the 13th chapter," I discovered my sister was right; I did not know what love was. God's word enlightened me then helped me to release my old way of doing things.

Taking a chance late in my third trimester, I waddled my big self, down to the courthouse, in hopes of being able to drop my child support case before having my baby. Instead, a new date was set for us to appear six months later.

GIVING BIRTH...

By the time my ex-fiance' had arrived at the hospital, our son was two hours old. I had developed a high fever to the point of delirium during delivery. Once the doctor notified my family of my condition, everyone prayed, including my son's father. For the next three days, he stayed at the hospital and took care of our son.

The nurse showed him how to feed and change his newborn son. He only went home to shower and change clothes. He slept in my room. I was not aware of his presence. On the third day, my fever broke. Awake, all I wanted to do was see my baby. I was unaware as to how long I had been sedated. After the doctor checked my vitals and determined it was safe to bring my baby to me briefly, I thought I was dreaming when my son's father walked into my room with a hospital gown and face mask on, carrying our son.

My sister rushed to my bedside, assuring me everything was alright. I was conscious, and my baby was fine. She quickly whispered, "he hasn't left his son or your bedside in three days," then she stepped aside. Tilting our son forward as close as he could, he let me see him. Delicately he whispered, "He's so handsome and strong, look at his chin!"

Who was this man holding my son? I identified a laugh somewhere within me when I realized he was in protection mode. Because my health wasn't one hundred percent, he did not want to let me hold him. He may have missed the birth and first two hours of our son's life, but he got a three-day jump of caring for him on me.

DISCHARGED...

Wheeling us out to the car was surreal. I was happy but exhausted. Once my son's father got us home safely, he stayed and helped us to settle in. Working evenings, he was there every day for the next two months to help. My mom and sister helped where they could as well.

Our son was the priority. He had everything he needed; milk pampers, clothes, and a whole lot of love. His father was there to take us to our doctor's appointments, and he made a couple of late-night runs to the pharmacy for medication. When our son turned five months old, I received a summons from the court set for the following month to finalize my disposition.

ONE MONTH LATER...

Here I was for the FIFTH time sitting outside the courtroom. It was the one-year anniversary of my son's brother's mother's prediction, not prophecy. I was indeed there as the plaintiff, but my reason for being there, she could not prophesy because only God knew the future. I wasn't there to request or enforce child support; I was there to release him from it. I had indeed come back, but our circumstances were different.

I was a different person, and so was my son's father. It was indeed my turn. He didn't show up with someone new on his arms because he was holding someone special in his arms, our son. After the clerk called our case, happily, I explained to Judge Deborah that my son's father had been supporting his child in every way he could. A motion for dismissal was granted, and the child support case was dropped. We left the courthouse together, in peace. My relationship with Christ and my son's father prevailed. Love had silenced the echoes from the walls of the halls of justice that day. Walking back to the car, pushing our baby's stroller, he stopped, looked at me, smiled, and said, "Thank You."

I smiled back and said, "Don't thank me, thank God for His love and His word." There was a question mark look on his face, so I shared 1 Corinthian chapter 13 from the Bible with him. By the time I finished, he laughed and said, "I'm going to have to read that. He looked at me and told me I was beautiful and that he loved me and wanted to know if I still loved him?

I told him I did, but I thought we needed to take some time and talk about things. We had a new son and a new relationship that needed to breathe and be shaped differently than what it had been before. His maturity became apparent with his next request. He had given it some thought; he wanted me to meet his oldest son's mother.

He said taking care of our son for the last six months was eye-opening. He realized he needed to reach out to his son's mother and apologize to her for abandoning their son. He wanted to ask her if he could be a part of his life. He was willing to take things slow, but he felt it was important that he be there for him. I told him I was proud of him and felt like he should work on his relationship with his other son before discussing a relationship with me. And let me tell you, it was a good thing I wore flat shoes that day!

I still loved him, and if we weren't in motion (walking), my knees would have buckled, sending me crashing to the ground. I said yes to his request to meet her, because I too, owed her an apology. He said he would arrange a meeting.

Curious, I asked what made him change so much over the last months. This is what he said, "When you left me I, it didn't feel the same as all the other times before. I can't explain it, but I knew you weren't coming back. At first, I wanted to believe, it didn't matter, and then I got mad. I remember thinking, 'How dare she let me live with the consequences of the choices I've made!'" I laughed; he didn't.

He said, when he talked to me, he could tell I was changing. It felt like my love for him had soured, and like spoiled milk, expired. He said he became convincingly afraid the day I called him and told him something might be wrong with our baby. He said fear made him respond the way that he did. And when he went to be tested and was told he had to return two weeks later for a separate hearing on child support, with me as the plaintiff, he got angry.

Sleeping with that anger for the next couple of weeks, the night before he was due back in court for the support hearing, he had a bad dream. In his dream, after being identified as the father of my child, I gave birth to our baby. When the time came for us to be released from the hospital, another man he could feel in his dream loved me picked us up, causing him to wake up in a cold sweat.

Frightened and not able to shake his nightmare, he showed up for court; I didn't. He said he had planned to apologize to me and ask me for another chance. So, when the judge rescheduling our hearing for six months later, shared the reason why I was not there, he rushed to the hospital to be with me. Still slightly feverish the day he brought our son to my bedside, I was right when I asked myself, "Who is this man holding my son?"

It was him! The man from his dream, a different man, who truly loved me. That dream scared him into chasing change; he, too, wanted a new reality. He told me the day he initially missed court he was taking his road test for his CDL license. He knew he needed to get a better job to take care of his children and prove himself worthy of my love. My heart was on fire!

THREE WEEKS LATER...

The arrangements had been made. His oldest son's mother agreed to meet us for dinner at a local restaurant. My sister agreed to babysit. My baby's daddy was nervous, and it was not about dinner but about leaving our baby. Watching his reaction was endearing. By the time we arrived at the restaurant, we were greeted with a pleasant surprise. His ex was seated close to her next. He was a handsome man with a warm smile. He stood up and shook our hands while she sat and smiled graciously. She was stunning, but so was I. Glowing, she looked like she was growing, in size.

Looking at her countenance, it took me sixty seconds to make the connection. She was pregnant and married! I was excited and happy for her. Sincerely and quickly, l apologized to her for my past behavior. She smiled gently and told me she accepted my apology. We shifted right into talking about her pregnancy.

She was having a girl! While we spoke, the men at our table talked. I found her to be such a kind soul. I told her all about my son and my new birth in Christ. I needed her to know I had changed but more importantly, who was now responsible for me, acting responsibly. After we ate, we got down to the business of visitation. This time, there, in the role of "supportive friend," I kept my mouth shut with a smile on my face. I was so pleased with the apology our sons' father gave her; it was heartfelt and long overdue.

They agreed he would be allowed to see their son in the company of her and her husband initially, and as time went on, they would gradually relax his visitation. She invited me to come and bring my son after a few father-son visits. Thankful to have been invited into the terms, by unanimous smiles, we all agreed. Sneaking peeks at her; I was happy she had met and married someone who loved her. Glancing at my son's father and thinking about all he had done for us over the last seven months, for the first time, I identified with the love settled on her face.

She was the kind of woman who deserved the love that found her; but so did I. I could tell our sons' father was happy for them. Before we left, we shared pictures of the boys. My mouth flew open when I saw the dark-colored crescent-shaped birthmark below her son's chin. Our son had the same mark in the same spot. His was tiny but unmistakable.

We all had a good laughed. We thanked the couple and told them we wished them all the love and happiness their hearts could hold. After letting me pray for them and their baby's health and safe delivery, I invited them to my church. Driving back to our son, I started thinking about that day in court when she said she had "been there and done that." Though the thoughts of comparison between her and I wasn't a guest at the dinner table, waiting for me outside the restaurant, thumbing a ride, it climbed on the backseat and was attempting to ride back home with us.

From the backseat, whispering the questions started. What did she see in their son's father? What did he see in her, and why didn't things work out between them? Sensing something was wrong, my son's father answered the questions I didn't ask. Keeping it simple, he told me, when they got together, we had broken up for what he thought was the last time. They ran into each other around that time. She had just ended her relationship with her fiance' of three years. She was pregnant at the time of their breakup. Unfortunately, the stress of her broken relationship caused her to have a miscarriage. He said because they were both in pain, they took advantage of each other. In between trying to figure things out, they were each other's convenience. They did not love each other. He said he thought she and her ex, rode the same merry-go-round we had, and when we were on-again, so were they.

So when she called and told him she was pregnant and he was the father, he did not want to believe her. She told him she needed time and that she did not want him to contact her. After she had the baby, he and I were back together. He said because he didn't know what to do, he chose to do nothing. That's when she started filing. He said he thought if he told me, it would have devasted me, and I would have never forgiven him. He told me he ran from his responsibility to her and their son and was preparing to run from his obligation to me and our son. He was wrong for how he treated her and me. Ironically, the nightmare he had was about her and me.

He told me he was happy she had married a great guy who loved her. Pulling over he stopped, turned off the car, turned to me and said, "Sweetheart, you are the one I lost sleep over, the one my heart was terrified of losing. I did what you suggested. I read 1 Corinthians the 13th chapter. I saw how much God's love changed you. I want God to show me how to love like that. I do love you, and I don't care what I have to do or how long I have to wait; I want you to be my wife. I want to spend the rest of my life loving and caring for you and my sons."

My tears were my acceptance speech for his honest apology. He held me, then playfully asked me if I would wait for him. He always knew how to make me laughed. Six months later, through consistency, counseling, and his commitment to Christ, he was ready; so was I. Having lunch with him one day, eating hamburgers and French fries, he got down on one knee and asked me to marry him. I said, yes! He presented me with a beautiful diamond ring. Smiling, he told me that was the only meal he could afford because he was working on getting us an apartment. I would have said yes to him, in a carryout or at a food truck. I was in love!

He knew I was there to help him and would, but I appreciated his initiative and drive. Just when I thought my heart could take no more, he slid a jewelry receipt in front of me; it was marked "Paid in full!" My smile turned into sweet tears of joy.

SCENE: COURTHOUSE...

We visited the courthouse for the SIXTH time. This time, we took the elevator to the third floor to give a cashier's check to the clerk for the purchase of our marriage license. That following Saturday, we pledged our love and exchanged our vows at our church in front of our family, friends, and our God.

To God Be All The Glory!

> "Love is patient; love is kind; it is not jealous; love does not brag, it is not arrogant. It does not act disgracefully; it does not seek its own benefit; it is not provoked, does not keep an account of a wrong suffered, it does not rejoice in unrighteousness, but rejoices with the truth; it keeps every confidence, it believes all things, hopes all things, endures all things. Love never fails; but if there are gifts of prophecy, they will be done away with; if there are tongues, they will cease; if there is knowledge, it will be done away with. For we know in part and prophesy in part; but when the perfect comes, the partial will be done away with. When I was a child, I used to speak like a child, think like a

child, reason like a child; when I became a man, I did away with childish things."

(1 Corinthians 13:4-11)

"But now faith, hope, and love remain, these three; but the greatest of these is love."

(1 Corinthians 13:13)

#6

THE GENERAL

Francis! Get up out of that bed right now, it's been three days!

Mama Kay had used her key to let herself in her daughter's apartment again. Francis heard her come in but did not move. Walking toward her bedroom, her mama yelled, "Whew! I'm sure when you step out of those pajamas, they're going to stand up on their own!"

Heartbroken, Francis had decided to lay in bed indefinitely. Mama Kay reaching the threshold of her daughter's bedroom door, pinched her nose and spoke quickly, "Girl, there are other fish in the sea, but the way you look and smell right now, they're going to swim away and tell all the other fish to swim for their lives!"

Francis looked up at her mom and rolled her eyes. She knew she was a drama queen, but her mama was the supreme drama queen. The apple hadn't fallen and rolled far from the tree. Thirty-six going on fifty, Francis had one goal, make that two, marriage and a baby.

She had gotten close three times in the last five years. Make that four, if you count the guy she met every other Friday night at the laundromat. Though she had a washer and dryer in her apartment, the evening

Francis met Roy, she was there washing her comforters. Once he made her acquaintance by speaking, they became friends.

On their second laundry date, she noticed he was about to take his clothes out of the dryer prematurely. It appeared he was short fifty cents, keeping him from completely drying his clothes. Offering him two quarters (which he readily accepted) bought them twenty-four more minutes to talk. He wasn't a "fold your clothes hot out of the dryer kind of guy," so as soon as the dryer stopped, so did their conversation.

Francis started dressing up every other Friday night to go to the laundromat. When her friends asked if she wanted to go out, she told them she already had plans. She did not tell them with whom or where. The one person she did tell, was her best friend, Ryan Baker. They had been friends since middle school. He was hilarious.

He never made her feel like she was behaving desperately when she told him the circumstances surrounding her meeting someone new. Her best friend was her go-to man when she wanted to get a male's perspective about what a man wants.

For example, the guy she met at the laundromat told her he was there washing clothes for his mama. Francis thought, "How sweet, a man who helps his mother, now that's a caring man with character." She thought highly of him until one Friday night. His mama pulled up, jumped out her car, and came in the laundromat, yelling, "Boy! I told you to fold these clothes when you take them out the dryer, so my uniforms won't get wrinkled! You won't work in a pie factory tasting pies, and here I give you one job to do, and you can't even do that right!

What's wrong with you, boy?" When she told Ryan, her smirk gave him permission to laugh hysterically. Ryan told her; the fact that she had given him fifty cents, and he didn't offer to give it back when they met again two weeks later, spoke volumes about his character and his pocket change.

He also reminded her, this guy had never complimented her or asked for her phone number. According to Ryan, Roy wasn't interested in friendship outside the laundromat. The thing that made them both crack up laughing together, was his mama's cameo appearance. She called him a boy and made it known; she had sent him to the laundromat!

Her love interest was almost forty years old, and his mama was still giving him chores. The other two times, Francis met what she considered potential mates; they just happened to be nice guys who were nice to her. She misinterpreted their niceness.

However, her last failed proposed prospect proposal held real substance. That was the one causing her to hold herself hostage in her apartment for the last three days. His name was William; they met at work. Both worked at an exclusive private assistant living nursing home for the wealthy. Francis had worked there for the last five years.

William, their resident chef, had only been there a year. She was the activity coordinator for a small group of seniors, five out of twenty-three living there to be exact. Residents, they were there for different reasons, from all walks of life. Some were placed there by adoring children; some had come on their own. A few were dumped there by uncaring family members to be shelved like an old un-interesting book.

For Francis, those were the ones she gravitated to the most. She loved the elderly. To her, they were more than old people; they were categorized characters, living books that housed history.

Eavesdropping, she overheard many interesting stories they shared among themselves. The seniors she was assigned to were quite a collection. As far as she was concerned, she had the best group in the home.

First, there was Sir Judah; he was a great dignitary from another country. He had three sons. His eldest was Shelah. His other two sons were twins, Zerah and Perez. His sons brought him to the United States to hide during a time of unrest in his country. When things calmed down, they came back to retrieve him.

He did not want to leave, so they honored his wish. What they did not know; there were two very special reasons why he wanted to stay. He was loved and spoiled by the staff (to include her), and he was a, "SSS" (Secret Smitten Senior). He was sweet on a pretty, elderly lady who sat across the table from him at mealtime. Her name was Di'andra, affectionately known to all who sat at their table as Lady Di.

She had been placed there by her daughter, who decided caring for her aging mother proved to be a burden and bothers to her life as a single woman. Her daughter rarely visited her mother.

Then there was Queen Ann; she was the mother of a renowned opera singer. Performing all over the world, her son wanted to ensure his mother received constant companionship and the best around the clock care in his absence.

Though he offered to hire an in-house caregiver for her, she wanted to live among her peers. Listening to her heart, he gave her what she wanted. Once a year, her celebrity son would come and perform for her and her fellow residents. He also spoiled her with jewelry and gifts from his travels.

Next, there was Sally. She was an Oscar award-winning actress who had starred in many films and on Broadway. When she started to show early signs of Alzheimer's, her attorney and long-time friend acted quickly and honorably. Liquidating her estate, he put the proceeds in a trust fund to ensure payment for her stay at the nursing home for the remainder of her life. He would visit her a few times a year.

Occasionally she would get a visit from an old movie star friend who would stay and join her for dinner. This was always an exciting treat for her group of friends. Getting dressed for those visits, Sally would put on one of her old stage costumes, then pack on tons of makeup as if she were preparing for an on-stage scene. In Sally's mind, she probably heard, "lights, camera, action!'

Last but not least, there was her favorite, "The General." He was a war veteran who wanted to be identified by his rank. He had no family. His room and board were paid monthly by the United States Army. For his service and sacrifice, he had received a "Purple Heart" medal and was very proud to have served his country. The General was also a believer in Christ. He always shared his faith with his friends. In the army, he served under and spoke highly and often of his last Commander and Chief, David.

The General kept those he dined with engaged with stories of battles he had fought and won alongside his Commander. The youngest of her group, she identified him as the oldest in wisdom, action, and resolve. Because of his faith, balanced, Francis thought him to be a great man of God.

She gathered and concluded from his shared stories and actions; he was a fierce, loyal protector. In her opinion, Commander David was blessed to have had a man of his strength and character serving under him. Francis felt honored to be a part of the team that took care of him.

There you have it; these were her senior babies. She called them babies because, in many ways, their behavior dictated as such. From squabbling, whining, and fighting with each other to protecting one another to a fault, sometimes they acted like sibling brats! Watching them have lunch one afternoon, admiring them, Francis remembered thinking, in the transitions of life how, "from the WOMB to the TOMB, man is once an adult and twice a baby.

> "Just as you do not know the path of the wind and how
> bones are formed in the womb of the pregnant woman,
> so you do not know the activity of God who makes
> all things."

(Ecclesiastes 11:5)

Conceived, babies grow in the "WOMB" in a fetal position. In most cases, if a man lives long enough, in the final stages before death, the body starts to curl back up into a fetal position, preparing for its departure. Once that last breath is exhaled from the body, separating man's spirit, he is then birthed into the eternal.

Thinking about man's beginning and end in detail, Francis thought about how, as babies, we exit the WOMB and enter the world crying, and when we're old, we leave this world whimpering, weeping softly. As babies, initially having no teeth, our food is served to us in the form of liquid. Later we advance to puree (baby food), then graduate to finely chopped table food.

As we grow, our teeth come in, giving us the ability to process our food by chewing on our own for many years. As we get older, after they have served us well, one by one, they fall out! Reversing; our food has to be chopped then pureed, and eventually liquified for consumption. When we are babies, we crawl, then pull ourselves up with the aid of nearby people or things (walls, furniture, etc.)

We practice walking by using baby walkers. And when our parents think we are ready, they take us out of the walkers. Standing, shaking, we take our first steps. Once we learn how to walk, off we go into our many adventures, only to (after aging) someday wake up with the desire to stay in our pajamas and go nowhere. Our once fast pace movement drastically slows down as we eventually become unstable, causing us to once again stop along the way to hold onto other people or things to steady ourselves.

Many eventually end up having to use canes, adult walkers, wheelchairs, or electric scooters to aid in movement. When we can no longer stand, back down we go. We lay, while (m) others' (minus the m') take care of us. From there, our bodies start the process of weakening. Shrinking, it slowly balls itself back up, preparing the body for its resting place, the "TOMB."

She thought about how babies wore diapers at the beginning of life and as they become adults, advancing in age as seniors, losing control of their bodily functions, adult diapers become necessary. As for hair (unconsciously running her fingers through her own), she thought about how some babies born with no hair, eventually grow hair, only to have it turn gray, then someday fall out as well. Concerning speech, in the beginning as babies we babble, then as we grow, we speak clearly what we are taught. Learning, we apply what we remember throughout our lives.

Sadly, as we age, we forget the sum of it all. People, places, and things we embraced or took for granted by ignoring or overlooking, becoming sentimental, regretful, or nothing at all, we no longer remember.

A lifetime of data holding our loves, lessons, accomplishments, and failures, evaporate into invisible clouds. Hovering, they are there, but in many cases, not accessible. Reflective in nature; between the squirm of the caterpillar to its transformed nature of a soaring butterfly, there is the process...

God, in His infinite WISDOM, has ordained the sun and moon in rotation, to rise and set timely. Like clockwork, He has ordained the same for man. Birth is the opening curtain that provides opportunities for many exciting acts in the play of life. Slowly fading, drawing, to a close in living, eventually the curtains close with no chance for an encore.

The breath of life is a gift (present) from God, no matter the circumstance. What we create in the time we are here (good or bad) is our opportunity to re-gift ourselves to others. The productivity of our lives is our show and tell offering back to the original Giver, God. That thought caused Francis to remember one of her mother's often quoted scriptures:

> "So then each one of us will give an account of himself to God."

(Romans 14:12)

Continuing her thinking process, Solemnly Francis marveled at these thoughts; from our diminishing eyesight, stamina, cognitive thinking, to the loss of elasticity and muscle mass, resulting in swollen or flabby wrinkled skin, the effects of aging will happen until we, pass away. Those thoughts caused her to remember yet another one of her mother's often quoted scripture.

"As for the days of our life, they contain seventy years, or if due to strength, eighty years, yet their pride is but labor and sorrow; For soon it is gone, and we fly away." (Psalms 90:10)

Shifting in thought, laughing under her breath, she remembered one afternoon during her senior's lunch, eavesdropping, she overheard Sir Judah (leaning on his staff) tell his four lunch companions how aging introduces you to unwanted family members. He said, "I tell you this; getting old, there's a royal pain in the behind family that's going to make your acquaintance, whether you want them to or not; it's the "Itis Family."

This inflammatory family of squatters, led by papa arthritis, mama bursitis, and their twins' tendinitis and tendonitis, bringing along their cousins' bronchitis, tonsillitis, gingivitis laryngitis, followed by a host of other related bodily ailments, will unpack their bags in your body with no plans to leave!" That made everyone at their table laugh. Ranging between the ages of sixty-three to seventy-two, barring a few of those uninvited ailments, most of Francis seniors were far from living in their full returned baby stage. She appreciated meeting them at this precious time in their lives.

Except for Sally's mental detours from time to time, Francis was grateful the seniors in her care still had their wits and dignity about themselves, making her job easy and delightful when it came to creating entertainment for them.

Their favorite three things to do were, playing Bingo, participating in holiday celebrations, and dressing up for their special dinners that featured live entertainment. This is where her best friend Ryan came in. Twice a month, he and his band would come and serenaded the entire group with songs from their era while they enjoyed their dinner. This gave them the feel of a senior supper club.

Some more sturdy seniors would dance to the music after they had eaten. Later she and Ryan would compare notes on the responses from his elderly audience. From where he stood, he could see them rocking from side to side, hunching their shoulders, singing along to the songs.

He especially enjoyed their smiles of obvious reminiscence. Stories of personal memories stored in their hearts made voiceless guest appearances, flashing across their timeless faces. Ryan always caught the winks Sir Judah made at Lady Di causing her to return a girlish smile.

That exchange was their substitute dance. It was indeed sweet to watch. Smitten, Francis often thought about the day Sir Judah's sons came to take him back home to his country. Because he did not want to leave, The General hid him in his room. The only problem with that was, protecting him activated The General's training from his days in combat.

After The General strapped on his old war helmet, he turned off the lights in his room, pulled his blinds down, then put a chair under the doorknob. He would not let anyone in. From behind his fort (door), He and Sir Judah could be heard yelling repeatedly, "We will not surrender!" As a result of their actions and war cry, three days later, remote controlled doors were installed in each room. Still, they won! Sir Judah sons let him stay. Dinner that evening was more than exciting.

Eavesdropping once again, Francis heard The General tell the ladies at his table the story surrounding their standoff, emphasizing his mission operation, "Save Sir Judah," had been accomplished! All she could do was laugh at his embellished version of events.

Wearing his medal of honor, issued to him by the United States Army to dinner that evening pinned to his chest, the story he told the ladies caused Sally and Queen Ann to gasp. He was their senior hero! Both ladies rewarded him by sliding their desert over to him. It was chocolate pudding, his favorite. Lady Di gave a different response. She was grateful to him, but her smiles of gratitude were reserved for Sir Judah.

She was glad to hear he fought to stay. She was sweet on him too. When they got up from the table to head back to their rooms that evening, The General had two escorts, Queen Ann, snugged up on one arm, and Sally on the other. As for Sir Judah, after Lady Di kissed him on the cheek, he grabbed his signature staff with one hand and her hand with the other.

Strolling out the dining area together, it was official. That evening they became each other's steady. Francis remembered thinking, she wished someone would be sweet on her like that. Just then, as if he was the answer to that prayer thought, Chef William popped his head out of the kitchen, then stepped out completely, surprising Francis.

He told her she had come out to see the looks on the seniors' faces. He had prepared a special Italian meal for them and was hoping to get some visual feedback from a dining room full of empty plates.

He told Francis the seniors in her group were the only ones who appeared to have picked over their food, and he wanted to know why? Francis gave him a lighthearted smile. She explained, their attention was captured by the re-telling of events that had occurred earlier in the day, and because of who the story was being told by, it was likely their appetites took a backseat because of The General's tall tale.

The General had captured the appetite of their imagination as he boasted about how he had single-handedly kept the old gang together. This made William laugh, then ask Francis what she thought about the meal. She told him she hadn't eaten yet. William told her to stay where she was. Disappearing through the double doors then reappearing a few minutes later, he rolled some saucy noodles on a fork and slid it into her mouth.

Having this handsome man with a chef's hat on fork feed her prompted her response of, "Delicious!" Not the food, it was seasoned a bit too much. Francis was thinking and talking about him. He was a tasty sight for her hungry eyes. Smiling, he asked her what she liked most about it?

Looking in his eyes, smiling seductively, she said, "It's creamy and fla-vorful," but in her head, she said, "Your eyes are creamy, dreamy, your lips are savory and full." Reading her eyes and her mind, this was his response in kind; "After work would you like to join me at "Happy Hour" for a drink, I like your smile and the way you think."

(Happy Hour with William, turned into five happy months.)

BACK IN HER BEDROOM...

Up on her feet, looking in the mirror, seeing what her mother saw, she understood why her mom said what she did. Minutes later, her nose confirmed her mother's sense of smell as well. Opening her bedroom door heading across the hall to her bathroom, she could hear the sizzle and smell the nice hot breakfast her mother was preparing.

Slipping into the bathroom, she turned on the shower. Stepping out of her pajamas, she smiled at the thought of them standing up on their own. Once she stepped into the shower, and the hot water hit her body, with the water gage set on jet streaming, that encouraged her to cry some more.

If there was ever a place, she could camouflage her tears, it was there. Stepping directly under the spouting water, she began to pour out her tears, ones she didn't know she had. After three days of crying, she thought she was all cried out. As the water washed over her hurt, it revealed another layer of emotional dirt. These tears were quickly identified as angry ones; she had let her senior babies down.

Preparing to serve a three-day suspension, she decided to take a few earned vacation days in front of them. Because of her unscheduled days off, she was going to have to tell her mother what happened. In the shower naked and exposed, she wanted the events of the last five months to go down the drain with the soap suds and her tears.

Twenty minutes had gone by; there was a knock at the bathroom door. It was her mother. "Francis, are you alright in there? I knew you were dirty, but good Lord, are you clean yet!" Her mom was sarcastic but right. She felt dirty and was attempting to wash away her mental, verbal, and physical participation in a matter. Fifteen minutes later, dressed and seated at the table across from her mother, she picked at the food her mom had prepared in silence.

Knowing her mother as she did, she was sure she had reached out to Ryan, and he had told her some of what had happened. Though he was her BFF, for the last few days, she had avoided him too. She did not answer his calls, text, or knocks at her front door. After her mother was satisfied, she had eaten enough to regain her strength, she started the conversation by saying, "Francis, you know I love you; whatever has happened will not change that. I spoke to Ryan. he said, 'I should talk to you'. He asked me to tell you he loves you, and you are still his best friend, and when you are ready to talk, he will be there to listen.

He misses you." Francis took a deep breath, but nothing came out. The only thing that could be heard was the minute hand on her wall clock. The look on Francis's mom's face changed from patient to a hint of fear; "What had her daughter done?

Was she going to jail?" Noting the change on mom's face prompted her to speak. This is what she had to said; "Mom, I know you don't like my friend William. After I tell you what happened, you're really not going to like him.

First of all, I am not pregnant; he has not cheated on me, hit me, or stole from me. It's worst; he used me to steal from my senior babies." Her mother's mouth dropped open. Was her daughter saying she was an accomplice to crimes against the seniors in her care?

Francis reading the rising panic on her mom's face rushing in, released this verbal response; "No, mom, I did not knowingly help him in his crime against my seniors." "This is what happened; William is the nephew of the previous head chef who had been with the nursing home for over thirty years. Upon retiring, he recommended his nephew for his former position.

Because his uncle was a great chef with integrity, as a courtesy to him for his loyalty and longtime service, they hired his nephew. Though William had just completed culinary school, they took a chance on him and hired him. Because of the seniors' health issues and tolerances, their food must be prepared per their dietary charts.

Everything needs to be prepared with low salt or no salt at all. Not even a bad chef could mess that up. A child cooking with an easy bake oven (following instructions) couldn't mess things up as bad as William did and he did so in the worst way.

Fresh out of culinary school, he was anxious to try some of the things he had learned. Unauthorized, he used different spices and recipes to prepare some of their meals and desserts. Going off-script, he caused some of the seniors' pressure, sugar, and cholesterol to go up.

His dishes invited members from the Itis (inflammation) family to jump on the seniors and make them ill. Over time, some experienced swollen legs, ankles, glands, and stomachs. Her mother's puzzling look suggested this question; "He did that, so why are you in trouble?"

Francis explained: "Mom, the afternoon William poked his head out of the kitchen, he was looking for feedback from what he had made the seniors for dinner. When he saw they were gone, he stepped into the dining area. He was not supposed to come into the dining area.

Because he was cute and came close, invading my personal space to fork-feed me a sample of what he had made, I did not remind him or report him for violating policy.

Also, after sampling his cooking, I did not immediately make mention to him or management the obvious; he had deviated from the seniors' individual and collective meal plans. Instead, I agreed to have a drink with him after work." Francis looked at her mother, who had relaxed in her chair.

None of what her daughter had said thus far was criminal. Continuing, she told her mom, it wasn't until after she had gone out with him a few times that she felt comfortable enough to talk to him about those two offenses that could have gotten him fired. If she was honest with herself, she didn't tell him right away because she liked him and didn't want him to take offense to her correction or see her as a company girl.

Francis told her mom, judging his response, he knew he was wrong. She shared with her mom what happened the first time he was introduced to her and the rest of the staff.

After being told by the "House Manager" at an open staff meeting how important it was that everyone follow the strict guidelines for the safety of the residences, which included their specific diets, William raised his hand. He asked if maybe once a month, he could introduce them to a new dish or a modified dessert.

Obviously not listening, everyone looked at him as if he were deaf. He was not Chef Emeril or Chef Boyardee!" Seeing her mother's facial expression change to slight indignation, the look on her face still wanted to know why Francis was being punished for William's crime. This caused her daughter to lay out the worst of what William had done.

"Mom, when William and I first started dating, he was always asking me questions about my senior's personals lives. He asked, who they were, if they have family, and how they ended up at the nursing home? I answered him because I thought he cared about who I cared about, them. To make a long story short, he went behind my back when I was not around and held private conversations with them; that was another violation.

Cozying up to them, he had each of them bring their most prized possessions to the dining hall for him to look at. Fawning over them, he asked if he could take the items home, show them to his friends, then return them. He got something from each of them. He took Sally's Oscar, a diamond ring from Queen Ann, and two things that belonged to Sir Judah. One directly from him and the other indirectly.

Under the pretense of borrowing, he took Sir Judah's signature ruling staff. It belongs to his country. Indirectly, he took Judah's signet ring, an heirloom he had secretly given to Lady Di. Of them all, the one that hurt me the most is what he stole from, The General. William stole his 'Purple Heart' medal." This was particularly disheartening for Francis because his medal, in her mind, held the equivalency of family.

His medal, memories of service, and his fellow residents were all he had. Francis told her mom she did not find out about the theft until the next morning. She was called into her supervisor's office and only given a few details. By the time she left, she had gathered; William had stolen their items, got caught, and had been fired.

Judging by what was told to her, they were investigating to see if she had knowingly or unknowingly assisted him in any way. Therefore, she was placed on suspension while her actions or lack thereof were being reviewed by upper management. Was she being considered as a suspect, a co-conspirator? Somewhere within, she did not care about being accused, suspended or worst, fired.

Her concern was her seniors, what they thought about her, based on what they might have been told. Just then, her phone rang. Glancing at her caller i.d. she could see the call was from her job. It was Mrs. Granger, her friend, who happened to be the facility's head nurse.

Scared to answer it, she chose not to. After the call cleared, her phone rang again. This time it was her supervisor calling from the nursing home on her private line. Not wanting to answer the call, in front of her mother, she ignored it. Just as she reached to silence her ringer, it rang again.

This time alarm arose within. Had something happened to one of her seniors? Pressing the receive button, she was right, except something was happening concerning all her seniors. The voice on the other end of the phone in mild panic advised her that The General, being the ringleader, had done it again!

Somehow, disconnecting the electrical wiring to his door, he had locked himself along with Sir Judah, Sally, Lady Di, and Queen Ann in his room. Forming a coup, she was told the women were crying, and the men were crying out, "Bring Francis back!" While listening, her doorbell rang. Shaking her head, signaling for her mother not to answer it, she could not stop her. Ignoring her daughter, her mother let Ryan in.

Looking at Ryan, horrified by what was being conveyed to her, waiting with bated breath, she wanted to know why they were calling her. Before Francis could ask a question, she was pleaded with. They needed her to come to work right away, in order to meet The General and his troop's demands.

Her supervisor's priority was to get him to open the door so they could get everyone out safely. Word had leaked out; William had been fired. It had also been quickly rumored that because Francis wasn't there, she had gotten fired too! After her supervisor finished speaking, she waited for her to respond. Francis told her she was dressed and on the way.

Running into the arms of her BFF, Ryan, she told him she needed him to drive her to her job right away; she would explain things on the way.

Grabbing her purse, she told her mom there was an emergency at work, and they needed her to come in right away.

Running out the door, she yelled to her mother; she would fill her in when she returned. Yelling back while closing the door, her mom said, "I will be praying for you!" During the fifteen-minute car ride, Francis did her best to fill Ryan in on the sketchy details. He listened intently, only making disapproving faces at the mention of William's name.

Once inside the nursing home, Francis was immediately met by her supervisor. She could see other spectating seniors had filled the hallways. Most had their eyeglasses on, and their hearing aids turned up as high as they could, trying to see and hear what was going on.

The closer she got to The General's room, the more she could hear loud audible voices. Standing directly in front of it, the voices coming from his room were chanting, "We want Francis! We want Francis!" Sounding like children, she could hardly believe her ears.

This was a serious moment, and all she could think was how she wanted to bust out laughing! Keeping her composure, she asked her supervisor if she wanted her to knock on the door and identify herself or wait until the senior protesters calmed down. The sarcastic look on her supervisor's face prompted Francis to knock on the door, first gently, then harder. They did not stop. Choosing to wait for a break in their chant, she shouted, "General! It's me, Francis!" It worked. The chanting stopped just as she heard a command for everyone to be quiet. Someone yelled, "Who is it!" From what she knew of their voices, it sounded like Queen Ann. She responded, "It's me, Francis."

The next voice she heard coming from behind their makeshift fort would not let her hold her laughter. It was Sally's. Clearly confused, she asked, "Who is Francis?" Francis thought the excitement might have been too much for her, causing her to forget.

Suddenly things became serious. She knew she needed them to open the door. Whispering through the crack, she said, "General, it's me, Francis. Please open the door; I want to make sure you're all okay."

The General was smart. He whispered back, "Are you back at work, or are you here just to get us to open the door and surrender?" Francis looked at her supervisor.

Rolling her eyes up at the ceiling, her supervisor motioned for her to say she was back at work. Francis said, "Yes, General, I'm back at work; I took a few vacation days off; that's all."

The General said, "I will open the door on one condition. Negotiating, he said, "I am the only one whose to be held responsible for these actions." Francis looked at her supervisor's face. It was blank. It was evident that was not a demand she could promise. When there was no response, The General spoke up and said, "Well, we're not coming out!"

Looking over at her supervisor, frantically, she nodded her head up and down, signaling, "yes." Francis relayed her answer. Just then, Sally could be heard asking again, "Who is Francis?" Standing in the hallway with his mouth opened in disbelief, Ryan watched the whole thing.

First, there was silence, then loud cheering as they shouted, "We won!" As soon as the click could be heard unlocking the door, two medical staff members rushed in to check on each of the seniors.

Escorting them out one by one (except The General), Francis could hardly believe they had done that for her. Each of them hugged her before being guided away. Sally hugged her because everyone else did. Francis could tell things were a little fuzzy for her and was glad she was being taken to receive medical attention. Stepping inside The General's room, she rushed to his bedside where he was sitting. He was in full uniform. Removing his hat, he motioned for her to come closer. As she approached him unafraid, he looked directly in her eyes and said, "I'm glad you're back.

You're like a daughter to me, to all of us." I did what I had to do to protect you. I wasn't going to let you be railroaded for something some Amalekite like fool did!" Just then, The General looked up at her supervisor and said, "This is a good girl right here. She shows her love for us by taking good care of us.

I know I broke the rules, but I had to right a wrong. Sometimes that means going up in the enemy's camp." For Francis, The General seemed to be talking in circles. Looking into his eyes, he appeared to be tired. Francis's supervisor raised her head slightly, signaling her to let Nurse Granger, who had stepped into the room, help her stand him up. The head nurse was there to take him to her office for a full examination and evaluation. Helping Francis lift him from his sitting position, she winked at her friend and whispered, "Don't worry, I will take good care of him." The General's focus was on Francis.

Looking at her, he said, "I served under one of the greatest commanders that have ever lived. He was brave, like King David from the bible. He was a fierce leader." Rising to almost full attention, he stood flat-footed and robust. With an unspoken code in his eyes, he told her to go home, open her bible, and read "1 Samuel 30:18-19," and she would understand. Afterward, The General winked, saluted her, then headed toward the door where he was met and escorted out of his room by another staff member standing by.

Staring into space, Francis stood still, stunned by everything that had just happened. She stepped out of The General's room just in time to see Nurse Granger let The General stop and speak with Ryan. Because of his height, her BFF had to bend his head and crouch down a bit to hear what The General wanted to say to him. It only took a minute. Ryan looked in her direction; she could not read the look on his face.

Whatever he said to her BFF, appeared to baffle him. Her thought, "we will compare notes later." Once The General turned the corner heading toward the infirmary wing, Francis turned her attention to her supervisor and asked what was going on concerning her?

Her supervisor told her they were still looking into the matter, but she could return to work the following day. Francis said okay, then headed down the hall to meet Ryan. When she felt she was at a safe enough distance away from her supervisor, she released a smile and personal laughter.

Her senior babies rattled their nursing home, turned it into a nursery, then turned it upside down, in defense of her! She was not told to come back to work because they were finished their investigation; they needed her to come because they were afraid of what her seniors might do next!

During the ride home, she forgot to ask Ryan, what The General had said to him that caused the unfamiliar look on his face. Instead, comparing notes, Francis started by telling her BFF what happened from the minute she approached The General's door, to her finally collapsing in his arms in laughter at the thought of being asked to come back to work the next day. She shared the scripture with him The General told her to go home and read.

When she told him, it was 1 Samuel 30:18-19, he smiled. It was obvious he knew the reference. Pulling up in front of her house, remembering, Francis asked Ryan to tell her what The General said to him. Skirting around the issue, he fed her some words that didn't make sense. She quickly assumed her long time BFF did not understand senior babble. Instead of being clear about that, he chose to be clear about something else.

Turning to her, he said, "Francis, I have two things I want to say. First, I need you to know that I waited in the parking lot for William to come and pick up his last paycheck, he never did. I was going to step to him for involving you in his mess. You know I'm not a violent man. I am a Christian. I try to love like Jesus, but I will fight you like Peter if you mess with my family. Pray for me. The Lord is still working on me in that area. This made Francis laugh. (ref: John 18:10)

While she was in a good mood, continuing he said; "Your mama and I never thought he was good for you. You started changing after dating him. I wasn't jealous, well, maybe just a little, but it was because you've always asked me what I thought about your potential dates, and with him, you didn't. I used to watch him through the small window on the kitchen door. He would look around to see if anyone was looking, then dump tons of seasoning in the food he was preparing.

Then he would stick his finger in the pot for a taste. Sometimes he took a drink from the liquor bottle he had hidden in one of the cabinets. But what really made me mad was the couple of times I walked up on him out back talking to other women on the phone, making plans to see them later. I knew he wasn't talking to you because you were inside working. The one time I tried to say something to you about him, you nearly took my head off! So instead of talking to you, I prayed for you.

You are my best friend, and I did not want to lose you and I did not want to see you get hurt.

When you were called into your supervisor's office and placed on leave, I called text and came by your apartment to tell you what I was told. Days before the incident, one of my band members told me he over-heard William say to your seniors that you trusted him.

He told them you said it was okay to ask them if he could borrow their precious items. That's what management is trying to determine, if it's true or not. Personally, I already knew the answer to that question.

Francis started tearing up. Before her first tear could fall, Ryan rushed in with the second and third thing he had to say. He figured she could cry one time for three different things. He told her he had done some inquiring, and because of the incident, Sir Judah's sons had been noti-fied and were coming to take him back to his country.

Also, because The General's had met their "three strikes you're out" incident policy, it was likely they were going to contact the Military and request he be transferred to another facility. She didn't realize this was The General's third incident! She had forgotten about the time he threatened another male resident for making Sally cry by calling her crazy because she (having one of her forgetful moments) accidentally sat down at the wrong dining table one evening during dinner.

Francis switching concern for herself to The General, speaking her thoughts out loud, said, "If The General finds out ahead of time, knowing him, he will probably round everybody up, pull the fire alarm and once everybody's out of the building, burn it down to the ground!

Both of them laughed. Ryan knew she was avoiding the first thing he had brought up to her, William. Facing the music, Francis turned to him and apologized for her behavior toward him when she was dating William.

She told Ryan she liked William a lot and thought he could be the one. Ryan looking straight ahead, said, "Francis, God knows your heart, He knows who and what is best for you. You are a wonderful, loving, caring woman. You had an old senior gang ready to risk it all, to protect your honor.

When somebody is willing to go to bat for you like that, you know you are truly loved. William did not love you. He enticed, exploited, then exposed you. Your seniors, in the name of love, covered you. They didn't care if you were guilty or not; their love leaped into action."

Francis, that's what God did for us. While we were yet sinners because of His love for us, He sent His only begotten Son to die for the sins of the whole world.

> "But God commendeth his love toward us, in that, while we were yet sinners, Christ died for us." (Romans 5:8)

> "For God so loved the world, that he gave his only begotten Son, that whosoever believeth in him should not perish, but have everlasting life. For God sent not his Son into the world to condemn the world; but that the world through him might be saved."

(John 3:16-17)

Ryan continued by saying, "Francis, Jesus loves you. The Lord knows everything about us all. He desires to help lead and guide us through every situation. He sees the beginning and the end and all that is in between.

I value you and our friendship. I have been praying for you for years. I do not want you to lose your job or your hope of getting married someday, but I must be honest with you. Until you lose your will, your way, by surrendering to the Lord, you are going to continue to repeat your actions and get the same results or worst.

Francis put her head down; between her mother and her BFF, she knew they had been concerned. Everything was a mess! Her heart and her thirst for a man was the culprit. Once again, giving oxygen to the wrong man, she had been deceived! Her seniors had jeopardized their residency for her, her mom was worried about her, and her BFF was prepared to catch a charge on behalf of her for planning to confront William.

Through tears of remorse, Francis asked Ryan if he would pray with her; she wanted to accept Jesus as her Lord and Savior. Ryan took her hands and prayed with her, leading her into a saving faith in Jesus Christ. He also covered her seniors in prayer and asked that the will of the Lord be done concerning each of them. After praying for his BFF, he took her out for her favorite meal, "fried chicken and waffles."

Over dinner, Francis told Ryan the heavy weight she previously felt had lifted off her during their prayer and had been replaced with a peace and a calm beyond her understanding. She felt as though everything was going to work out fine.

Ryan confirmed her words with his declaration by saying, "Francis, by giving Jesus your heart, you have given Him control of your life. Let the Holy Spirit go about making every crooked place straight and lets you and me enjoy these delicious waffles and chicken wings!"

TWO WEEKS LATER...

While working, without warning, Francis was summoned to an in-house hearing. As for William, she was told he had been fired. Because she had been allowed to resume her position (after her seniors staged their protest) and no one had said anything more to her about the incident, she thought the matter had been resolved. Fear swept over her as she stood in front of three board members; she was on TRIAL.

Remembering what her mother told her to do after she shared simultaneously her new birth in Christ and her fear of being reprimanded, Francis closed her eyes and whispered a prayer. By the time, the hearing was over, she had received a warning with a three-day suspension held in abeyance. She was grateful.

The Lord had moved on her behalf. She gladly accepted the board's rendered verdict. She needed to take some responsibility for her actions and inactions. Emerging from the meeting, shaken a bit, immediately she called her BFF.

Near tears, she left him a voicemail message telling him everything, including him being right about The General's fate.

During the hearing, they informed her that because of the incident, Sir Judah's sons were planning to come and take him back to his country the following month. They also told her they were in the process of finding a new home for The General.

Francis, ending her voicemail message, asked if he could meet with her, she needed him. Within minutes he responded by text. He was in a meeting but would come as soon as it was over.

Used to him dropping whatever he was doing and coming when she called, Francis was not sure how she felt about him not being able to do that this time. She realized she trusted and relied on him more than she knew. Ryan had always been there for her.

Thinking about her need for him made her think about what she must have meant to him. Here was a man who let himself be used in helping her screen potential dates for herself. And when the ones she selected without his approval turned out to be failed attempts at love, he was there to help pick up the broken pieces of her heart and heal it through encouragement and sometimes laughter. He always reaffirmed her by telling her she was beautiful and by the Hand of God, "Fearfully and Wonderfully" made. (ref: Psalm 139: 14)

Instead of letting anxiety lead her into a dark place, she went and sat in her car. Closing her eyes, what she was feeling inside, made its way out, in the form of her tears. Silently she wept and prayed for herself and her seniors. Those five seniors had become family.

They loved each other very much and were about to suffer a devastating break up, one, not even The General could stop from happening. Waving her white tissue in surrender somewhere between her tears and sleep, Francis felt a stir in her belly. From a place within, she heard softly, "Everything is going to work out just fine; "Trust Me."

Those comforting words coasted her into a sweet light car nap. Awakened by a light tap on her window, it was Ryan. With a look of panic on his face, he motioned for her to unlock the door. By the time she pushed the button, he was already on the other side of her car, waiting to get in.

Once inside, his panic was met by her calm. The Holy Comforter had already done for her what he was used to doing for her. God had brought His peace to her mind and her situation. Sensing this from her beautiful smile made him smile, then speak his heart.

Two months later...

Mrs. Baker, would you like any refreshments? The flight attendant's voice brought her out of her blissful daze. Francis responded, "No thank you, but can you tell me where my husband is?" The attendant told her he was in the front cabin of the plane, talking with the other passengers. Just then, she heard a loud familiar laugh.

Looking at the clouds outside her window, Francis heard a voice say, "I told you everything would be just fine; 'Trust Me.'" She did, and they were. Things were more than fine. Reminiscing over the events leading up to that moment, between clouds, Francis engaged her thoughts.

The day Ryan found her asleep in her car was the day he shared his true feelings for her; he not only loved her; he was in love with her. She realized she was in love with him too. Ryan was not what some women would consider handsome, but she realized she loved him, inside, out, not the other way around, proving "beauty truly is in the eyes of the beholder." In this case, she was the blessed beholder.

A few days after they revealed their love for one another, Ryan expressed his further, by asking her to marry him. She said, "Yes!" Ryan finally told his fiance' what The General whispered to him the day he was being escorted from his room after his protest.

The General whispering to him about her said, "She's a rare blooming flower from God's garden. I see the way you looked at her. Son, you have found the one God has planted for you. Pick her before it's too late." Then General, slowly walking away, dropped his shoulders in defeat and whispered, 'Don't be like me and wait until it's too late.'"

Francis smiled at the thought of hearing God tell her to "Trust Him." She did not know He had already worked out His plans for Ryan, her, and her seniors. The loud voice she heard coming from the front area of the plane, was none other than the voice of The General. She got up to go and hear him tell his story again. Hiding behind the partition, she listened quietly with a smile on her face.

He told everyone how he knew what William was up to when he lied and said I told him it was okay to ask them if he could borrow their heirlooms and precious jewels. The General said, "That scoundrel got Sally's Oscar and Queen Ann's priceless diamond necklace.

He got two things of Sir Judah, his important scepter (ruling staff) from him, and his signet ring from Lady Di. Because, besides them and me, no one else knew, Sir Judah had given it to her as an engagement ring.

That's why I fought so hard the first time to keep him there. He loved Lady Di and needed more time to tell her." The General said, "When it came to me, I tricked that old fake chef. I gave him a duplicate copy of my "Purple Heart" medal for bait.

The evening we brought those things to the dining room for him like he asked us to, I knew he was planning to steal them. Looking through the kitchen door window, I saw where he put them. I waited until he went out back for a smoke, then I snuck in the kitchen and went right to the cabinet where he hid them and took them back!

He didn't know I was profiling the profiler! He was a bad thief and a lousy cook! I left him a note; it said, "Not Today Devil!" I would've love to have been a fly on the wall to see the look on his face when he realized, the things he stole from us, somebody stole them from him! I was surprised he came to work the next day.

When he did, management approached him; he was dumbfounded. He didn't know they had placed a hidden roving camera in the kitchen, in hopes of catching him in the act of violating their dietary rules and restrictions in preparing our meals.

The thing is, they had him on camera, stashing the items in the cabinet but not me retrieving them." Changing his voice, The General said, "I'm telling you, I might be old, but I move like a ninja.

Timing the movement of the camera, when it roamed to the left, I got in, got our stuff and got out!" He went on to say, "I recognized the camera because it was just like the one, they put in my room. They thought I didn't know it. God had my back. He did it for me like he did it for King David and his men against the Amalekites. (ref:1 Samuel 30:18-19)

The General finishing his story, said, "When I gave everybody back their stuff and told them what William was planning to do could potentially harm our precious Francis, we all agreed to show management our items and plead the Fifth Amendment.

We exercised our right not to answer any questions. I didn't have to coach Sally because she didn't remember giving William her Oscar in the first place. We all said the same thing; that's why we're still together.

He was right. Except for Sally, Sir Judah, Lady Di, The General, and Queen Ann, along with her and new husband, were all aboard that plane on their way to Sir Judah's country. With his sons ruling in his absence, he was returning to his homeland to live out the rest of his days with his soon-to-be bride, Lady Di. Francis and her new husband were on their way there to witness the royal wedding of Sir Judah and Lady Di and a lower court wedding for The General and Queen Ann.

By God's grace, it was not too late for The General. Because he had no family, he was strong when it came to protecting those he loved, but when it came to sharing the vulnerability of his heart, he was weak. He did not know how to tell Queen Ann what he felt for her; that is, according to him, until he saw the love Ryan held in his eyes for her. By then, he thought it was too late for him but did not want the same thing to happen to Ryan.

Weeks before Sir Judah's planned departure, a lot had secretly gone on between her seniors. When Sir Judah's sons finally came to escort their father home, he introduced them to his fiancee' Lady Di, his newly trusted, "Commander and Chief," The General, and his fiancee', Queen Ann.

And because Ryan and Francis had gone to the "Justice of the Peace" and gotten married, newlyweds, they were invited along for an all-expense-paid honeymoon. While there, they would have the opportunity to witness the weddings of her seniors who were still in their adult stage of living and loving.

When Sir Judah gave Lady Di his signet ring, she was unaware of its value, though he was not unaware of hers. Unbeknownst to her, he had placed his country, on her finger, signaling he was prepared to give her everything.

When Lady Di's daughter was told, she was in utter shock. The mother she had so carelessly discarded was engaged and moving to another country, where she would officially be title "Lady Di" and treated like royalty.

She would live out the rest of her life in the company of people she knew loved her, a family she mattered to. As for Queen Ann, her son gave them his blessing. His mother was marrying a decorated man of honor, who had proven his love by protecting her, a man of God, like him.

He was pleased to be adding a new venue to his list of places in the world to perform, starting with his beloved mother's royal wedding. As for their host, Sir Judah's country was breathtakingly beautiful. His castle was like something out of a fairytale.

Her and Ryan's quarters were majestic, something she could have never imagined. From the food, entertainment, and exploration of Judah's country, the three weeks they spent there were beyond amazing. Francis stood in as the matron of honor for both weddings, crying tears of sheer joy.

The official ceremony honoring and naming The General as "Commander and Chief" of Judah's small country made her shed tears of reverence and gratitude from her soul. She loved him like a father and was happy that not only had he been given the blessed opportunity to pick his flower (Queen Ann) because of his love, confirming wisdom, strength, and courage to protect and lead, Sir Judah, picked him!

> 'Wisdom is with aged men, with long life is under-
> standing. "With Him are wisdom and might; To Him
> belong counsel and understanding." (Job 12:12-13)

Watching her seniors love, value, and look out for one another was their gift to her heart. She had learned so much about love in caring for them. Days before Mr. and Mrs. Ryan Baker were scheduled to leave, Sir Judah, his wife (Lady Di), The General, and his wife (Queen Ann) summoned them to the royal court for a private meeting.

Once greeted and seated, the newlyweds were told they were welcomed to visit anytime. One by one, her seniors expressed their love and appreciation for her. Sir Judah went last. By the time strength and comfort from Ryan's arms could be felt, Francis reeling from what Sir Judah said, understood how much her seniors meant to one another. He told them they wanted Sally to come for the weddings, but they were not able to reach the executor of her estate in time to get travel approval for her.

He told them it was later discovered that when his son Perez spoke with her executor, he was told Sally was out living her funds, and once they were gone, he was not sure where she would be placed. The executor further advised his son, he had been trying to find a grant or get placement for her through a government assistant program. Sir Judah told them; "Whether Sally was or wasn't in her right mind, she did not deserve to be dismissed or discarded; she mattered to them.

After sharing his heartfelt comments, he shared his proposal with them. He (Sir Judah) was wondering if she and her husband would be interested in managing a small five-unit nursing home facility he had purchased back in the United States before leaving. Sally would be the first resident.

Following that disclosure and request, he made this profound statement; "How dare she be penalized for living beyond her financial gain!" Since when did living a long life become a debt! Francis was speechless. Ryan was not. He asked Sir Judah what made him purchase a nursing home? Answering, he said, "Initially, I bought it for one reason. I had planned to ask The General to come to my country with me. If he said no, knowing the nursing home was planning to move him (because his eldest son Zerah told him), I wanted him to have a place where he could go and be free.

The General had been good to me, and he has protected us all at one time or another." He went on to say he had planned to ask her if she would check in on him from time to time. He told them when The General surprised him and said yes, to his offer, he decided to sell the home. Smiling and looking at his new bride, Sir Judah said, "My wife asked me not to." She had her own ideas as to what to do with the home.

Lady Di asked him to ask Francis and her husband if they would be interested in managing it and owning it someday. Everyone's eyes landed on Lady Di. Literally far away from her past but with a faraway look cast in her eyes, she said, "I never want any senior to feel unwanted like they are a burden or bother.

Still looking at a framed picture only she could see, solemnly she said, "After we have lived our lives taking care of others, to include family, sadly when we get older, in some cases those we have loved, nurtured and provided for, giving them the prime years of our lives, don't want to honor, let alone take care of us." Francis knew Lady Di's invisible drawings were from her own experience. God hearing her heart, had given her an unexpected end. Here she was making one of her first decisions as Sir Judah's accepted and respected "First Lady."

> "Show respect for old people and honor them. Reverently obey me; I am the Lord."

(Lev 19:32)

Married, Francis looked to her husband for a response. She wanted to say, "Yes!" However, she knew she could not, without his input. Ryan's smile said yes for them before his mouth did. Like her, he loved seniors and understood all too well what it meant for this special group of seniors to have Sally taken care of; she was their sister.

While they (Francis and her husband) could have just agreed to let Sally live with them, this was more about creating an environment where the forgetting and forgotten fruitful could thrive. For Francis, she could be free to created and managed an atmosphere of love for the elderly. Over the next three days, Judah and Ryan met to go over his business proposal in detail, while the new brides spent their time indulging in pampering.

Though nervous, Francis felt this was an excellent opportunity for her to work with who and what she loved, seniors, and their lives. With her loving, handsome, intelligent husband at the helms and God on their side, she was excited about the future He had planned for them.

When the time came for them to leave, as one of his first duties, they were driven to the airport, escorted by none other than the new Commander and Chief, The General.

This was fitting. Francis cried and hugged her seniors before leaving. The impartations she received from them were gathered and locked away in a special treasure box in her heart.

Undetectable to the naked eye, there would be no need to declare it through customs once she was back stateside. Carrying it within, she would hold everything they taught her in her heart. Among her collectibles was this thought; "People hold value their whole lives, but there is something special about making it to your senior years." This group taught her to love fiercely and faithfully and never to underestimate God. They taught her to live life to the fullest and, most importantly, to prepare yourself in this temporal life on earth, for your eternal rest in the hereafter in Him (Jesus Christ), in heaven.

The General taught her to be a fighter and to share her faith in Christ boldly. She watched as he fought for and led each one of his senior siblings to a saving faith in the Lord, ensuring they would all be together in spirit forever. With her seniors accepting Jesus as their Lord and Savior; she deemed them to be among the WWW's (World's Wealthiest Wonders). Because man is born into sin and shaped in iniquity (ref: Psalms 51:5), passing through this world, seniors can genuinely testify of life's ups, downs, ins, outs, wins, losses, joys, and sorrows.

For those seniors who accept the Father's gift of salvation through Christ, preparing themselves for their eternal rest, Francis felt if people would stop, take a seat at their feet and listen, they would be blessed with words of wisdom as they share the keys of life, love and the pursuit of true happiness;

starting with acknowledging their need for a relationship with Jesus as Lord and Savior.

EIGHTEEN MONTHS LATER...

Taking turns feeding their twin boys they named after Sir Judah's sons Zerah and Perez, Francis laughed at the thought of The General's last words before boarding their plane for home after their honeymoon. He prayed over them, saluted Ryan, then hugged her and whispered; Don't forget to read the bible to Sally; Ecclesiastes is her favorite book." Then with a sly grin on his face, he said, "Promise me of the three, you'll name the protector after me."

Then he smiled, kissed her on the cheek, and said, "I love you, daughter." Just then, his name's sake came running in the dining area, barking; someone was at the door. It was another package from abroad. Queen Ann and Lady Di had sent some more things for their god-grandbabies. The General had sent a special whistle and chew toy for their family's furry protector, their German Shepherd. He was given to her as a puppy, Francis named him "The General." He was Ryan's welcome home gift to her.

A mother now, she and Ryan agreed she would stay home with their sons while he ran the nursing home. Elated, her mom pitched in to help where she could. Before giving birth, she helped to manage things at the nursing home. Per Sir Judah's approval, they went about making renovations. They hired a highly qualified staff, which included her friend Nurse Granger from the nursing home.

She accepted their offer to be the Head Nurse on site. Renovating, Francis and Ryan made some wonderful changes to the facility. She wanted to make the home safe, with a feel of intimacy. Sally was their first resident. She was happy to be there. Some days her mind was sharp as a needlepoint; others, she was not sure who she was or where she was. Francis always knew how to make her smile.

She would read to her from the book of Ecclesiastes or show her pictures of her old friends. When she sat at the table to eat with her new senior siblings, Francis could see, though she never said anything, she was somewhat confused. In Francis's eighth month of pregnancy, she sent a telegram regretfully informing the others of Sally's passing. Within days, Sally's senior siblings traveled back to the states for her homegoing service. It was not a sad occasion. It was a joyous one. Each of the seniors speaking shared words of love and kindness concerning Sally.

The General was the last to give his acknowledgments. To everyone's surprise, he did not tell one of his many stories. He simply said, "Sally gave this world her mind and her passion through art. She received many awards to include an Oscar for that exchange, but our dear sister gave us her love, friendship, and allegiance. It does our hearts good to know she received her most prized gift of eternal life. Being of sound mind, body, soul, and spirit, she gave her life to the "Author and Finisher" of her faith, Jesus Christ. Sally, we love you. We will all be together again someday. And when we meet in spirit around the throne, we will lift our voices and declare through God's SON, "We Have Won!"

'then the dust will return to the earth as it was, and the spirit will return to God who gave it.' (Ecclesiastes 12:7)

'And as it is appointed unto men once to die, but after this the judgment:'

(Hebrews 9:27)

The sum of it all...

The conclusion, when all has been heard, is: fear God and keep His commandments, because this applies to every person.

(Ecclesiastes 12:13)

FOOTNOTE:

Francis's Request...

> "Even when I am old and gray, do not abandon me, O
> God. Let me live to tell the people of this age what your
> strength has accomplished, to tell, about your power
> to all who will come. Your righteousness reaches to the
> heavens, O God. You have done great things. O God,
> who is like you?"

(Psalm 71:18-19)

God's Response...

> "Even when you're old, I'll take care of you. Even when
> your hair turns gray, I'll support you. I made you and
> will continue to care for you. I'll support you and save
> you. To whom will you compare me and make me
> equal? To whom will you compare me so that we can
> be alike?"

(Isaiah 46:4-5)

ENDING SCRIPTURES...

"And we know that God causes ALL THINGS to work together for good to those who love God, to those who are called according to His purpose".

(Romans 8:28)

"For He rescued us from the domain of darkness and transferred us to the kingdom of His beloved Son (Jesus), in whom we have redemption, the forgiveness of sins. He is the image of the invisible God, the firstborn of all creation: for by Him (God) all things were created, both in the heavens and on earth, visible and invisible, whether thrones, or dominions, or rulers, or authorities—ALL THINGS have been created through Him and for Him. He is before all things, and in Him all things hold together. He is also the head of the body, the church; and He is the beginning, the firstborn from the dead, so that He Himself will come to have first place in everything. For it was the Father's good pleasure for all the fullness to dwell in Him, and through Him to reconcile all things to Himself, whether things on earth or things in heaven, having made peace through the blood of His (Jesus) cross."

(Colossians 1:13-20)

GOD BE GLORIFIED!

Biography

Deidra Bynum is the founder and CEO of the Titus 2:3 TCT Ministries (LLC). Retired from the Washington D.C. Police Department she relocated to N.C. There is where she, as led by the Lord, continues to write. She is the mother of two beautiful young adult daughters. With four amazing books, "Jacob's Leah (In Her Shoes)," "King David's Abigail IHS (And Today's Brides), "Abram's Hagar IHS (Diaries)," "Judah's Tamar IHS (Trials)" and a fifth book, "Samson's Delilah Dilemma IHS (Confessions) in the works from her anointed library of "Unsung Characters of the Bible," Deidra continues to add stories that educate and enlighten readers all over the world. Each book from her first series (Unsung Women of the Bible) is uniquely written in two parts. "Part One" identifies and expounds on a woman from the Bible, while "Part Two" consist of a collection of created modern-day stories of men and women encountering God in search of satisfying their thirst for love.

God Bless You,
Deidra

CONTACT INFORMATION:

Titus2:3 TCT Ministries P.O. Box 49645
Greensboro NC 27419
E-mail: titus23tct@gmail.com
Website: intheirshooes.com
E-mail: contact@intheirshooes.com

Facebook:
Deidra Bynum (Author Page)

Instagram: intheirshooes2021
Twitter: Deidra Bynum
@jleahinhershoes

CPSIA information can be obtained
at www.ICGtesting.com
Printed in the USA
BVHW081814260421
605867BV00006B/1426